MANCHÁN MAGAN

TRUCK FEVER

A Journey Through Africa

BRANDON

A Brandon Original Paperback

First published in 2008 by Brandon
an imprint of Mount Eagle Publications
Dingle, Co. Kerry, Ireland, and
Unit 3, Olympia Trading Estate, Coburg Road, London N22 6TZ, England

www.brandonbooks.com

Copyright © Manchán Magan 2008

ISBN 9780863223891

Mount Eagle Publications/Sliabh an Fhiolair Teoranta receives support from
the Arts Council/An Chomhairle Ealaíon.

2 4 6 8 10 9 7 5 3 1

Cover design: Anú Design
Typesetting by Red Barn Publishing, Skeagh, Skibbereen
Printed in the UK

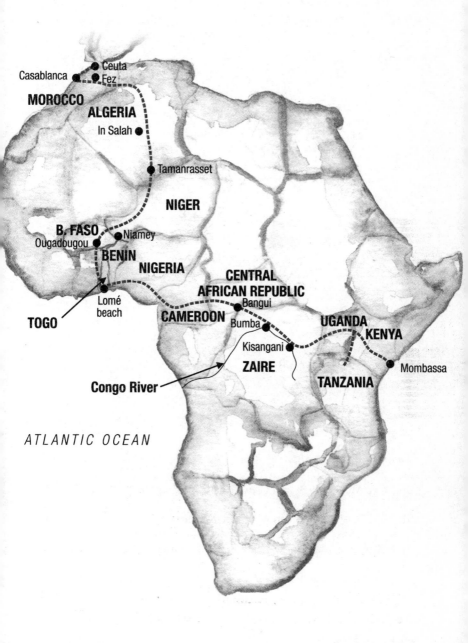

Ceuta
Casablanca
Fez
MOROCCO
ALGERIA
In Salah

Tamanrasset

NIGER

B. FASO
Ougadougou
Niamey
BENIN
NIGERIA
Lomé
beach
TOGO

**CENTRAL
AFRICAN REPUBLIC**
Bangui
CAMEROON
Bumba
UGANDA
KENYA
Kisangani
Congo River
ZAIRE
Mombassa
TANZANIA

ATLANTIC OCEAN

Thanks

To Steve MacDonogh and Cleo Murphy at Brandon.

To Marianne Gunn O'Connor for her imprimatur.

To Orla Coleman and Rikki Tahta for the writing sanctuary.

To Mullingar Public Swimming Pool – a crucible of literary epiphanies and a womb of retreat when the writing doesn't flow. To the Dublin and Westmeath library networks for feeding my ever-changing interests.

"Before the Congo I was just a mere animal."
Joseph Conrad

Chapter 1

JOHAN OPENED THE leather buckle of his rucksack, pulled out a length of rope and threw it over the boathouse rafter. He tied it off a joist, leaving one end dangling. Two large doors opened out on to the lake and the early sun poured in, brightening up the clutter of old kayaks, cracked skis and long-forgotten gramophone discs that lay scattered on the ground. His children were away at college now, and no one bothered much with the place any more.

A chill wind blew in across the lake from the Swiss Alps, and he pulled the lapels of his heavy felt jacket closed against it. The step-ladder was rusty and gave a sigh as he set it underneath the rope, slid the noose around his collar and kicked outwards. The squeal of the fibres grinding into the joist circled out across the water. Johan's face drained of life, his sharp features losing their great resolve.

I woke suddenly with a crick in my neck. I was in the back of a truck – an old troop transporter – on my way to Africa. There were eighteen people crammed around me, all of them jumbled together trying to sleep. The girl on whose shoulder I had been resting sensed my fright and opened her eyes, looking around her blearily.

"You OK?" she muttered.

"Fine," I managed.

We were going to Africa; going to spend six months driving across the continent: through the Sahara, through West Africa and right across the centre to Kenya. There was no real reason for the trip: we were going because we needed to be somewhere; we needed to get away. I had only met the others that afternoon, and although I knew little about them, I could see from their eyes they were uneasy. We all had that vague, lost expression – the shifty, hollow look you see in the faces of army recruits staring out from the back of a wagon-roof truck. There's rarely any sign of commitment or resolve, instead a disquieting absence, a dull sombreness. Nonchalance. We were a bit like that, life's also-rans. If there had been a war on we probably would have been over there instead. As it was, our generation was robbed of that opportunity. We had no easy avenue to glory, or adventure, or escape. We had to make our own.

It was freezing cold – mid November. It never occurred to me that to reach Africa in winter I'd have to cross sub-zero stretches of Europe. I suppose I hadn't thought about it all that much. I had been diligently stacking shelves in a hypermarket in Germany when suddenly I realised I had £1,000 saved and no idea what to do with it. I was barely twenty years of age. I knew little about anything. My dad had just died a few months before, and I had been having terrible dreams. I felt I had to get away – things couldn't be so bad anywhere else.

The rain was dripping through the truck's canopy, finding its way into my hair and down my neck. Through a ripped eyelet in the canvas, I caught sight of a sign pointing to Mantes-la-Jolie, but I had no idea where that was. I guessed we were somewhere between Rouen and Paris. Looking around at the strangers huddled on the two benches running either side of the truck, I longed to know what sort of people they were. We were going to be crammed into this space for some time, battling through some of the most desolate parts of the world, so it was kind of important that we get on.

What I had been able to find out so far was that most of them were British, with one or two Australians and New Zealanders too. Three were nurses, one was a locksmith and another a soldier. There were two young girls fresh out of an elegant London school, their ingénue eyes revealing a radiance that I suspected stemmed from innocence and gave me a tiny, but genuine glimmer of hope. I had assumed that the whole group was feeling the same mix of desperation and adventure as I was, but, in truth, I had no idea. All that was certain was that they felt a degree of the desperation. I could see it in their faces. I just had to hope I was right about the adventure too.

I tried closing my eyes again to grab some more sleep, but within seconds I was straight back into the dream. It was the next part; it always came in the same order, in threes, like some macabre altar triptych. I knew it backwards by then: Johan would hang himself in the boathouse, he'd swing there for a while, moaning gently for what seemed like for ever, until finally the boathouse and the lake and everything around him disappeared and he fell, plummeting downwards either to the ground or else endlessly through a void, never hitting bottom. I think it was like this because that was how my father had told it to me: the story of a ghost he claimed inhabited the boathouse of a climbing refuge he had stayed in in the Alps. It was one of many stories he told about his time hiking in Europe just after the war. Back then, he said, everyone had a secret to tell, and they regarded him, a bright-faced, Beethoven-haired Irish man straight out of medical school, as the perfect repository. He would accept a glass of wine from them and listen as they told their stories in French or German or bad English. He would simply listen and nod as he had been trained to do.

I got to know the stories well as he retold them again and again when we were hiking together in the Wicklow hills in the years before he died. There was one about a minor aristocrat he had rescued after she had fallen unconscious in the bath near Annecy, and another about a Jewish cobbler who had stitched his rucksack, and instead of taking money as payment wanted to share his story with a passing foreigner whom he would happily never see again. But it was Johan's story that my father kept coming back to. He had always loved ghost stories, had frightened us as children with tales of will-o'-the-wisps and banshees. He knew that the manner of Johan's death disturbed me, and it made him all the keener to return to it. Fear and fun were linked in his mind in the most innocent way. When we were young, he would throw a sheet over his head and chase us down the corridor with a carving knife.

When the group first met at four that afternoon on the harbour in Ramsgate in the south of England, we had all been too nervous to talk very much. This worried me more than any other fear my family or friends had tried to instil in me about the trip. We were heading into the complete unknown; all that was certain was that we would be tested to the limit –

no one makes it through the heart of Africa without experiencing real difficulty. I knew that much. And so, I felt it would probably be a good idea if we got to know each other's names soon at least. But I kept this to myself. I was hoping to attract as little attention as possible. Just from the way we were eyeing each other up, smiling at some, ignoring others, I could already feel the dynamics of the group asserting themselves. The jockeying for position in the pack began before we had even uttered a word. Sniffing around like animals. We were in danger of falling back on our basest instincts, retreating to the laws of the pack, and in any such hierarchy I was bound to find myself near the bottom. I had always been an outsider, had never played team sports or joined other group activities. I did things in my own way and in my own time. In a more sophisticated community, it might have made me a leader, but here I sensed I was as likely to end up the runt. If I weren't careful, I would become their patsy, their pliant bitch. My plan was to keep my head as low as possible for as long as possible.

A more hopeful voice inside me tried to explain away their frigidity as mere shyness. We were all simply overwhelmed by what lay ahead, and in the morning everything would look brighter. Their exuberance and bonhomie would shine through. These defeated cast-offs of the modern world would expand into wise, compassionate human beings who would take me under their wings and teach me all I needed to know about the world. We'd teach each other, look out for each other, create a community that nurtured us all, that carried us through the challenges ahead.

Unfortunately, all the evidence so far was stacked against it. The only real conversation we had had was over tea on the ferry to northern France. One of the nurses had mentioned something about disease and everyone had suddenly perked up, pitching in their own gruesome details about killer illnesses we were likely to encounter: malaria, river blindness, dengue fever, bilharzia. They competed with each other on the goriness of ailments and the comprehensiveness of the first-aid kits they had brought to combat them: who had the best antihistamines, antibiotics, syringes, suppositories and IV-drips. All I had was a box of paracetamol and some malaria tablets. The locksmith, whose lips were crusty with chap, started telling stories about the rusty scalpels they used in African hospitals and how people routinely had their kidneys ripped out in hotel rooms after being slipped a laced drink in the bar. Between each sentence he'd run his tongue around his lips in a bid to keep them moist, to stop the scales from falling off. I wondered why he didn't use lip balm – unmanly, I supposed.

Eventually, their pessimism got the better of me, and I couldn't help myself blurting out, "Look . . . sorry, excuse me . . ."

They all looked over, but I didn't go on. I was afraid my voice would let me down. A quiver had entered it, and I feared I might actually end up in tears. I inhaled deeply and, after a moment, pasted a nonchalant smile across my face and continued.

"Yeah, look, we've just left it all behind, right?" I said, trying to sound jocular. "We don't know what's ahead, but it's got to be more than dirty needles, yeah?"

They didn't say anything, just stared. The whole restaurant fell silent – or at least the two other diners who were finishing off ketchup-streaked platters of steak and chips did. These were the only other passengers on board: tattooed truckers, one bearded and bald, the other with a ponytail.

"It's just good to be prepared," one of the nurses said testily.

They all agreed with that and nodded heartily. I couldn't think of anything clever to say and so got up and walked away. I had alienated the whole group in one go, everyone I would be spending the next half year with. I bolted to the sanctuary of the lavatory and berated myself eye-to-eye in the stainless steel mirror. The place smelt of vomit and felt strangely reassuring. What had I let myself in for? I was bound to these people now; there was no way out. When I finally calmed down, I went back outside and found them talking about guerrilla kidnappings in the Congo. They paused mid sentence to stare pityingly at me, and I tried flashing an unconcerned smile.

We drove on through the night, and in the morning, with the sun shining in through translucent patches in the canvas, we jolted to a stop at a lay-by. Suzi, our leader, came around from the cab. Even after driving all night she still looked fresh and perky. Along with Joe, the mechanic, she would be driving us the 16,000 kilometres to Kenya. Suzi was one of those indomitable, fiery women who had formed the backbone of the Empire during the colonial days. She was the only thing about the trip that I had confidence in. This was her sixth trans-Africa crossing. There was nothing she didn't know; every route through every country and every local bird, tribe and animal. She oozed grit and resolve. I imagined she could get us through anything. Despite the freezing weather, she was wearing only a tight T-shirt and spandex leggings with a skull cap pulled low over her forehead. In a gravelly, obstinate tone that belied her thin frame, she announced that from here on in we'd be sleeping in tents. She had ten army-issue tents between the nineteen of us. We were to divide them up, choosing our partners with great care, because we would be sleeping with that person for the next six months. We also had to choose our cooking partners right away, for from now on two people would be responsible for all the cooking, shopping and cleaning every tenth day. The most important piece of advice she could give us, she said, was to avoid having the same cooking and sleeping partner, as we were bound to end up hating each other before long. All pairing up had to be done immediately, as someone needed to start making breakfast straight away.

A sort of panic took hold of us on hearing this. We eyed each other suspiciously, trying to work out who among us might be the most incompetent, the most insufferable. It was a bit as if she had told us that someone on board was a psychopath and we had to find out who was least likely to murder us in our sleep, or molest us, or poison us. Now was the time to assess who might suffer from flatulence, insomnia or kleptomania. Who could we possibly manage to share our lives with for half a year without ending up hating them? As the long-reaching consequences of our choices impinged on us, it became ever harder to choose. We still didn't even know each other's names, for pity's sake. I could see Suzi getting a degree of pleasure from all this. Either she enjoyed wilfully inflicting torture on innocent people or else she had already managed to develop a grudge against us in the sixteen hours we had been together. I had a feeling that this whole ritual of humiliation was her vendetta for all the trouble we were bound to cause her later on. She had been criss-crossing back and forth across the continent for a decade and she knew everything there was to know about it. She gave the impression that it was depressing for her to be faced with yet another group of ignorant, awkward punters full of the same stupid questions she had been asked countless times before.

I had never put up a tent in my life before, and so I looked around for anyone more rugged-looking than me. There was an Australian with a marine haircut called Wayne who I thought was bound to have camped out at some point, and so I nabbed him, while a reassuringly well-fed nurse named Stella chose me as her cooking partner. In a matter of minutes, our fate was sealed for better or worse.

The November sun, mustering whatever meagre heat it had at its disposal, shone down upon us, raising our spirits somewhat, and through awkward exchanges I got to know a few of the others. The three nurses – Stella, Felicity and Dorothy – were all rather similar: women in their mid thirties, each brimming with common sense and low self-esteem, taking a year's sabbatical. There were two brothers from Cornwall, Duncan and Norman, both fat, one squat, the other less so. They were brash, cheery men, with a marked scatological bent. They reminded me of background characters from a Grimm's fairy tale or a cheap pantomime – duped citizens of Hamelin shouting after the piper, or a conniving wig-maker preparing Cinderella's sisters' hair. Norman, the Tweedle-dum to Duncan's Tweedle-dee, had the suitably medieval occupation of locksmith. He was the one with the cracked-earth lips who had revelled in stories about people's kidneys being ripped out. His brother Duncan was a market gardener. He had expressed his intention to bed every woman on the truck, and as a result had been left with neither a sleeping nor cooking partner. They had had to buddy up together.

I thought it endearing that two brothers had come away together and mentioned something about it to Duncan.

"The only reason he's here," he replied, pointing to Tweedle-dum, "is 'cause my ma went down on her bended knees and begged me to bring him. She didn't want the big hulk lumbering around the house all winter."

None of us seemed to have any firm reasons for being here, but Stevi's was the most nebulous of all. He had accepted a place on the trip in lieu of a long-owed gambling debt. Stevi was from northern Germany originally, but you'd never tell it from his strong Birmingham accent. He had been raised on a pig farm on the coast up near the Danish border in a place associated with pale, anaemic light and sharp breezes. He epitomised the area, with egg-white eyes that blinked a lot and clammy, grey skin, coloured only by angry red rashes around his hairline. He had no lips to speak of, nor much by way of eyebrows either, but he managed a flimsy fair moustache and that spiky hair common in the Teutonic gene pool.

He was here because a friend had paid for two places on the trip six months earlier – in fact, his friend had been the first to sign up, but was then arrested soon afterwards. Subsequently, his friend was released on bail and had been planning on going ahead with the trip, but his lawyer had convinced him that skipping bail would not endear him to the judiciary. Stevi had magnanimously stepped in and agreed to take the tickets in place of the gambling debt. He had no interest in Africa, but he had always liked the man's girlfriend and thought that six months away with her was an attractive proposition. Unfortunately, the friend had doubts about letting his girlfriend go and in the end he forbade her, which left Stevi with two grand's worth of unwanted tickets. He tried to get the company to refund him, but they refused, and so he thought, *fuck it*, he might as well come along for the laugh.

We pitched our tents in gravel that first night on the side of the *autoroute* somewhere in the middle of France. As well as the nine I've mentioned – Suzi and Joe (leader and mechanic), Wayne (my tent partner), Stella, Felicity and Dorothy (the nurses), Duncan and Norman (the Cornish brothers) and Stevi – there were Lucy and Natasha (the young London girls), Rita and Vinnie (a couple formerly based in Tasmania), Henry and Mildred (middle-aged retirees), Luke (an athlete and market seller), Holly (a cartography student), Rodney and Marsha (an ex-army couple) and Dudley (a Welsh divorcee.) I bent five tent pegs trying to lay the groundsheet, and Wayne took it badly. Disproportionately so, I felt: he called me an ass-wipe. I considered asking for an apology, but he was older than me and his crew-cut and hard eyes gave him the air of a mercenary. We were cell mates now, and I realised the only way we would get through this was if we both stuck to our allotted roles, and it was clear he wasn't going to be the submissive one.

"Wayne Wyatt is the name, bro," was how he introduced himself to me. "Spit 'n vinegar is the family crest!"

He paused waiting for the usual guffaw that greeted the remark and when it didn't come, he added, "That's a bit of a joke, mate – it's what we always say, yeah?"

"Oh," I managed. "Ha."

I didn't sleep well that night. I was aware of Wayne's heavy breathing and the cloying fug emanating from his sebaceous skin. When I closed my eyes, I could see Johan hanging there. I tried my best to push him away, but it seemed to just bring him closer. When the rope broke and he came hurtling downwards, I felt like I was falling too and I cried out in anguish. Wayne kicked me and I was brought back to earth, but not for long; as soon as I drifted off again I was back with Johan. He had finally reached the ground and was looking around him, frightened. I felt concerned for him and then saw my father as a young medical student in a brightly starched housecoat rushing towards him. He bent down over him and stared, until a disarmingly pretty nurse, who looked the split of Lucy, the young private school girl, came to tell him that a young boy was waiting to see him. It was me, aged eight, in tight blue shorts and a helmet of blond hair, but he didn't recognise me. He poked at my kidneys in a desultory manner, and I was about to shout something, to tell him who I really was, and perhaps I did, as Wayne kicked me again.

Chapter 2

WE CAMPED FOR the next few nights along the motorways of France and Spain. Over breakfast one morning, we watched on as the stark reality of all that lay ahead dawned on one poor couple. The sudden realisation of what it meant to be cramped in the back of a truck, sleeping in a tent, cooking on a fire and relieving oneself in the woods for the next six months proved too much, and they lunged at each other – clawing at one another's throats like cats. It happened seemingly for no reason, like the way a forest fire erupts in summer. The couple – Rita, a cranky Tasmanian with a forehead like boiled ham, and her partner Vinnie, from the Isle of Man, whose eyes were stony and cold – piled into each other like demented pit bulls. It seemed to have been sparked by a comment he made about a dint on the lip of her enamel mug. He accused her of not looking after her things. It seems inconsequential now, but we all had so few possessions and were going to have to look after them for so long that we became obsessive. We had been given one mug, plate and set of cutlery each that would have to do us for the entire trip. Rita had already lost her spoon, and the chip in her mug seemed like the beginning of a pattern. When Vinnie made some comment under his breath about it, she just turned around and lunged at him, giving him a sudden low tackle which sent him hurtling out the back of the truck. He lay there slightly concussed for a moment until Joe, the mechanic, helped him to his feet, and then he came back at her, lashing out with his arms flailing. A few of us came forward and managed to pull them apart, but not before they had done each other real damage. Vinnie's cheeks and scalp were bleeding, and there were bits of flesh beneath Rita's nails. She swore she was going to leave the trip, and he said he would be glad to see the back of her and called her a whore. It turned out to be the highlight of the day.

Things had got so grim in those first few days that we had all considered leaving at some point. The tents had to be pitched and latrines dug in frozen earth, and it was proving impossible to find enough dry wood for the fire in the desolate lay-bys in which we camped. Most mornings the fire took for ever to light, and when it finally did flicker into meagre, spluttering life, there weren't enough logs to keep it going long enough to cook the porridge properly, so we had to swallow it back cold and lumpy.

From a purely selfish perspective, I would have been glad to get rid of both Rita and Vinnie. Neither was the sort of person you'd choose to go on an extended expedition with, and we would all have appreciated the extra space. There was very little room on board for nineteen, not including leader and mechanic, especially since we had not yet learnt to pack the tents properly and there were rods and flysheets severing the space like a cat's cradle. I suppose I hadn't given much thought to the sort of people who would be aboard the truck, but if I considered it at all, I presumed they would be open and adventurous. People keen to explore other cultures and new experiences. I was already realising how wrong I had been. Each of us had very different reasons for being there – most of them negative. What united us was the desire to escape.

Henry, a sixty-year-old quantity surveyor, was the oldest amongst us. He was so drugged on sedatives that he appeared genial at first, avuncular almost, but one glance at his flickering eyelids showed he was liable to erupt Vesuviusly at any moment.

"I'm telling you . . . I've worked hard, I have – damn hard to make myself what I am today," he'd say in the commanding voice of middle management, "and now it's time to let my hair down."

I prayed the sedatives would last him until Kenya. He had brought with him a divorcee named Mildred. She was tiny and rotund, and had once been a well-regarded sign painter in Glasgow. Now bankrupt and bitter, she had somehow convinced Henry to pay for the trip to escape her creditors. The two of them appeared to be locked in some type of mutual pact that I longed to know the terms of. It must have been the reason why they were both so highly strung. I liked to imagine they had pulled off some terrific stunt or scam before leaving and were using the trip as a hideout. Who would ever think of looking for them here, on a truck crossing Africa? Or, perhaps, they hadn't actually committed anything yet, just set it up; put in motion some dastardly plan that would only come to fruition once they were safely away and untraceable to it. If they were ever found out, the rest of us might eventually be called in as alibis. I found it suspicious how they both had a neurotic need to know the date at all times. The further we got into Africa, the more urgently they needed to know, and the harder it was for us to be sure, since there were no newspapers and no decipherable radio signals where we would eventually end up.

Of course, I may have been completely wrong about the two of them. It was just a hunch, mainly triggered by the fact that elements of their back story didn't add up. If they were involved in something, it definitely revolved around Mildred, as she was clearly the more anxious of the two, but that might have been simply due to the fact that she took fewer prescription drugs. Henry's shiftiness was further heightened by his attire. He was always impeccably dressed, as though he had been teleported directly from his office to the back of the truck, or else that he expected to be hauled up in front of a judge at any moment. He had a butterfly-collar shirt complete with cufflinks that he wore on Sundays and special occasions, but even his normal daily shirts were tailored and sometimes monogrammed. It made the whole trip seem like an extravagant incentive-type event that he'd organised for his employees.

"It is important that we present the right front to the world," he said in his sonorous, managerial tone when someone questioned the suitability of his clothes. "First impressions are half the battle. Furthermore, nothing gives one a feeling of inward stability more than being well dressed."

He tucked his chin in broodingly when he said this and chortled like a hen for added emphasis.

I suppose we were all clinging on to some safety blanket for reassurance. Stella, my cooking partner, had had a quilted, eiderdown dressing-gown made especially for her for the journey, which she spent all day snuggled up in as though preparing for hibernation. I noticed I was becoming overly dependent on the "fun pack" of mini Mars Bars in my locker. I had smuggled them in in outright violation of truck regulations, which stated that all food was to be kept in the communal larder underneath the chassis to prevent rat infestation. The Mars Bars were my sedatives, and I would sneak off once a day to eat a few when no one was looking.

It's unfair to say the group was without any modicum of a sense of adventure. It was just that what was there was feeble and undeveloped. We were the runts of the adventuring world. In previous generations our sort would probably have made up the foot soldiery of the Crusades, or the Scramble for Africa or the Conquistador expeditions. We were simply too unimaginative, too weak, to be adventurous in our own right and thus were forced to pay a thousand pounds to a company in Wales to provide us with the experience. They supplied the truck, the driver, the mechanic, some tents and pots and pans, and enough fuel to get us across Africa. The rest was up to us – to sit still and be quiet, to savour the hardship, debasement and muted glory such a trip entailed. I suppose there was a masochistic streak in all of us that wanted to test ourselves, probably fuelled by a desire for approval, or at least attention. Low self-esteem was the one thing we all had in common. We hoped Africa would be an alembic that would convert our vapid hearts to those of heroes. The letters home would be a vital element in this. It was through these we would prove ourselves to those that mattered most – the unaffectionate fathers, disparaging work colleagues, indifferent siblings, dismissive ex-girlfriends – all those who didn't value us for the superheroes we occasionally believed we could be. We were like children swinging ever higher on a faulty swing, showing off to Mummy, unaware of the catastrophe that was bound to befall us.

To be fair, things were a little bit different with me. There was no one at home that I really wanted to impress. I would not be sending many letters home, nor, for that matter, would I be receiving many. I simply needed to get away. After my dad had died, nothing made sense any more – not that it had made all that much sense before either, but now things had become unbearable. On top of that were the dreams that had been messing with my mind for months now. I had to find some answers to who and what I was, and I knew I was never going to find them at home. I had to get away, to go out and explore the world, and this was the cowardly, ham-fisted way I had chosen.

Lest I paint too bleak a picture, I should make clear that by the time we had reached southern Spain I was beginning to enjoy certain elements of the trip. There was a great freedom to our odd existence of sitting passively with no purpose other than to be driven south across the planet for as long as it took to reach Nairobi. It was almost Zen in its futility; a sort of childlike existence where you take each day as it comes, happily going along with whatever you're told to do. For the first time in years, I had no agenda. I had given over my power and returned to an infantile state. Each day was spent sitting on a bench being gently lulled by the truck's motion into a lobotomised stupor, only becoming animated again at night when we had to pitch camp and cook dinner.

I was reassured by the fact that we were beginning to be more at ease with one another as we got to know each other a bit more. We began to meld a little, not so much in harmony, but more in apathy. We become inured to each other. Things that had seemed annoying at first became less so as we lost touch with the triangulation points of our previous lives. We cared less about our appearances and hygiene – mirrors, hairbrushes, make-up, soap were stowed away as the common smell and look of the tribe took over.

Within a week, we had reached the Costa del Sol, which in the grey November drizzle had the tragic air of an auditorium in daylight. Everyone had stories to tell about previous holidays there – half-remembered drunken exploits that all seemed to have been either "fucking mad" or "awesome". I had never been here before and found it in equal parts fascinating and unsettling – like the feeling you get seeing an ant's nest, or cattle copulating. The others seemed so at home in the grim bars and stale dance clubs that lined the streets, and I worried about what would happen when we got to Africa – when we were finally, and irrevocably, rent from the umbilical cord of all we knew. I felt the nurses would be fine – they had survived everything the NHS could throw at them – and Henry and Mildred had age on their side, but for the rest, myself included, I was genuinely worried. We savoured our last fry-up in a Union-Jack-bedecked sports bar, and in a copy of *The Sun* posted above a urinal, I learnt that Margaret Thatcher had resigned the previous day. Her talons had at last been wrenched from office, and in her entrails I conspired to read an omen for the trip.

That evening a boat ferried us out from the Rock of Gibraltar and across the Mediterranean through heavy rain. It was still pouring as we docked at an expanse of concrete stretching a mile into Africa. This was Ceuta, a last relic of Europe's colonial stranglehold on the continent, and now principally a duty-free port run by Spain. It was now a focus of attention for immigrants looking for a chink in the bulwark of fortress Europe. It was incredibly ugly, with concrete silos and corrugated hangars bristling with razor wire and bathed in eerie, phosphorous floodlight. Infra-red cameras followed our every move, and I noticed tiny shreds of clothing snagged in the high chain fences, and even the tattered shoe of some poor girl.

Suzi pulled up at a twenty-four-hour store which had patrol dogs circling menacingly outside. She told us to go in and buy as much alcohol as we could afford. The journey ahead was going to be tough, she said. Some of the countries would be Muslim and therefore dry, and we would need as much alcohol as we could carry to make it through. One of the nurses asked if it wasn't against the law to bring alcohol into Muslim countries, and Suzi, by way of reply, pulled up a floorboard revealing a hidden cavity beneath.

"It fits sixty litres, if packed right," she said. "It's up to all of you to make sure no one finds it. Do whatever you have to."

"What do you mean?" said Felicity, a fastidious district matron from the Peak District, who always sought clarification on every remark, like an overly eager apprentice or insecure mature student.

"What?" Suzi snapped.

She was fast losing patience with all of us, particularly Felicity. She loathed our ignorance. She loved Africa and appreciated being paid to travel through it, but hated the fact that she had to bring us along the way.

She grimaced at Felicity, breathed in deeply and began to explain in a remedial tone: "At almost every border, I'll be up in the cab dealing with the carnet" (the *carnet de passage*, the truck's documentation). "I won't be with you. A guard might come back to you and ask for a quick inspection. If he finds the drink, every other overland truck that comes after us will be searched. Their floorboards will be ripped up and their drink confiscated. They will never forgive you. Your names will be up on the message board at the Thorn Tree Café in Nairobi even before you reach it, and they will beat the shit out of you when you turn up. Is that clear enough? When trucks coming from Nairobi realise that we are the ones who screwed it all up for them, they will come after us. They'll slash our tyres, smash our windows, whatever . . . inflict misery. Do you understand yet, Felicity?"

Felicity snorted peevishly. I think she was imagining being back in her own environment and Suzi coming to her asking for a home-carer's allowance for her dying mother and her ticking the *no* box out of pure malice. She was used to getting her own way and, furthermore, was used to having the bloody obvious explained to her in moronic detail over and over again, and in turn explaining the bloody obvious to other morons.

"I am not pissing about here," Suzi shouted. "This is serious shit. You will not get through the months ahead without alcohol, OK?"

We nodded.

"Don't screw this up."

We nodded again with increased conviction and filed off into the store like chastened recruits determined to do the right thing. By pooling our last *pesetas*, we found we had enough for two cases of no-brand gin and vodka and a case of whisky, and we stored these in the cavity just as Suzi instructed. Afterwards she explained that since there was nowhere we could pitch a tent in the concrete-covered port, we'd have to bed down underneath the chassis of the truck. I didn't fancy the idea of waking in the night with an oily axel looming over my head and instead found an old cargo crate over by a stevedore's hut and lay out my roll mat there, pulling a tarpaulin over me for warmth.

I was confronted by Johan again. He was just setting up the stepladder beneath the rafter, lining it up with the rope. It was the moan that escaped from him afterwards that frightened me the most. It reminded me of the sound my father had made in his last days in hospital.

At some point, it was impossible to tell when, as the sodium glare of lights fooled the sky, I woke to find a rat scurrying across my feet and leapt up in fright, throwing the tarpaulin off me as I watched the rat's horizontally erect tail recede into the darkness. My heart pounding, I didn't stop to look around me, just ran towards the opening until I tripped on something

– some object near the entrance – and came crashing down on to the metal floor. The crate rang out, resounding across the port like a gigantic bell. I pawed about frantically, trying to get back up, but my knee was bruised and numb. Suddenly my fingers touched something warm and fleshy. I cursed, shooting to my feet again as fast as I could, but a stab of pain jolted through my thigh, and I thought I might fall at any second. It was only when I was outside the crate and looking back that I noticed the body, reluctantly shaking itself awake and getting to its feet.

"*Pardon, monsieur. Pardon,*" it said, coming out after me, cowering, one hand above its head.

It was a boy, about sixteen. We stared at each other as he emerged into the blinding orange light. He was wearing flip-flops and a ragged cotton T-shirt. I guessed he must be a local street child or a migrant, but it was clear he had no idea who I was, or what I was doing coming at him from the back of an empty crate.

"Don't send me back," he was saying in French.

I sighed, collapsing on to a large mushroom-shaped mooring and rubbing my sore knee. The patrol dogs were still barking, edgy from the noise of the crate.

He squatted at the foot of a hexagonal mast that went soaring into the sky, raining light back down on us from six massive metal-grilled bulbs. His skin was mottled with pale blotches and he was very thin.

"Where are you from?" I asked.

"Burkina Faso."

It was somewhere south of me. That was all I knew, although I was aware that I would be travelling through it in the months ahead.

"Ouagadougou," he said.

I mimed incomprehension. Later I found out that this was the capital.

We sat looking out at the Mediterranean in silence, and after a while I asked what he was doing here. He told me eight of his friends had set off from his district months before, but most got separated along the way. At the Moroccan border, there were only two left: himself and a distant cousin who was heavily pregnant. They had been chased by guards, and she had collapsed and gone into labour. Her baby had come out feet first. The guards had wanted to help; one of them had tried turning it, but he failed, and they had to bury the two of them under a layer of dead grass.

The boy just laid out the story coldly, looking out toward Europe the whole time. Dawn was coming up, and he said he had better find a new place to hide. He sneaked off, and I was left looking around the empty port, trying not to cry. I unlocked the axe from its clasp at the back of the truck and began to chop wood for breakfast – slamming at the logs blindly, furiously; missing with every second blow.

"Whoa there! Wha' you up to, mate?" Norman said hoarsely, rolling sleepily out from underneath the back suspension leaves.

"You're late," I said, mid swing of the axe. "You're on breakfast duty and there's no kindling, and the jerry cans need to be filled."

"Yeah, yeah," he said dismissively, "don't go getting all uppity, you twit. Everything in its own time. Get your knickers untwisted there like a good boy and go put that bloody axe away before you do yourself some damage."

Chapter 3

WE DROVE STRAIGHT up through dry scrub and barren hillsides into the Atlas mountains. Above us were peaks bathed in a brilliant pageantry of colours: blushing rose, glowing gold and mauve. Below were mud-brick Berber homes built on terraces near rivers fringed with date palms, and all around them were narrow cultivated strips of almond trees and sashaying patches of wheat. As the truck swung around hair-pin bends, sending the rear body lurching over the edge, we could look down and see, far below, magnificent palm-filled gorges nestled in crevices gouged out of the earth's crust.

We reached Chefchaouen, a quiet blue and white Berber village, by evening. It seemed a place out of time, with cobblestone streets, narrow alleyways, an ancient *medina* and oil lamps. Up until the Spanish invaded in 1920, only three Europeans had ever been there: two missionaries, one of whom was poisoned, and a journalist who was attacked for being a "Christian dog". It had been a haven for revolutionaries and smugglers for centuries, and still seemed full of shady Moroccan mobsters in cheap Seventies leisure suits. I watched as they loaded up the boots and roofs of rusty Mercedes cars with heavy sacks and amorphous bundles wrapped in hessian. These might have contained rice and beans, but the smell of hashish in the air made me wonder. With its twin industries of drug and immigrant smuggling, and its dry scrub landscape, Chefchaouen reminded me of a Mexican border town – Tijuana or Juarez – as if all First World societies needed shady, vice-ridden border towns at their southern extremities to cater for the illicit.

We pulled in to an olive grove above the town to camp for the night. Shepherds were herding under trees, and a young girl was sorting chickpeas and singing an Arab pop song. In the distance, lush patches of hemp swayed in the breeze. The shepherds stared on as we pitched camp, one eye on their flock, the other on us. The sight of them, dressed in traditional clothing – *djellabas*, *burnouses* and leather sandals – astounded me. It was the first time I had been confronted with the timeless existence that was continuing all over the world – as if an old storybook had come to life.

One of the shepherds approached us hesitantly, offering firewood and herbs while his friends looked on eagerly, goading him with quiet mutterings. A *muezzin's* wailing call to prayer echoed in the distance. I noticed the nurses clinging warily together as the man approached, and Vinnie made some joke in a stage whisper about "ragheads wiping their arses". That was the only acknowledgement anyone made of the man; otherwise we ignored him as he quietly proffered his gifts. He looked around him anxiously now and again, at one point turning back to his friends for moral support, but they signalled to him to stay a while longer, urging him with plaintive faces to be bold and engage us directly. I watched as he steeled himself and finally went over towards Stevi, who was pretending to busy himself doling out measures of whisky into our enamel mugs. The shepherd walked right up to him and tapped him on the shoulder. At this Stevi spun around suddenly, raising his hands in a comedic way as though surprised to see someone there. The group tittered. Stevi stuck out his hand with an exaggerated, foppish flourish like a jester or a camp comedian in a music-hall show, or those humiliating variety performances the British put on for their queen.

"Hiya, mate," Stevi trilled in a jocular sing-song. "How's the shepherding business going, then?"

Everyone burst out laughing, except the shepherd, who stared in incomprehension.

"Baa, baa," Stevi mimicked, wagging a false tail and doing the thumbs-up sign to try and get the point across.

Everyone found this hilarious, but the shepherd was lost. He looked around him with concern, trying to make sense of it. I could hear his friends urging him on with the same sucking sounds they used to soothe their herd. Finally, he lay the bundle of herbs down beside us and stepped backwards.

"Look, mate," Vinnie said, "we don't want any of your knickknacks, right? We're not interested."

"Not interested," Felicity enunciated helpfully.

The man turned and backed away, leaving the herbs on the ground for us.

"Bloody A-rabs, they'll try and sell you their granny, eh?" Henry said jovially.

Once the shepherd had made it back to his friends, they gathered around him encouragingly, patting him on the back and murmuring things, trying to make it all seem OK, to make it seem as though he hadn't just publicly lost face. An ominous feeling took hold of me. I knew Morocco was famous for its hawkers, and I could understand why we might have been a bit wary of them; it was all new to us after all and we hadn't come to terms with things yet. Still these were the first Africans we had encountered on the trip – ordinary country folk trying to be friendly, a welcoming party from Mother Africa perhaps. Our behaviour didn't augur well for the rest of the trip.

I was still mulling over the incident an hour later, wondering what the others had been expecting; had they hoped Africa would be like it was in colonial times when you never needed to have contact with locals if you didn't want to? There was always an underling to act as an interlocutor. Perhaps they hoped we'd create a tiny bastion of Britishness on board the truck – a citadel on wheels.

Luke, an amateur athlete in his mid thirties, sauntered over from the fire and laid a hand on my shoulder.

"How's it hangin', boy?" he said.

He was from the East End of London and made his living selling second-hand pianos in the Old Brampton market. From his long Samsonesque curls and the ruggedness of his cheeks, I thought at first he might be a fisherman. I imagined him battling Hebridean seas on a listing trawler – that was until I heard the accent. His clipped London accent always made me think of Ovaltine and nylon stockings and the whole Dunkirk spirit – the dauntless optimism of Cockneys during the Blitz, or at least the image of them portrayed by Ealing comedies and caricatured by Monty Python.

"You don't look so dapper," he said. "Are you in the dumps?"

I shrugged and he settled himself down beside me.

"See that star over there," he said, "shepherd's star – the first in the evening sky. Just you watch how those woolly blobs on the mountain all came hurrying down now. The first time I saw that was with my mum in Kent – it must be thirty years ago now. We were off hop picking and she pointed up and says, "You just watch, son, that star will pull every sheep around down the hillside. It's 'cause it's got a magnet inside," she said. Every night from then on, we'd be sitting around the fire, our hands cut from the hops and our spines sore, and we'd watch the flock trailing home. Most summers, I still go to Kent, but there ain't many sheep there no more, that's for sure. Bloody big motorway built right through."

This was Luke's first time outside England. He had come because of a few stray lines in a Van Morrison song about a "sense of wonder". Something about coming to "lift your fiery vision bright . . . to bring you a sense of wonder in the flame". The idea had intrigued him, and he became convinced that he could find his own sense of wonder in Africa. He had looked for the cheapest way of getting here, and his search had led him here, to this truck. I tried quizzing him on what he thought a sense of wonder actually entailed, but he'd never say, except that the nearest he had got to it up to this was when he was running: towards the end of a 100-metre sprint when he was certain he was about to trim milliseconds off his previous best, a feeling of potency would surge through his veins, a wild, untrammelled feeling that brought new reserves of energy with it. It came only after he had broken through every pain barrier, overcome every fear. He would emerge the other side feeling as though he could merge with the wind. It was frightening and exciting, he said, and made the rest of life muffled by comparison.

Luke was a dreamer, an idealist who wasn't prepared to play other people's games. Within a day of leaving Ramsgate, the others had labelled him "the clown" because of his bold, jolly features and boisterous manner. They called him "hippy" too because of his long hair. He was a bit of a joke as far as they were concerned, and although he didn't seem to react in any discernible way to their taunts, on the evening of the second day he suddenly fell silent and didn't utter another word until we touched land in Africa a week later. It was an act of sublime resistance, so subtle that the others didn't even see it for what it was. From the odd glance between us during the week, I could see that he shared some of my disenchantment with the trip.

He looked across at the others now sitting hunched over the fire and then at the herbs, which still lay where the shepherd had left them.

"It's not good, Mocha," he said, shaking his head and grimacing.

"No," I said.

Mocha was the name the group had given me after trying half-heartedly to pronounce my real name once or twice. I had never had a nickname before; up until this everyone had always been happy to call me by my given name. Although the nickname bothered me a little, I had enough sense not to protest. At least it wasn't the clown, or the patsy.

Luke stared into the fire, frowning for a moment, then broke into a mischievous smile.

"I think I know what we can do," he said.

"What?" I asked.

He gave me one of the frequent winks that accentuated his talk and gestured for me to follow him. I raised my eyebrows questioningly, but he wouldn't explain any further. He just set off, bounding across the hillside on his angular, hare-like legs, never once looking back to see if I was still coming.

"Where are we going?" I tried calling as he disappeared over the brow of a hill.

Finally, he stopped at a rough stone hut and waited for me to catch up. An old moss-cushioned olive tree with its bark badly gnawed by goats was growing out of the side wall. I had noticed a few of these huts, used by shepherds for shelter at night, scattered across the mountain. Luke knocked hesitantly on the plank door, and a hollow-faced man with a moustache peered out. He eyed us suspiciously at first through a narrow chink, but then flung back the door, ushering us in. The bare stone walls were held together with crumbling patches of plaster, leaving large gaps where the wind blew straight through. Four of the shepherds from earlier were crouched on the ground around a meagre fire. They were sharing a large pipe of pungent hashish and immediately offered it to us. I hesitated, but Luke winked, and I realised the pipe was as much a gesture of friendship as a door into their world – or a stepping stone, at least, to help ford the chasm.

It tasted of sweet smoked apples, but had an acrid, earthy undercurrent that reminded me of a peat fire. I coughed a bit, and they handed me a cup of mint tea, smiling broadly, and then we just sat there for a while as they talked among themselves. Finally, one of them, who had a bit of English, asked me what we wanted. I had no idea and looked to Luke. Already the drug was beginning to kick in, casting its spell on the surroundings. Luke explained that we just wanted to say hi. When this was translated they all laughed, and I found myself laughing too. The eldest of the shepherds began telling us a story about how Africa was like a lion, or at least that's what I thought he said at first. He was speaking in French, and I was having to translate for Luke and couldn't always keep up. He was halfway though the story before I realised he wasn't saying lion at all, but onion, and I had to go back and retranslate the story. He said if you cut it with a knife it won't bleed, but instead will make you cry. (I was wondering why a lion wouldn't bleed if you cut it, or how it could make you cry without killing you at the same time.) He went on to say that if you care for it and cook it gently, it will be sweeter than caramel. It will feed you and nourish you and protect you from disease. He told us we would never understand this place – you can keep peeling it back layer after layer, and even when it's all gone, what you're left with is still Africa.

We sat by the fire for a few hours, not speaking much, just gazing dreamily into it, until a dog began to howl in the distance and the elder Berber shook the others to their feet and told them to go check the flock. We watched as they disappeared into the bold, blue moonlight, and then decided it was time to head back.

We were walking back along the trail and were almost in sight of the truck when someone sneaked up and snagged my arm from behind. It was one of the younger shepherds. He had called into the cabin earlier but hadn't stayed long. He was wearing a red Mod-like cardigan over his *djellaba* and looked about seventeen, his moustache more fuzz than bristle.

"You wan par'y?" he hissed in barely discernible English, with his finger up to his lips conspiratorially.

Luke and I looked at him uncomprehendingly, our minds still addled by the evening.

"Party?" he hissed again.

We looked at each other, shrugged and set off with him back up the hill. I was about to ask him more when a battered Mercedes with broken headlamps came careering down the track, stopping only inches in front of us.

"Get in," said our friend, pushing us in on top of a boy and a girl squashed into the back seat. He got in after us, holding the door open so that we would all fit, and with his other arm shook hands with us and introduced himself as Mustafa. As we bumped our way along the track, the five of us melted into one sweaty organism, until eventually we clambered out at a dishevelled-looking shrine and descended down a track into a low gorge. We were walking through quite dense forest, and from down below the sound of rhythmic drumming and hand clapping was filtering up. It mingled with the sweet-smelling junipers and the busy murmuring of the others. I began for the first time on the trip to feel genuinely excited about what lay ahead, as though this whole thing really was a great adventure, and not some military manoeuvre or grim migration. The closer we approached, the louder the music became, and I could hear words being sung over it – rough, wild singing in a high voice, repeated by others in a call-and-response fashion. The words were slurred and resonant, and seemed pleasantly out of syncopation: someone would call *Allah El Awaldin,* followed by a general reply of *Ah-Haweyeh,* a beat and a half later.

The base of the gorge was flat and lush, and at its centre was an encampment with tents and a gas generator and stalls selling food. We headed for the largest tent, which was filled with people dancing. Inside, the singing and clapping remained constant, luring my mind into it like a metronome. Mustafa beckoned us to sit down on a rug near the musicians and fetched skewers of lamb for us.

"*Salaam!*" he said with a joyous grin, handing us each a skewer and lighting a long slender pipe of opium for himself. The music, though repetitive, sent currents of passion and exuberance sweeping through me like breath. Women in birthday-candle-pink *djellabas* and men in more sombre robes were dancing furiously in a line; the men's hats were covered in beads and cowry shells with long tassels that spun out frantically as they danced, carving halos in the air. The women flicked their wrists like radar searching for signals, and as their passion grew their heads swayed, sending their braided hair flying out around them.

I looked around the tent not quite believing I was really there. An older woman broke through the crowd and marked out a space on the floor with an invisible line. She pulled out two knives and started slashing her forearms with them.

"Under spell," Mustafa said. "Feel no pain."

I raised my eyebrows dubiously.

"Or, not too much," he corrected himself.

A series of red welts rose on her skin, but no blood – they were like bad jellyfish stings. At the end she collapsed in a heap on the floor. Mustafa suddenly pulled Luke and myself to our feet and told us to dance. A young girl with henna tattoos showed me how to move my body. In spite of her veil, I could tell she was beautiful by the way her eyes shimmered, dancing like damsel nymphs trapped in an inkwell. We exchanged awkward smiles – two uncomprehending cultures signalling good intentions.

I noticed the woman who had been dancing earlier collapsed in a corner, the welts on her arms still raw and sore-looking.

"Is she OK?" I asked Mustafa.

"Yes, she has much practice. She is just tired now. It is very spiritual, very draining."

"Why does she do that to herself?"

"Showing she is in the hands of Allah – nothing can hurt her. It is best if people don't crowd around now; they must leave her in peace. Often people try to touch the blood to get the blessing. This is not good. You can get very sick and even die because of infection. Maybe the knife is dirty or someone has many germs when they are touching you to get *baraka*. A girl in my village was sick like this, very sick. I spent three nights with her telling her to get better."

"Oh," I said, not understanding.

"She went into deep sleep, between life and death," he said, "and I had to tell her that she could come back if she likes . . . or not. In the end her body cleaned the poison and she came back."

A little while later the generator broke, and Mustafa decided we should be getting back.

Everyone was asleep at the campsite. I sneaked in beside Wayne and lay there for hours, dazed and enthused, listening to him snoring sonorously beside me. It was my first real night under African stars – leaving aside the previous night on the nasty, Spanish-owned dock. I was already beginning to see how I might be able to circumvent the claustrophobia of the group – to play whatever game was required of me, but on *my* terms.

Chapter 4

I WAS STILL seeing Johan most nights. He had a remarkable ability to
insert himself into any dream. I suppose I sort of knew what he was
doing there, what my mind was trying to tell me, but I hadn't come to
terms with it yet. I had rarely dreamt with such lucidity and presumed it
must have had something to do with the uncertainty of life here, or possibly it was a result of sleeping out in the open. I asked Luke about it, and he
claimed that the filaments of our cheap army tents acted as dream weavers.
He said the gypsies who used to pick hops with him in Kent always claimed
they dreamt more intensely out of doors. Houses made them sick, he said.

I realised, of course, that the dreams were connected with my father.
Relatives had told me that I might feel like I was going out of my mind at
times in the months ahead. It was quite normal, they assured me, during
the first year of bereavement. I had never lost someone close before, but
the one thing I did know was that it could bring you to the edge. I could
see there was some slight connection between Johan and my father. It was
my father who had told me about him after all and they both had a love of
the Alps, but there the similarity ended; in every other respect, my father
could not have been more different. He was a donnish, ascetic character
with a love of antiquity and a weakness for good food and wine. He had
none of the sternness or athleticism that I imagined Johan had. They were
definitely different people. I wasn't simply dreaming of my father. At least,
I didn't think I was.

It was around about this time that I began keeping a note of the dreams. Each morning, having written my account of the previous day in my diary, I would jot down a few notes about the night before. I suppose I thought it might help make sense of things, put them in context. I had read Carlos Castaneda in school and had been impressed by his accounts of training the mind to become conscious in dreams. He claimed that if you could awaken your mind during sleep you could actually control what happened in the dream. I had always liked that idea, and I suppose I felt that if I could learn what he had meant by it, I might be able to get closer to my dad. But I soon realised that becoming conscious in dreams wasn't as easy as Castaneda made it out to be. In fact, it was near on impossible, and I gave up trying. I still kept on writing the dream diary though, partly so that I could tell the stories to Natasha and Lucy, the young London girls, later. I had happened to mention Johan to them one morning, and they were so intrigued that they insisted I keep them up to date on everything that happened. I tried explaining that things weren't always sequential or even coherent (these were dreams after all), but Lucy dismissed this and launched into a riveting account of a dream she had had before her French A-level exam in which she had murdered a man. All through the exam she could still feel the lingering sense of the barrel of the gun between her fingers and smell the odour of smouldering gunpowder in the air – she could even taste that familiar gagging fireworks taste at the back of her throat. I was amazed by the intensity of her recollection. She was such a sweet, refined girl, with a genuinely loving heart and the face of a baby marmoset, yet she could talk assuredly about murdering a man, even about where she had got the gun and how she made sure to point it towards the left side of his brain to ensure maximum damage.

The night of the knife dance was the first time I became aware of myself in the dreams. Johan was cowering on the boathouse floor, and I noticed a figure climbing up the hill towards him. It was Lucy again. She occupied a certain proportion of my thoughts during the day, so it was no surprise that she would appear at night too. She was wearing tight blue shorts and no shoes. She looked nonchalantly at Johan, and then, turning determinedly away from him, she spotted me climbing up after her. The day was hot and her long thin legs shimmered with a sheen of sweat. She wiped her brow, ignoring Johan completely, and came hurrying towards me, saying something that I couldn't remember when I awoke.

"You took drugs last night, didn't you?" Norman said when I stuck my head out of the tent in the morning. "You stupid pillock!"

"Is he right?" Suzi said, striding over as soon as she heard. "Did you smoke with the shepherds?"

Luke was standing behind her rubbing his brow wearily. I was thinking of saying that it was really only a stepping stone to help ford the chasm, but thought the better of it.

"They bloody did an' all," Duncan said. "Luke as good as told me. Look at the faces on them: guilty as shit, bloody dope-heads."

"I'm serious," Suzi said. "I've told you what I'd do if I caught anyone taking drugs on the trip."

In Ramsgate she had laid out her cardinal rules, and top of the list was no drugs.

"Maybe," I muttered.

"Maybe, what?" she said. "Think about your reply, 'cause if you smoked you're gone."

She waited for a reply. I looked at the ground, and Luke began whistling the solo harmonica tune from *A Fist Full of Dollars*. Enraged, she spun around to him and jabbed him in the shoulders.

"I mean it," she said. "If you get kidnapped or stabbed or arrested, I have to deal with it. It's up to me. I have to get you idiots across Africa in one piece; and if you screw it up, I'll dump you in the middle of nowhere, I swear I will."

There had been unfortunate incidents on almost all of her previous trips. People had died, or almost died. She had had to ring home and tell parents their child had been swept away by rapids or contracted hepatitis B or lost sight in one eye. She had had to ring children, too, to tell them their parent had suffered a heart attack in the desert. She was determined this time that things would work out. Nineteen of us had signed on in Ramsgate, and she would bring all of us back no matter what. To achieve this we would have to submit unquestioningly to her rule. It was the only way she could keep us safe, she said.

"If you get busted here, you're in prison for life," she had explained. "They don't mess around. You're just rich white bait to them, and they'll dangle you over your parents or government until they get what they want."

As punishment, she told Luke and me to go dig the rubbish hole, insisting that it be the full metre square and at least a metre deep. Up until now we had been digging shallow trenches and barely covering them with soil. Suzi claimed that this was the sort of shoddiness that would kill us later on. Once the weather hotted up further south, she said, a shallow pit would lure snakes, rats and killer spiders right into the camp. If we wanted to survive, we would have to cop ourselves on.

It took the best part of an hour for Luke and me to dig the hole with pickaxes and shovels to Suzi's satisfaction and fill it again once we'd thrown in the few empty tins and packets from the night before. By the time we had it all done, everyone else was on the truck waiting for us, and some locals were already poking at the hole to sift through whatever we had discarded. We locked the shovel and pickaxe in their clasps and banged on the roof, signalling we were ready to move out. Suzi had asked us to use the intercom that was connected to the cab to communicate with her, but we preferred rattling the roof bars. It made us feel more gung-ho, more like the adventurers that we definitely were not.

We had driven less than a kilometre when Suzi buzzed through on the intercom to ask whether Joe, the mechanic, was in the back with us. He wasn't. (Neither he nor Suzi ever sat with us. We were the punters, the live cargo, and beyond making sure we were fed and watered, they had as little to do with us during the day as possible.) Joe had gone missing before, but he normally turned up again before we pulled out of camp. Before leaving Australia, he had worked for years as a goldmine restorer. Companies would airlift him into old mines which had been abandoned due to low gold prices, and they'd leave him there for months at a time to overhaul all the machinery. He would have no contact with anyone or anything except the insides of old machines: crushers, scrubbers, diggers, winches. He'd take each one apart, replace every worn hose and cog, and undo the damage of years of dust storms and harsh sun. Other than the occasional airdrop of food and supplies, he'd be on his own for months, and so it was no surprise that he found life on the truck a little claustrophobic. As soon as we parked up for the night, he would head off on his own, walking far into the bush, sometimes only returning at dawn. He seemed to be able to survive on very little sleep and almost no food for days at a time. He was by far the most unassuming character on the truck, and in fact rarely spoke to anyone unless he had a few drinks taken. The only time I saw him at ease was when he was under the chassis of the truck or inside its engine. He loved our old Bedford M3, calling it his *Habibi*, which a local had told him was the Arabic for darling.

Suzi now went around us all asking us when we'd last seen him, but no one had a clear idea. She turned the truck around and headed back to the campsite. I could tell she was angry. She liked to think she was in control of everything, but in truth we were all completely dependent on Joe. Without him, the truck would hardly last a week. It was old and had already suffered a lifetime's abuse at the hands of ignorant cadets in the British army. By rights it should have been retired long ago, but the army had been too greedy to let it die gracefully and had sold it on to Suzi's boss for a song. The idea was that it would be reconditioned, then driven across Africa and shipped home, only to have to endure the same ordeal the following year and the year after that endlessly until it finally fell apart and was sold for scrap.

Without Joe's constant intercession, none of this would happen; none of us would be going anywhere. Only he could coax it to go where we needed it to.

"Maybe the ragheads took him," suggested Felicity when we reached the camp and found no sign of him. "Maybe they want a ransom."

"Hardly," said Suzi witheringly.

"No need to be crabby," Felicity said testily. "Constructive input, that's all I'm trying for here. We're a team now, Suzi, and we had better start acting like one."

I don't think Felicity had any idea how close to the edge she was skating. You simply did not answer Suzi back. Had Felicity had any social awareness skills at all, she would have known this. I imagined the trail of frustration and fury she must have left behind her in her place of work; the wounded egos and offended underlings that some poor HR officer was left to mollify. (Having said this, I nevertheless admired Felicity's sheer courage in standing up to Suzi. Certainly none of the rest of us would have dared.)

Suzi decided to send a group of us down to the town to look for Joe, while another group was told to make a quick count of the bottles under the floor to make sure he hadn't taken any and gone off to get drunk somewhere. Luke and I decided to make a detour via the shepherds to check whether they had seen him. But none of us had any luck. There was no sign of him, until finally around mid afternoon a pickup pulled in to the campsite driven by a man dressed in a grey canvas jacket and jeans with suspicious grass stains around the elbows and knees. Joe was crouching in the back, looking triumphant.

"Can you please pay this man whatever he wants?" he said cockily to Suzi, jumping out.

"Where the hell were you?!" she screamed.

"Looking for this," he said, holding up a threaded bolt exultantly. "And these!"

He threw her a bag of steel washers which she caught one-handed and hurled straight back at him, missing his mouth by inches.

"I woke in the night with that song," he said, catching the bag calmly in his palm, "you know the one: 'I'm going to wash that man right outta my hair . . .' You know it? 'I'm going to wash that man right outta my hair, I'm going to wash that man right outta my hair, and send him on his way.'"

"Are you insane?" Suzi exclaimed.

"So, I thought to myself, that's odd . . . why that one? And then it clicked – the washers, the 2 2/5 imperial washers! That's when I decided we had better replace the mounting block."

"What?" Suzi said.

"For the camshaft," he said, "obviously!"

He spoke with the assurance and ease of an indulgent monarch when he was discussing mechanical matters. It was remarkable because it was so at odds with his normal awkwardness. He knew he was in his element – a prodigy in a world of dunces.

"But it's fine," said Suzi.

"Maybe, but I reckon it's about to get crook."

"There's nothing wrong with it, Joe. It's perfect. Not even a rattle."

"Not now there isn't," Joe said airily. "But later. That's what the song was saying . . . it was a hint to get the washers."

There was little she could say to this. She paid the grey canvas man what he was looking for, and Joe set off to overhaul the mounting block.

He said it would take him the rest of the day. I was intrigued by the whole thing, not because it was weird that Joe regarded songs as being prophetic, but because I did too. Ever since I was a child, I would find myself humming a song over and over in my head and only later realise it had been trying to tell me something. Up until this, I had thought I was the only one.

So as not to waste the day completely, Suzi ordered us all to collect as much firewood as we could. We would need as many logs as would fit in the fuel racks for the Sahara, otherwise we'd be relying on a single gas cylinder strapped to the roof. At dusk when we all got back to the camp with our piles of wood, she ordered Luke and me to saw it up as a further punishment. She watched over us the whole time, bellowing out instructions as we tried to strap it securely to the chassis with chains.

I went to bed that night with my hands blistered from the saw and I slept fitfully. I tried reading for a while, but Wayne said my torch was keeping him awake. He said if he didn't get a full night's sleep he'd be crabby in the morning; *more* crabby I felt like saying, but I kept it to myself.

Despite the pains in my back and shoulders, I managed to sleep through most of the night until finally, sometime before dawn, I was woken again by Johan's screaming. When he hit the ground, he let out a roar and it woke me; I could feel the pain stabbing up his legs as if it were me who had fallen. I got such a bad cramp in the back of my shins that I had to drag myself out of the tent, pulling my lower half after me like a wounded animal.

Staggering to one foot, I cursed blindly, patting my sole tentatively on the ground to bring the blood back. Everyone was still asleep, oblivious to the vague glimmer of light in the eastern sky and the first lonely twittering of birds. I sighed resignedly, still scraping at the earth like a colt testing its muscles and rubbing my calves to make sure the spasms had fully passed. Once the pain had gone, I began making my way back inside the tent again, careful not to wake Wayne as I slipped in beside him. I was just zipping up the flysheet when I noticed a figure sitting alone at the fire staring straight at me. I was surprised that I hadn't seen him until now. The few smouldering embers of the fire which were left could hardly have offered the man much heat. From his clothes it looked like he was local. I glanced nervously back, a little embarrassed at having been observed in my ground pawing ritual. It was only when he pulled the hood off his head that I saw it was Mustafa. I unzipped the flaps again and clambered back out.

"What are you doing here?" I hissed.

"I didn't know which was you," he said, pointing at the tents.

I stared at him.

"I think, maybe I fell asleep for bit," he added.

I didn't say anything.

"My uncle says you should come with me," he said. "Maybe you can understand better the onion, yes?"

"Come where?"

"To my aunt. She is living further up – just one hours away, maybe two."

"We're leaving in the morning," I explained. "We're going to Fez."

He nodded for a while, considering this, then said, "I will take you there after, no problem."

"To Fez?" I said.

"Yes, yes," he said dismissively. "It's only over the mountain. Come now."

"Why?"

"We are friends," he said, as though that explained everything. "You will be seeing the farming in the hills. It is very beautiful, and my uncle too – other uncle up in mountains – very funny man."

I was trying to work out what was in it for him, why he was willing to drive me the whole way to Fez, or even if he actually meant it. I knew the route over the mountains was a lot shorter than by the main road, but I also knew it was not recommended for foreigners. It went straight through the main cannabis growing area and was controlled in parts by drug lords.

"Your friend comes too," Mustafa said, as though it was all sorted.

I decided to leave it up to Luke whether or not we should go and went over to his tent to wake him. Peeking inside, I found him lying wide awake, leaning up on his elbows looking at Holly, his tent partner, who was sleeping soundly. He was staring at her, awestruck by her beauty. She was by far the most beautiful of the lot of us – a slender, sallow-skinned, twenty-six-year-old from Suffolk, whose almond eyes and high jawbone reminded me of a gazelle. She had studied cartography in college and now wanted to get a more three-dimensional view of the world she had been poring over in 2-D for years. We all fancied her a bit, and by some fluke Luke had managed to wangle her as his tent partner on the first day. He was the only single-ton among us who had managed to get a partner of the opposite sex.

I pinched his toe, and reluctantly he tore his eyes away from Holly's chalk-textured breasts, which were rising and falling softly as she slept. He blinked dramatically at me, his eyes refocusing themselves, an expression of pleasure across his face. I whispered Mustafa's offer to him.

"Sounds great," he said immediately. "Let's get going."

He was already shimmying out of his long johns and putting on hiking pants as he spoke.

"Shouldn't we ask Suzi first?" I said.

Luke stopped to consider a moment and then said, "How about we leave her a note?"

"She won't like it," I said.

"Suzi is the *man*," Luke said after a moment. "I've spent my life running away from the *man*, and I'm not about to start kowtowing now."

Holly stirred, puckering up her face adorably as she did so.

"What's going on?" she said, dozily.

"We're just going away for a bit," Luke cooed. "We'll see you in Fez."

Holly frowned as she considered this; her wide eyes looking around her.

"You can have the tent to yourself for a bit," Luke said, soothingly. "Enjoy!"

"No," Holly said determinedly, her voice still hoarse with sleep. "Don't."

"Huh?" Luke said.

"Don't go," Holly said. "Or at least let me come . . ."

This surprised us. Holly had been noticeably reticent to connect with anybody or take part in any activities since the start. It was as if she had been left raw and wounded by something in the past and was now hiding out from the world, like an elegant Persian recovering under a hedgerow far from home after a bad injury. It had amazed everyone when she agreed to share a tent with Luke. No one could quite guess what her motivation was, and she just shrugged when Felicity had been tactless enough to ask.

We waited while she quickly threw on a fleece and some leggings, then we brought her out and introduced her to Mustafa. I could see a slight hesitation pass across his face, but he didn't say anything. He was still crouched over the embers, wrapped in his heavy wool cloak, picking the dirt out of his nails with a knife. I wondered again why Mustafa wanted us with him and why he had sat outside my tent waiting, but I put it behind me; at that stage I was looking for any excuse to get away for a bit. None of us needed much encouragement.

In the car on the way out of the camp, Mustafa explained that we'd be staying in his aunt's old house in the hills. He said it was a bit rundown, but the location was really beautiful. We had to go into town first to collect something from his uncle's and then we'd be on our way. At a cut-stone building with blue shutters which Mustafa said belonged to his cousin, we stopped for about twenty minutes while he went inside. He came out again in the company of a woman who was carrying two well-stuffed sleeping bags. He took these from her and put them into the boot. I pointed out that with Holly along we might need a third, but he told me not to worry.

We were hardly out of town before we came across the first roadblock, a haphazard sun-shelter with a strip of spikes thrown across the road. The fat, triple-belted officer got up from his bench and looked us over warily, asking to see our passports and check our belongings. Mustafa got out and politely led the guard off a few paces, and when he came back everything was a lot more friendly. The guard seemed meeker and treated Luke, in particular, with real deference, insisting on shaking hands with him and with me. When we tried showing him our passports, he waved them away magnanimously. When Mustafa asked him politely whether he wanted to check the boot, the officer insisted that there was no need. An expression of benevolence, or possibly relief, spread across the officer's face as he waved us off and wished us a good journey. More or less the same thing happened at the next two roadblocks: Mustafa got out, had a quick word with the guard, who then insisted on paying his respects to us and congratulated us on how pretty Holly was and sent us on our way. I had no idea what Mustafa was telling them, and when I tried asking him, he just said that the roadblocks were of no real importance, just a temporary measure to appease foreign governments. The king had always turned a blind eye on cannabis cultivation in the Rif Mountains, as it was the only crop that grew well in the barren soil; every other plant turned out as stunted and sick looking as the few pine trees that clung to the ridges. The crop was vital to the local economy and had transformed a poor, backward region into the primary source of Morocco's hard currency. "Green oil" was what the locals called it.

It was noon when we reached the village, pulling up outside the old farm house, which was damp and basic and had no electricity other than a solar panel connected to a big tractor battery. I noticed further up the hill an elegant new villa that Mustafa's uncle and aunt had built. A few days spent there would have been wonderful. Nonetheless, even this old place was a big improvement on our army-issue tents. I noticed that our beds were already made up with clean sheets and blankets, and, oddly enough, we never saw the sleeping bags again. Mustafa was right about the views though – they were beautiful, revealing valleys terraced for kilometres with fields of gently swaying hemp. A grove of pines crowned the ridges like a parapet, and beneath them were Alpine meadows speckled with wildflowers. Donkeys laden with hemp stalks trailed through narrow gullies, while the odd gleaming pillar-box red tractor put-putted back and forth along the inclines.

His aunt was a jolly, rotund woman who was so proud of her thick, hennaed hair that she refused to wear a veil or headscarf. She kissed us on both cheeks in the French style and invited us all to lunch in a place that specialised in pigeon *tagine*. I noticed she got breathless once or twice on the way to the restaurant, but she said it was nothing to worry about, just a pollen allergy. She said it got steadily worse the more cannabis that was grown in the area and the more pesticides used on it.

The smell of the plants hung in the air across the whole valley. On our way through the back lanes of town, it was impossible to ignore the fug wafting from the tiny rooms where hemp leaves were being pounded in vats with wooden pestles. A yellow veil of what I presumed must be resin hung over everything – even the obligatory portrait of King Hassan on every wall. The workers looked remarkably clear-headed considering the amount they must have inhaled. The only visible effect I could see were bloodshot eyes, which could well have been from dust irritation. Mustafa's aunt explained that the workers went to great lengths to avoid breathing any of it in, as they considered it of such poor quality. The main crop was a fast-growing strain for the export market. Locals preferred to keep well away from it, favouring instead their own more traditional varieties, which they grew at home without fertilisers or pesticides. There was increasing concern in the area about cross-fertilisation of the old strains with the new super-crops. Ideally, they wanted the industry to be regulated, so that the traditional varieties could be maintained and fostered – a bit like the system of *terroirs* in France. More importantly, they wanted the shady middlemen who added binders of motor oil or condensed milk or mashed bananas to be stamped out.

The pigeon was surprisingly tasty. There were so many almonds, prunes and olives in it that one didn't notice the type of meat. Mustafa's aunt said the flavour was down to the cook's alchemic talent at mixing *Ras el Hanout*, the traditional spice blend that contained up to one hundred different elements from belladonna leaves to rosebuds and even, at times, a special variety of beetle called Spanish fly. His mix was so good that she swore it could transform rat meat into rump steak. Dessert was pastry and pecan nuts wrapped in sugar syrup and dripping with more toffee. The aunt ordered two for herself, while I had difficulty finishing the one I shared with Holly. The aunt was about to order a third when she began to feel breathless again. Mustafa fetched her a glass of water and helped her to her feet.

We walked slowly back up the hill to the farmhouse, and while the aunt went for a lie down, Mustafa opened a cupboard crammed full of whisky bottles and brought one into the garden with four juice glasses.

"My uncle brings them back from Spain," he said when he saw me looking back at the cupboard. "For bribes."

"Do you go often?" I asked.

"To Spain?" he said. "Never. I don't have the money."

I raised my eyebrows.

"Really," he said. "I am just a shepherd. My father is a post worker. It is my uncle who is rich. Up here in the mountains, everyone is rich. Some even have tractors! My uncle, sometimes he offers us little presents if we do things. He is buying for my sister tiny buttons when she is sixteen so she can hear. She has sickness – her ears don't work. He is buying them when she stops growing because these things cost more than a tractor, even though they are only the size of a *dirham*."

"Why don't you move up here and work with your uncle?" Holly asked.

"I used to," Mustafa explained. "This is my village, but then we had to go . . ."

He paused a while, before continuing, "My father was lucky to get a postal job. It is hard to find work. You must know someone. Best if you know someone in the army. If you have a friend high up, everything is possible. It is like a string for the puppet: you can get it to dance when you want."

He mimed jiggling the strings of his hand, making it slide into Holly's pocket and smiling innocently as he groped her thigh. She yanked it out again.

"That is how it is," he said, raising his hand innocently and standing up. "Come on, follow me. We will go to the café."

At a corner table in a street café, we settled beside some old men playing dominos, who looked around at us whenever we talked too loudly. We felt we were bothering them, so we moved to another table, near a group of boys huddled over a large pewter pot of mint tea. Mustafa knew one of them and he embraced him, kissing both cheeks. They weren't locals, but students up for a weekend break from their Koranic studies in Casablanca. They were eager and innocent, asking us the sort of questions that Dick Whittington might have asked a Londoner. Was it true that people in Europe had many telephones in one house, and many televisions and cars? Did we really have machines in the walls that gave out money when you put a card in? One of them said he was going to Marseilles soon to work. He had wired money to his penfriend to get a room ready for him. He was amazed that it could cost £1,000 just to paint a room. It had taken him a year to scrape that amount together, but his friend had said not to come before sending it. He was now planning to get a job as a painter as soon as he got there, if it were really the case that they were paid so well. The only problem was that he had sent the money two months before, and his friend hadn't been in contact since. The phone was never answered now, and the lovely penfriend letters that had been arriving each week for years had suddenly stopped. He hoped his friend hadn't become ill.

"Was it usual to pay to have a room done up before you rented it in our country?" he asked.

The old domino players were joined by a few revellers on their way back from a party. They were pretty drunk and swaggering noticeably. Wrapped in their Berber cloaks with their peaked caps swirling and tee- tering in the murky glow of the shaded wall lamps, they looked like sor- cerers, dizzy and disorientated at having been summoned from the pages of a long-forgotten storybook. One of them shouted something at us which Mustafa tried to ignore, but the man kept repeating it. Eventually Mustafa eyed me with embarrassment, saying the man was insisting I answer a question for him. I was chuffed and said, "Certainly," but Mustafa was reluctant to continue.

"He wants to know . . ." he said, pausing, seemingly lost for words.

The man came lunging towards us, repeating the question straight into my face.

"He wants to know . . ." Mustafa tried again.

The man grabbed my face, turning it towards him and repeating his question, slowly and louder, as though that might help. He smelt musty, like he might actually have come from the pages of a book – an old book soaked in cheap alcohol. A shower of beery spit spattered my face and I went to wipe it off, but he thought I was going to hit him and he grabbed my wrist and bent it backwards.

"He wants to know," Mustafa said desperately, "if your penis really has skin over the top like a newborn baby. He has heard that in Europe you don't cut the dirty layer away."

I laughed, but then seeing how serious he was, I stopped.

"Tell him . . ." I said, pausing as I decided how best to reply. "Perhaps."

"You don't understand," Mustafa said. "He wants to see for himself."

I laughed again. I didn't mean any offence by laughing – it was just an odd request and I was surprised – but he took it as an insult. He raised his arm and came hurtling forwards, shoving me hard in the shoulder so that the chair tilted and I fell backwards. The others, the old men and the Koranic students, just looked away discreetly. It was a matter of honour between the two of us now, and it wouldn't be right to intervene. It was between ourselves and Allah. *Inshallah.* Before I had a chance to get up again, he had kneeled on top of me, pinning me to the ground, and all I could think about was how odd the whole situation was. Was no one going to step in? I tried shoving him off by heaving my chest upwards, but his knees were tight against my ribs. He was staring at my mouth, pulling his arm back aiming at it when Luke finally stepped in, grabbing him by the scruff of his neck and squeezing until he was forced to collapse downward and roll off me. Luke then yanked him to his feet and hurled him towards the door. Only then did the others come forward, gathering around me, fussing and apologising on his behalf, saying he always got a bit *derangé* after drink.

A woman I hadn't noticed before, sitting at a copper inlaid table, spoke up above the din in hesitant French, saying the whole thing had been largely my fault.

"Sorry!" Holly, who had a smattering of French, said indignantly.

"Your friend has bad *djinns* inside him," she said in French. "They are attracting trouble."

Holly didn't respond – I don't think she understood – and I decided to let the comment pass, but the woman was determined to press her point home.

"Bad *djinns,* foreigner," she repeated.

I was annoyed that someone would try putting the blame on me.

"I was just sitting here," I said.

"Maybe," she said doubtfully, "but you bring trouble. Certainly."

I turned away from her, back to the others. She repeated the word *"certainment"* with such conviction that it made me stop and think. Perhaps she really did know what she was talking about. It left me feeling disconcerted. *Djinns,* which God is said to have created out of fire once he had finished moulding mankind from clay, were like the fairies that we had given up believing in back home. It made me uncomfortable to think she could see something about me. I turned back to her.

"How do you know?" I said defensively.

"They are there, working against you," she said. "Go to the *fikh* in the morning and he can help."

I looked questioningly at Mustafa, who shrugged. A *fikh* was a type of witch-doctor, he explained. They tended to travel between towns, setting up in a market for a few days before moving on to the next one. This transient practice was ostensibly so that they could share their gifts with as many people as possible, but in truth it was more likely a precaution in case people began to suspect their abilities.

The woman had tired of our conversation and returned to writing in an old ledger spread across the table. She was the only woman in the café, and I imagined she might possibly be the owner.

"What do you think?" I asked the students.

"Perhaps," one shrugged. "He did come straight up to you – to no one else but you. You have to ask why. Have you felt life working against you before?"

"I don't know," I said.

"You should go to the *fikh*," he said. "Better to be safe. Explain it to her and she will look after it."

I nodded absently.

"Whatever happens, give her respect and don't haggle," another of the boys said. "If she puts a hex on you, you are in trouble."

We stayed on in the café all evening, snacking on olives and *pita* bread when we got hungry. The waiter tried to claim that I had completely misread the situation and that the man actually only fancied me.

"He was wanting to kiss you. He sat on your body like making love," he said.

I didn't know if he was serious or not, although one of the few things I knew about Morocco from the novels of Paul Bowles was that homosexuality was quite common. Up until the 1930s, boy auctions were held in market squares, where farmers could pick up a stray waif or orphan to take home with him while stocking up on tools and provisions.

Chapter 5

A T AROUND ELEVEN o'clock we went back to the house and finished off the end of the whisky bottle before going to bed. Sometime in the middle of the night, I woke needing to go to the lavatory and pawed my way down the corridor to the hole-in-the-floor outside. On my way back, I happened to glance out into the courtyard and saw Mustafa's aunt slumped against the wall. The night was unseasonably warm, and at first I thought she might be out getting some air, but when I thought about it more I realised it was hardly likely. Earlier on, we had dropped her off at her new house, agreeing to meet again for breakfast. I saw now that her head was bent at an odd angle. Opening the double doors, I called out to her, but she didn't reply.

"*Madame?*" I tried again.

I approached, moving slowly so as not to frighten her in case she was deep in concentration. She didn't look around.

"*Madame?*" I said more urgently, but still she made no sound.

I bent down and shook her shoulder gently. There was something rubbery about it. Her skin wasn't fleshy, but more like putty or day-old dough. I noticed the tip of her tongue peaking out from the side of her mouth and it frightened me. It reminded me of a stopped pendulum.

"Are you OK?" I said loudly, letting her arm go and stepping away in fright as the limb slumped back with a heaviness that seemed to confirm my fears. Her eyes were wide, but she couldn't see me.

I ran to Mustafa's room, and before I had even opened my mouth he had jumped out of bed and was staring at me expectantly, like a relay runner waiting for the baton. It was as if he knew why I was there before I had said anything. He was looking around him anxiously, raking his fingers through his tousled hair. He knew something was wrong, but didn't know what.

"OK," he said, before I had managed to utter a word. It was as if he half understood what I was about to say, but was waiting for me to fill in the details.

"It's your aunt," I said finally.

"Yes," he agreed, and after grabbing a blanket went running out to her.

I was left standing in the corridor with that strange feeling of being caught up in someone else's world.

"Can you bring me a stool?" Mustafa called after him, and I set off looking around the house.

It was an old place with rooms full of hidden nooks and dusty cubbyholes. I found a dark wooden loom down one corridor. It was draped in swathes of muslin, bristling with nervous moths that fluttered in agitation when I turned the light on. Hanging behind the door, I noticed three more sleeping bags like the ones we had brought – all of them with their seams ripped open like the discarded cocoons of giant cousins of these same moths. I brought the stool out to Mustafa, who was crouched on his hunkers in front of his aunt. He had his hands outstretched on her forehead.

"Is she . . . ?" I asked.

"She is fine," he said, "just disorientated."

He laid the blanket gently over her and stroked her hair. I looked away.

"My uncle says she has been doing this a lot. Coming home to her old house. She walks the whole way in her sleep. I think she is getting ready to pass – they are calling her back."

Mustafa said he would bring his aunt home and told me to go back to bed.

At breakfast next morning, the aunt met us as though nothing strange had happened. She was as bright and focused as ever. When she heard what the woman had said about the *djinns*, she insisted I take it seriously. It was always better to be on the safe side when it came to *djinns*, she said.

The consequences of not addressing these things could be serious. I was still doubtful, but I asked her who she would recommend if I did decide to go. I certainly didn't want to waste my time on some charlatan. It depended who was in the market on the day, she said. The bad ones got run out of town pretty fast.

Luke reckoned I had nothing to lose by going to see one. He said he had seen the gypsies who used to pick hops with him do things that defied all logic. They had powers, he said, whether you believed in them or not. Even the most dodgy crystal ball gazers, he said, had floored him at times with their insight.

I decided to visit the market after breakfast and see what we could find. And fortunately within minutes of arriving there Mustafa was able to point out to us a *fikh* sitting on a rug in the centre of the square with seven women waiting patiently on a step beside her. When I approached them, they began giggling and murmuring amongst themselves. I wondered whether they had heard from the people in the café that I might be coming. I joined the end of the queue, but they insisted that I go straight in, and before I knew it I found myself sitting cross-legged in front of a tremendously bushy-eyebrowed woman, with dark lines of powder accentuating her cheekbones. She asked a series of short questions in Arabic, and I gestured to Mustafa to come and translate. Her enquiries were vague at first; about my general well-being and some coy questions about my home life, which I took to refer to my marital status and sexual experience. She seemed to want to make sure that I wasn't under the spell of any love potion. She then directed her focus on my diet, but seemed to only half-listen to my replies, busying herself with pinching tiny portions of various spices and powders in response to what seemed like inner whims. There were dozens of plastic bags of powders lined up in front of her which she mixed up spontaneously into something presumably appropriate to my condition. She worked in a cursory, harried manner and seemed to be just about finished when she asked one final question about my sleeping patterns. I mentioned the dreams, and immediately she froze, staring down for a full minute before tipping out the contents of the mixing bowl on the ground and looking up in exasperation.

"These are nightmares?" she asked intently.

"No, dreams," I assured her.

She shook her head.

"Nightmares," she said adamantly. "It is serious. Death *djinns*."

She waved a hand dismissively over the bags.

"Huh?" I shrugged.

"No good," she said, wiping the last of the powder from inside the bowl. "You must find leather for soles and also some copper, small grindings of copper, as small as dust and with no green rust. Bring these back to me and I will see what to do."

"She's not serious?" I asked Mustafa when he had translated all this.

"Very," he said, his face solemn.

The whole thing struck me as rather bizarre. I got up without saying anything and backed away from her. As I did so, I tried offering her money, but she refused to accept it, saying I should pay when I came back with the materials. I had already decided that there was no way I was coming back and I tried explaining this, but before I got a chance to, the next woman in line came bustling up and squatted herself down, pushing me firmly aside.

When we got back to the house, we found the aunt collapsed again on the floor beside the breakfast table. She smiled meekly when she saw us. She seemed to be more embarrassed than in pain. Mustafa tried to lift her, but as soon as she put pressure on her foot, it went from under her and she slumped back down in a heap on the kitchen tiles. Mustafa tried to lift her again more carefully, but she had fainted out cold and was now a dead weight. He tried to revive her but she didn't respond. I went to help but he waved me away, shaking his head brusquely and telling me to "get away". Then he looked up apologetically and said this was something he needed to do on his own. It was best if I left him. His aunt was approaching the end, he said.

Holly asked should she call for an ambulance, and he laughed weakly, saying there was no such thing.

"A doctor?" she said, and he shook his head.

"Her mind is having little shut downs," he said. "She will be frightened if she doesn't know the people around her. It is always this way. They get confused."

We took the hint and turned back outside. As we filed out, I saw him grip his aunt by her arms and pull her across the uneven tiles. It felt uncomfortable being in the house at such a time, and we arranged to go out on a hike into the hills so as not to be in the way. Holly spotted a grove of overgrown mandarin trees with a heavy crop of late-season fruit in the next valley, and we made our way slowly over there and picked the few that weren't full of wasps and insects. By the time we got back to the house around mid afternoon, everything seemed different. The house was full of neighbours and cousins. The aunt had taken a turn for the worse; her pulse was erratic, and they feared she might be on the way out. No one seemed to know exactly what was wrong with her or what they could do about it. There was still no sign of a doctor or a nurse. They seemed to accept that she was old and it was her time. We felt uncomfortable staying on at such a time and decided we should pool our money and pay for someone to drive us to Fez.

It took a few hours to find a taxi and agree a price, and it was evening before we finally set off. By then the house was full of neighbours, and it was easy for us to slip out unnoticed. The taxi was an olive-green Renault 4 that wheezed up and down through the mountains like an overworked sewing machine. It made far slower progress than Mustafa's Mercedes had, particularly since we got delayed for long periods at every roadblock while our car and bags were thoroughly searched. I was increasingly suspicious about what had been inside those sleeping bags and wondered what Mustafa had told the guards about us to make them back away each time. I wondered whether he had brought us on the trip to act as decoys. But that didn't seem to make much sense, as it hardly seemed like a foolproof plan. What would he have done if we had refused to come? The taxi man hinted that drugs were constantly being ferried down the mountain and cash was coming back up. I suspected that we may have played some role in it, but I may be maligning Mustafa.

The driver had said we could make the journey to Fez in one go, but a suspension leaf broke just before midnight, and we had to stop in a village and wait for morning when a new one could be hammered out in the forge. We got rooms in a newly widowed seamstress's home, who also had a loom draped in swathes of cloth. No sooner had I laid my head on the pillow than Johan returned and I was back in his boathouse. This time I heard noises coming from the climbers' refuge next door to the boathouse, and when I went to investigate I found most of the group there. Rita, the

Tasmanian with the phenomenally broad forehead, and her husband Vinnie were knocking back schnapps, while the nurses, Stella, Felicity and Dorothy, were wearing the blue overalls that I wore in the German hypermarket. Stella told me that the canteen was serving bratwurst and kohlrabi for lunch and that I should hurry as it was closing soon. Felicity and Dorothy said it was my own fault if I missed out, and Stella stared hard at them and threw her eyes to heaven. I remember thinking how odd it was that she was the only one of them who had the caring capacity that nurses were meant to have. Rita and Vinnie began to bicker and I told them to be quiet. They turned on me. I backed away, but then noticed Lucy coming at them with her gun, and I screamed, "NO!" and she said, "But they're going to hurt you," and she pulled the trigger.

It was by far the most intense dream I had had. I had no idea where they were coming from, but I knew that they couldn't continue. It was getting so that I feared going to sleep. At least this time I was on my own; I didn't have Wayne to contend with.

While we were driving next day, the taxi man asked us did we not think it was odd that Mustafa's aunt happened to fall sick just when he was there.

"Why?" I said. "Were they close?"

"No," he said. "Not that, but because of who he is."

He went on to explain that in the community Mustafa was regarded as a death chaperon, or at least that's the best translation he could give. He played a role at people's death. From what I could gather, he in some way helped to escort them out of this world and into the next. It wasn't a traditional thing or anything, just something he had always done. Even when he was young, the taxi man said, he used to turn up when someone was dying and help them – steer them through the unfamiliarity to the other side. People were very suspicious at first. It worried them to see him hanging around the sick and the elderly, but over time they grew to accept it. He would be ushered in and allowed to get on with his work.

The taxi man told us how he had seen him in the early years sneaking in and hanging around until the dying person called him over – that was, if a neighbour or relation hadn't noticed him first and shooed him off. They all thought he was a bit of a nuisance, that he might be odd in the head. It was only later they came to realise that the dying person actually liked having him around, and they let him be. Occasionally, he was called out of school or woken in the middle of the night and hurriedly brought to a neighbour's home to stand by the bed of someone who was very frightened. They often wondered what he did for them, but he was never very good at putting it into words.

The taxi man said that problems began to arise when Mustafa started arriving at people's houses a few days before they even got sick. This frightened people, and his parents warned him not to do it. There was a thin line between a death chaperon and the Grim Reaper. He stopped, claiming he couldn't foresee death any more, but the taxi man always wondered whether this was because he had allowed his senses to atrophy, or if in fact he could still tell, but had the sense to keep it to himself.

I wished I had known all this about Mustafa earlier. It sparked a thousand questions that I wanted to ask him. I wondered whether the taxi man was exaggerating. He was clearly enjoying recounting the story, and I wondered if it were merely a way of passing the time or of practising his English. He talked half in French and half in English and wanted me to translate any French words that he thought might be useful to know in English.

The idea that someone could help steer you across the chasm was alluring, principally, I suppose, because of having watched my father wrestling with the journey over weeks in the hospital, plummeting into frightening realms which no drug could reach. Since childhood I had been intrigued by exploring the boundaries of reality. The first time I was allowed go to the library on my own, aged nine or ten, I went straight to the huge marbled catalogue to hunt out the class numbers of anything mystical: 133 – Parapsychology & occultism; 131 – Occult methods for achieving well-being. When I was twelve, the Royal Dublin Society allowed me become a junior member, and I scoured their archives for works on mystic cabals and first-hand accounts of Madame Blavatsky and Le Count de St Germain. Since I had a feeling that these interests would not be considered healthy by adults, I had the good sense to keep them to myself.

My supposition was proved correct by an encounter I had with a lay brother on a train going to my cousin's farm in the midlands. He spotted me reading a book on ESP and demanded to know where I had gotten such a thing. I told him about my junior membership of the RDS, and he shook his head anxiously and began to harangue me regarding the dangers of the paranormal, saying that anyone espousing direct communication with spirits was just luring you into the devil's clutches. These books were only for the lost and the fallen, he insisted. Fortunately he got off at the next station and I was free to continue reading in peace, but his words had made me all the more intent on keeping my interests private.

I asked the taxi man whether Mustafa might have been referring to his special abilities when he told me about helping the girl who had contracted an infection from the knife dance. Mustafa had mentioned something about talking her out of her coma. The taxi man was surprised that I knew about this incident. The girl had come from his village and at the time, he told me, it had caused quite a stir. Up until then, Mustafa had only offered help to the old and the dying, and they were rarely in any fit state to discuss exactly what he did for them, but this young girl had made a full recovery and was keen to tell everyone what had happened – how Mustafa had come to her when she was unconscious and reassured her, laying out the various options and opportunities that were open to her.

This was the first clear sense the community had of what Mustafa did, and it worried them. They called a meeting at which the *shaykh* declared that Mustafa was a liar and a cheat, and that it was impossible that anyone would feel fear or confusion on the path towards paradise. The taxi man seemed to agree with him.

"In death we are safely under the guidance of Allah," he pointed out decisively. "We feel ecstasy and delirium as we enter paradise under the merciful gaze of the Prophet Mohammed."

I felt like saying that it wasn't like that for my dad, but of course he wasn't Muslim. The taxi man said the *shaykh* decided Mustafa was a charlatan and was possessed by *djinns*. His father decided it was best to move the whole family away, and Mustafa's uncle helped him find work in the postal service near Chefchaouen. By this stage the taxi man, it has to be said, was revelling in the intricacies of his story – adding all sorts of irrelevant details. He reminded me of the narrator from *A Thousand and One Nights*. The narrative had become more about verbal flourishes and repeated motifs than Mustafa's actual experiences. I wanted to believe so badly in what I was being told. I latched on to the frail connection between

Mustafa's supposed abilities and my dreams. Was there really a way of connecting with the dead? Could my dreams be more than just subconscious expression of my anxiety? I wanted to make sense of it all, to know what the hell was going on, and I found myself rifling my memory banks for anything I could recall from the old library books.

Chapter 6

TRACKING DOWN THE truck in Fez was not a problem. There was only one big campsite in town, and as soon as we approached we could hear the tortured strains of Dire Straits blaring from its stereo. The group had raided the drink stash again and everyone was drunk. Fortunately Suzi wasn't around; she had picked up a mechanic from another truck and had gone off to his tent.

"Here come the fudgies!" Vinnie announced when he saw us, and everyone laughed.

"Fuj-what?" the taxi man enquired as I was handing him the money. I shrugged and gave a long sigh, resigning myself to being back.

"Fudgie numero uno!" Vinnie said as I approached.

"What?" I said wearily.

"Fudgie," Vinnie repeated. "You know? Fudge packer."

"What are you on about?" I said.

"You know," he insisted. "Uphill gardener, chocolate plumber. You and Luke – you like it up the rear, right? That's why you keep going off together. Is Holly like your little fluffer, yeah?"

Loud guffaws came from the others. Dorothy and Felicity, the nurses, who were the only ones more or less sober, sidled up to me with relishing leers across their face.

"Just wait till Suzi sees you," Dorothy said, miming a throat cutting. Felicity nodded approvingly.

"Don't mind them," Henry, the quantity surveyor, said, in his typical grandiloquent tones, giving Luke and me a jovial slap on the back and Holly one on the bum. "Rabble scum, the lot. You kids just keep enjoying yourselves; don't mind the rest of us."

He put his arm amiably around my neck and wrestled me into a headlock with boisterous hoots of laughter, tousling my hair and saying, "You guys, what *will* we do with you! You need a nursemaid to keep you out of trouble!"

I laughed good-humouredly and he let me free, pushing the bottle of vodka to my chest with a munificent wave, before launching off after Rodney and the others who had gone to the far end of the campsite to taunt the passengers of a rival overland truck – a more expensive and luxurious one, with its own chef and high-tech dome tents and folding directors' chairs, and a trailerfull of luxury goods. The passengers from this truck were all safely tucked up in bed, and Rodney was having trouble waking them.

He was shaking their tent poles, and shouting, "Come on, lads, come have a drink with us . . . don't be shy. Plenty of time to sleep when you get back home. HELLO! Is anyone there?"

Rodney, like Henry, had just walked away from a constricted career and was keen to enjoy every moment of his new freedom. He had served in the British army for twenty years, including two tours to Northern Ireland, and this was the first holiday he and his wife Marsha had had in all that time. He was a willowy, carrot-haired man with a neat moustache, sinewy arms and skin as open-grained and deeply veined as sea-washed timber.

"They think they're too good for us," Rita called out loudly.

"You're probably right, Rita," Rodney shouted. "Just because they spent three grand on their poxy camp gear makes them all high and mighty."

"Wonder if it's really all that waterproof?" Norman said.

"Good question, Norman!" his brother Duncan, the Tweedle-dee character, said, unzipping his fly. "Should we test them and see?"

"Better be safe than sorry, I always say," Norman replied, and the brothers began urinating on the nearest tent.

Vinnie tried to join in but he could coax only a meagre spatter.

Eventually, the beleaguered occupants of the tent realised the taunting would continue until they reacted and a torch light flicked on warily inside.

Henry came hurtling back towards us, leading us towards his own tent and out of the way of the fight that would inevitably erupt.

"Scum," he said breathlessly, "I'm surrounded by scum . . . You boys are lucky you missed out on Casablanca."

"It's a cesspit," Mildred, his middle-aged partner, agreed, putting aside her knitting as we approached. "Waste of space."

"The way I see it," Henry slurred, "I've seen enough filthy polluted cities in my time without . . ."

He was having trouble standing up at this stage, and all of a sudden he fell over right in front of us, sprawling out on the ground with his pleated Marks and Spencer's pants somewhere down around his ankles. He was looking up into the stars with a blissful expression, as if his whole life had been leading towards this point, this apogee of retirement.

The nurses were always careful to only drink in moderation – or at least Felicity and Dorothy were; Stella, my cooking partner, was more laid back. They were clucking censoriously over the shouting and swearing that was coming from the posh truck now. They were coming to the end of a game of pontoon, and Felicity was trying to interest them in a get-to-know-you game which she had swiped from a bonding weekend she had organised for the NHS. The group had been playing the game a few times over the previous nights, but restricting themselves to ten questions a night so as to draw out the fun. Stella got up from the game and came over to us. I apologised for being away for our cooking night, and she insisted it was no problem. She told us to ignore the snide remarks of the other nurses' criticism and insisted that we bring her along if we went on any more adventures.

Next morning, I managed to avoid meeting Suzi and made my way straight to the *medina* in the company of Natasha, one of the two young London girls whose incandescence I had noticed on the first day. She had sidled up to me as I was leaving the campsite, looping her arm through mine like someone out of Jane Austen.

"I know something you don't know!" she said in her beautifully crisp accent. "Something about somebody who might just fancy you."

"Who?" I said, in a rush of embarrassment.

But she wouldn't say any more, just propelled me through the onslaught of smells – fly-carpeted meat, cedar shavings, newly sheared fleece – that made up the laneways of Fez.

"Well, not so much fancy," she corrected herself teasingly, stepping quickly to keep up with me as I continued through the tangle of lanes that stretched out around us, "but maybe who likes you just a little."

Her language, her attitude, her whole way of being was so at odds with the rest of us. She and her friend Lucy still wore the patina of the exclusive school they had left just a few months before. Their world was a mix of Harvey Nic's and *Bunty* comics, full of treats and little courtesies. Since arriving on the truck, they had spun a mini self-contained universe around them, as precious and elite as a Fabergé egg; they had their own endearing customs and ways of caring for each other, and even their own language, in which the words "iggle" and "wiggle" replaced alternate syllables, making the English incomprehensible to the rest of us. I was entranced by them, but I didn't quite know how best to convey it, how to crack the shell.

"Can't you guess?" Natasha persisted and I blushed again. This was how I normally reacted to them. I didn't know any other way. I had been at an all-boys, Catholic school and didn't have much experience in their coy, coquettish ways of relating to the world. It was so innocent, so endearing, that it was hard to know how best to respond to it. It was pretty obvious that she was referring to Lucy. She was the only other person in her world. Over the weeks I had been watching them both cuddling up against each other, nuzzling and nurturing each other like puppies, and I had longed to be included in their play.

"Maybe you two should go on a date," Natasha said to me.

"A date!" I exclaimed.

Although I wanted to be friends with them, the idea of going on a date with someone you shared the same one metre by three metre moving cell with was not something I found appealing.

"Why not?" Natasha cried, ducking into a doorway to avoid a heavily wrapped woman carrying trays of rising dough to the municipal ovens. "It'll be a chance for you to get to know each other."

Natasha could not see how impossible this was; the teasing that would inevitably follow. One of the things I loved most about the two girls was their obliviousness to the outside world. The general level of maturity in the group was equivalent to that of inmates at a reform school, but the girls were so confident in their own little universe that they took no notice of it. The fact that people sniggered and made crude remarks when they cuddled didn't bother them in the least. Their confidence reminded me of the British in India, creating entire Home Counties villages complete with tea shops, croquet matches and summer fêtes without any regard for the local derision it attracted.

"Come on," Natasha teased. "Are you a man or a mouse?"

I shrugged, and eventually found myself agreeing to call for Lucy later that day when she had finished her guard duty on the truck. In the intervening hour, I headed back into the maelstrom of the market to look for a blanket for the cold Saharan nights.

Finding the weaving quarter wasn't easy, and after numerous dead ends, I paid a local boy to guide me through the labyrinth to a central square surrounded by a dozen identical stalls with a dozen seemingly identical carpet sellers, each sitting on an identical intricately woven pouffe. It had the appearance of a refractive vortex, with sun flooding into haphazard spots, giving the place a mottled look. Along lanes in each direction were more carpet sellers, each sitting on his own identical pouffe in a similar carpeted cubbyhole. In tiny niches carved into the mud walls above them, children and women sat weaving cloth with their fingers and toes.

I had set out that morning determined to learn the language of bargaining so that I could finally begin to engage with Africa a bit more. It seemed that it was at the root of everything here, from conversation and relationships to trade. In Ireland it's largely a silent affair, a reel of winks, nods and meaningful stares, but in Morocco I had noticed that it needed to be accompanied by a torrent of gesticulation and voluble protest. It needn't make much sense, just as long as it was loud, its purpose being principally to indicate resolve. The final price had to reflect the extent of passion exerted by both sides during negotiations. I had noticed all this, but I had yet to put it into practice.

As I approached the stalls, a young girl with a lemon-slice smile and a burgundy dress grasped my finger and pulled me towards her uncle, who grabbed my wrist and sat me down on a pouffe that magically appeared from nowhere.

"Welcome, where from? *Alleman? Wie Gehts!*"

"Irish," I mumbled.

"*Céad míle fáilte,*" he gushed, petting my hand reassuringly. A glass of mint tea was placed before me, and he asked as though his life depended on it what he could do for me, signalling to his nephew to unfurl carpets at my feet.

"A blanket," I managed.

"A blanket!" he cheered. "Yes!"

He signalled to the nephew who was already pulling down bolts of cloth from a high shelf.

"Look only, not buy," the man reassured me. "You look, you like, you buy."

I told him that I didn't want to spend much, and his face bloomed like a lotus.

"As you like. No problem. Pay as you like," he said, still kneading my hand.

The process went on for an hour, and eventually I handed over four Duracell batteries and a fiver and took my blanket back to the truck with me, confident that I had taken another tiny step towards engaging with the continent.

Lucy had been primed by Natasha about our date and was waiting when I reached the truck. As always, there was a trace of a smile across her face, and her jet black ringlets framed her pale thin face. She was all cheekbone and jutting chin, but it was the shy curve of smile that most defined her. A trace of it remained no matter what the circumstances, running up through her left dimple towards her ear. It was something to hold on to at even the gloomiest times, though quite regularly it was bursting forth in full beam, setting the world alight.

As I led her away from the truck, I began to regret having agreed to Natasha's request and felt quite awkward about what I might have let myself in for. Although we had all been living on top of each other for weeks, like nuns and convent-school children, we rarely spent time in twos. It was an unusual situation to be in. I felt like a suitor from another age and found myself asking rather stilted questions.

"It's good," she replied, smiling broadly, when I asked her what she thought of the trip so far.

"And what about the group?" I continued.

"Yes, it's good too."

"Yeah?" I said.

"Yes," she said, brushing her thighs to emphasis the point.

"And what about Suzi, what do you think of her?"

"She's good," she nodded happily.

"Right," I said. "Is there anything you don't like?"

"Hmmn," she said, thinking. "Nope, everything is peachy so far."

She reached out to touch wood and giggled nervously.

We both fell silent. I could think of nothing else to ask her, or at least nothing that might coax a more insightful reply. Her mind didn't seem to go in much for evaluation or criticism. Everything was good, and if it wasn't, she was too well-mannered to draw attention to it. We walked on in silence for a while, and suddenly I felt her fingers brushing mine. They reached around and soon we were holding hands. I blushed again and we continued walking, swinging our arms like in some schmaltzy American movie. It was sweet, and I should have been touched, but in truth it made me feel nervous. Although she seemed to be unaware of the prevailing atmosphere on the truck, I knew exactly how ruthless the others could be. They fed on weakness, on sensitivity – picking at it with the voraciousness of inmates anywhere, of people cooped up together and forced to submit to a regime, of the institutionalised. I could just imagine the jeering and crass remarks that would greet any budding romance, and I knew I wasn't up to it. It's hard to convey how oppressive the atmosphere was. Maybe I was just cowardly.

Already, Dudley, an unfortunate Welshman who had come on the truck to escape a broken marriage, had been made a virtual outcast as a result of his craven need for our attention – no matter how negative. He lied, he boasted, he nitpicked and whined until we had all given up on him – even the nurses, Felicity and Dorothy, who took a masochistic pleasure in supporting the underdog. Within a few weeks, he reached the point where he had no allies left, and things turned very nasty. Everyone ganged up on him. We used him as our personal and collective punch bag, our scapegoat for every minor frustration. It was tragic to see how he suffered, and it was only a matter of time before he would break.

Having a relationship with Lucy would have left me open to the sort of taunting that Dudley suffered daily, and I knew I wasn't strong enough for it. Also, I didn't really believe I could have a proper relationship with her. I admired her greatly, but we were simply too different. It was bound to break up after a while, and we'd still have to sit cooped up together for the rest of the trip. I was attracted to her, but it was mostly physical. It was hard to relate to her in any other way. She was still a child with a mind full of her furry toy collection back home and which was her favourite coloured sweet in a packet of Smarties. Although only two years older than her, at twenty I was already relatively cynical and hardened. At least compared to her I was.

"Tell me, what *don't* you like about the trip?" I asked her at last, slipping my hand casually out of hers.

She thought for a second, puckering her little face up like a baby chimp's.

"I miss my home," she said at last, "especially the kitchen with the Aga and Mummy and Squibbles. When I used to get back from school, Mummy always let me help with dinner and I'd play with Squibbles – he's a Siamese. He's seventy-seven in cat years. I'm worried he'll get sick when I'm away. Dada has put up a big map of Africa right beside the Aga, and every day they mark out where they think I am with pins and coloured string. We had to go to two different shops on Charing Cross Road to find the right colours. It's why I'm so keen to get to the *poste restante* – to catch up on everything."

Pins on a map! It was so poignant. The image it created in my mind was enough to wrench my heart. I'm sure that at some level my family cared about what happened to me; it was just that they were too caught up in their own lives, their own loss, to show it. Things were hard for everyone at the time; I wasn't the only one coming to terms with losing my dad.

"Mariah, my big sister, has had her baby," Lucy continued. "He's so cute, and I'm hoping there'll be lots of pics."

Thoughts of home made her more loquacious, and she recounted in detail her games room and tree house and the wood-burning stove that had been especially installed in her room so that she and her friends could hang out after school, lounging on beanbags on the thick lambswool carpet, gossiping and drinking cocoa. Her brother carried sacks of logs upstairs whenever she needed them. They all spoiled her rotten, she giggled. Her father even squeezed orange juice for her every morning before school and brought it up on a tray.

"In February, when the first crocuses come," she said, "he puts one on the tray too, in a tiny crystal thimble."

Her life sounded unreal, like something out of a fairy story. I wondered what the hell had made her leave it all behind. But before I could ask, a man put his arm around her shoulder and pulled her off down an alleyway – a Moroccan man, tall, but with a bad stoop and a frayed collar that pushed against his hairline. I followed in a panicked run, but it was hard to keep sight of them as he steered her through an onslaught of feathers and chicken shit into what must have been the poultry section of the market. I heard him say to her, "Come quickly, it's this way," but looking around all I could see were bamboo crates and scrappy panniers stuffed with squawking ducks and chicks. Finally, I caught sight of them rounding a corner and tried to grab at her, but she was being pulled along by the man. She glanced back at me, but with more bemusement than concern on her face.

He made a sharp turn down a lane by a kebab-vendor who was roasting skewered chicken wings on a smouldering brazier. I lost sight of them then for a moment until I saw a door swing back into its frame at the end of the alley and I rushed towards it.

Inside, he was waiting for me.

"Come," he said, "you are too slow. Upstairs now."

He pointed to the far wall where a series of steps were notched into the adobe.

"Up there?" Lucy asked.

He nodded and she started skipping up, taking two steps at a time. We rose up through a house, the steps becoming narrower as we went until suddenly we were on a flat roof and the man shoved sprigs of mint under our noses, telling us to be sure not to breathe in. I resisted him at first, but then registered the stink and was suddenly glad of the mint. I could feel my stomach heaving; it was almost overpowering. Below us a series of enormous round vats had been hollowed out of the earth, each filled with a different brilliantly coloured liquid. There were men teetering on the edges of the vats carrying mounds of animal skins on their shoulders, which were dripping with the different colours. Mainly reds – oxblood, ruby, cochineal. It was the intensity of them that made the scene so star-tling. The man explained that the colour came from poppy petals. There were other shades too, made from mint, cedar and cinnamon. The smell was from a different series of vats which were filled to the brim with a shocking white liquid of lime and pigeon shit and the urine and brains of various animals. These vats were used to strip the hides of grease and flesh and hair, the man explained. There were men standing knee-deep in them, scraping the skins with blades.

Lucy was staring down, utterly captivated. She had a keenness to her, a sharpness, that beguiled me. I imagined that somewhere inside her mind must be an intelligence to match this crystalline gaze, and it saddened me that she never expressed herself more. She seemed to be clinging on to the thought processes of a child, which I couldn't blame her for. It's what privilege bought you in London – an extended innocence. I was impressed by how easily she accepted even the most bizarre and exotic sights. While the rest of the group reacted in either horror or pity, she just took it all in, processing it without prejudice. Nothing fazed her. I felt oddly proud of her and longed to know what effect these experiences would have on her in a few years' time when she matured. I know there was only two years between us, but it felt like so much more. If my life had been sheltered, hers had been positively hermitic.

"It's mad, isn't it?" I said.

"Yeah," she said, wistfully.

"The smell is pretty bad," I said.

I felt I was going to retch.

"It's OK when you get used to it," she said.

"Let's get out of here," I said, leading her back down the stairs and handing the man some money to get rid of him, but he refused to leave and instead coaxed us into his cousin's leather shop next door where the bags and coats smelt of the same pigeon shit.

"You know, there's been something I wanted to ask you," I said to Lucy.

"Yeah?" she said, looking up at me.

"It's about hugging?" I said.

"Huh?" she said

"You and Natasha," I said.

"Oh," she said, "that's not hugging, it's cuddles."

"Cuddles," I said awkwardly.

"What do you want to know?" she asked primly.

"I dunno," I said, "it just seems unusual."

"Not to us," she said. "All the girls at school do it. It makes everything better."

"I suppose," I said.

"It does!" she gushed with added conviction, "I swear! Natasha's got a book at home – *The Little Book of Hugs* – and it says that cuddles cure depression and ease stress and even help you recover from cancer."

"Yeah?" I said.

"Oh yeah," she said eagerly. "Don't you hug your friends?"

"No," I said. "Not really."

"Oh," she said, then paused. "Not ever?"

I shook my head.

"That's a shame," she said contemplatively.

I was half hoping she would stretch out her arms there and then, but instead she pulled a didactic frown and said, "You know, there are many different types."

"Oh."

"There's the back-to-front and the heart-to-heart, and the sandwich and the big squeeze and the cheek-to-cheek and . . ."

"Really?" I said.

"Oh yeah, really!"

"Can you show me?" I said.

She made no reply, just looked at me strangely, then eventually said, "You want a cuddle?"

I nodded.

"Now?" she said warily.

I shrugged and looked around me.

She reached her arms tentatively around my bum, pulling me in close to her and began to breathe slowly and deeply into my belly. Her body was rake thin and hard with knobbly protrusions, but open and seemingly full of kindness. She clung to me with such rapt tenacity, burrowing her prominent little chin into my clavicle, gently swaying me back and forth and allowing herself to swing with me. From her belly I could feel a rumble, almost a purr, as her breath spread out into mine, and she looked up beaming her tightly sown, little teddy-bear smile at me. An image flashed through my mind of me licking her breasts and I was just about to bend down and kiss her when I stopped myself. It wasn't right. She may have been practically the same age as me, but in most other respects she was still a child. She still read *Winnie-the-Pooh* in bed, for pity's sake. All I could think of was those furry toys back home – the different Eeyors and Tiggers she had told me about and the rare princess doll her father brought back from Malaysia. She needed to be protected. She and Natasha were going to need all the help they could get in the months ahead. They were prime targets, not just for me, but for all of us. Already Duncan, the Lothario who had promised to bed every woman in the truck, was making advances on them both, and I could see signs of Natasha beginning to weaken, succumbing to his occasionally witty asides. She had no experience of such predatory behaviour and was throwing girlish glances back at him whenever he cynically slipped in a reference to loving baby animals and wanting to care for all the little mal-nourished children in Africa.

"Aawh, bless," Natasha would sigh reverently. She seemed to ignore his other more frequent comments that were almost always at least partially offensive or racist.

Duncan was a hyena searching for meat; anything would do. Following his claim about regarding the women on the truck as his personal harem, the other, older ones were steering well clear of him, but Natasha was too young to know better. It was clear Duncan was aware that he had a six-month stretch ahead of him and would need some action on a regular basis, it didn't really matter where. At eighteen, and with the early stirrings of a crush, there was little chance Natasha would listen to anyone who tried to warn her. She was a grown-up now, she felt, and she would make her own decisions. We were powerless to intervene. Duncan could see this clearly, but he had enough guile about him to take things slowly. He had time on his side. He would reel her in inch by inch. She would be worth it – fresh and unspoiled.

Chapter 7

VULTURES WERE CIRCLING close to the sun at the border post into Algeria, waiting with the patience of undertakers for the sight and smell of frailty. Their telescopic eyes scanned the ground. We were leaving the sweet mandarin and sour olive groves of Morocco and crossing into the semi-desert of northern Algeria. It was dawn and cold, the land still in the grip of the night before. The plan was to cross the border early in the hope that the guards would have sobered a bit from the night before and not had a chance to start drinking again. We had got up especially early to make it here on time as Suzi had warned us that these crossings – remote outposts of bored soldiers with nothing to do but drink the contraband alcohol they confiscated – could be one of the greatest dangers we faced in Africa. The two guards who halted the truck were surprisingly courteous, cleanly shaven and dressed in impeccably starched uniforms. They apologised in advance for the few minutes delay while they entered our details into the ledger. They pointed out that although trucks were supposed to pay an entry tax, if we liked they would allow us claim ours was a bus to save the expense. Within ten minutes, our customs declaration and *carnet* were returned, and Suzi was being waved through the barrier without having paid a single *franc* extra to anyone. We were just pulling out on to the road again when the guard came sauntering back out of his kiosk, saying he ought to take a quick final count of our passports just to check they tallied with the list he had been given. We let down the steps at the back of the truck and he jumped aboard.

"Very nice," he said, looking around him. "Home sweet home. All your beds and tents so neat and tidy – very good!"

We laughed as he walked up and down the truck taking a quick look at our passports as he went.

"I wish my guards could be so neat and tidy," he said, and we smiled with pride at ourselves.

"It is all very clever," he said, pointing at the hi-fi speakers strapped to the roof-bars and the intercom hooked up to the cab. "Everything is shipshape and in order."

He stood for a moment marvelling at the ingenuity of it all, running his fingers along the neatly bevelled hinges of our lockers. The cabinet-work was excellent – Joe had spent four months preparing it all before we left England. He had been given the chassis and engine of an old Bedford M3 bought from the Ministry of Defence for £3,000 and had transformed it into an overland expedition vehicle with jacked-up suspension, massive all-terrain tyres and seating and storage for twenty people. He had even added a safari seat over the cab to provide a lookout for later on when we were in the game parks. He regarded the truck as a work in progress and was constantly tinkering with it, adding little touches, like an air compressor and a tape deck built into a sealed alcove to protect it from floods and sandstorms.

"And what is under there?" the guard said.

He was pointing at the long banquettes running down either side.

"Sleeping gear," Mildred said, getting up and lifting the cushions to show him her sleeping bag and roll mat underneath.

"Ah yes!" he said delightedly. "Everything so neat and tidy."

I noticed activity in the sky above us as the vultures spotted something and began winding down through the eddies.

"And in here?" the guard said, with a curiosity that showed no sign of abating. He was pointing at the lockers behind our backs where we kept everyday things like cameras, medicine, plates and cutlery.

From where I was sitting, I could see the first vulture landing, folding its great wings around itself and plunging its head into a red and grey heap on the roadside – a road-kill rabbit. The others soon followed him down, their wings furled in tightly and their necks craning into the rabbit's viscera.

Mildred opened her locker.

"It is like nineteen snails all in the same shell," the guard said brightly, undoing a few of the locker clasps and peering inside as he talked.

He did a little tap dance on the plywood floor.

"And under here is more again?" he said, looking downwards. "More nice things?"

Our smiles suddenly stiffened. No one replied.

"More food and blankets, yes?" he said eagerly.

No one said a word; eventually Rodney, the carrot-haired, ex-soldier piped up, "No, mate, that's just the floor there."

"Just the floor?" the guard said doubtfully.

"Yeah," said Rodney. "Sure."

"But what about food?" the guard said, concernedly. "In the desert you will need food."

"Oh yeah, don't worry, there are a few tins of stew and spam under that first floorboard, all right," Rodney conceded, "but that's all. It's just the chassis."

"The *shazy?*" the guard said dubiously.

"Yeah, the chassis – the frame of the truck," Rodney clarified.

"The frame?" the guard said with a frown settling over his bright features. He was just about to bend down to investigate when Stella began to make furious choking noises from the back of her throat. We turned to her as one. She was holding her neck at an angle and trying to stifle a raspy moan that sounded like a Buddhist invocation. It was an unusual and disturbing performance, and we were all a bit worried for her. Suddenly Felicity cottoned on and leapt to her feet in a flurry of activity, grabbing Stella's shoulders and performing the Heimlich manoeuvre violently once or twice.

The guard looked around him anxiously.

"What is the matter?" he asked.

"She gets sick," Felicity said. "She needs medicine and gets very sick."

I thought as a trained nurse Felicity could have come up with something more medically detailed, but the guard seemed convinced nonetheless. She pumped Stella a few times before reaching into her back locker and pulling out some water sterilising tablets, tearing one out of its foil wrapper and popping it into Stella's mouth. Stella chewed it until foam began fizzing out of the sides of her mouth. She was still flailing and gasping, and making weird cooing noises in the back of her throat like a dove in distress.

The guard was about to signal to his companions for help, but Luke insisted that all that was needed was to get her lying down, and we all eagerly agreed. It had at last dawned on us that Stella was just trying to distract him from the floorboards. Rodney helped Luke lift her on to the floor and she immediately quietened.

"You're bringing *her* into the desert?" the guard said.

"Oh, yeah, she'll be fine," Rodney said brightly.

"She is sick," the guard insisted.

"It'll do her good," Rodney chirped. "Promise!"

The guard looked reluctantly around him and backed out of the truck.

"God be willing," he said.

We were proud of ourselves for having handled the situation so well. It gave us confidence that we could deal with incidents ourselves. None of us were really sure what would have happened if our alcohol had been found. Would our names really have been posted on a board in Nairobi? We just had to take Suzi's word for it. More than anything, we wanted to avoid incurring her wrath. We had only a vague idea of the possible dangers Africa might have in store for us, but we had a far better idea of how dangerous Suzi could be. Her leadership was becoming ever more trenchant. She still told us wonderful stories at night around the fire about the animals and landscape around us, but rarely bothered to explain her actions any longer. At the beginning of the trip, she had initiated a practice of weekly Sunday meetings at which issues could be brought up and discussed, but these were gradually changing in format. She rarely bothered to explain herself at them any longer or even take much notice of our opinions. At one meeting a group had come together to complain about her choice of campsites, which had become increasingly erratic. Such was Suzi's rush to get us through Africa in one piece that she insisted we cover as much ground as possible as fast as possible before we reached the equatorial regions where the terrain would get immeasurably more difficult and we might end up stuck for days at impassable roads or washed-away bridges. As a result, she had got into the habit of driving until nightfall. It meant we were left casting about blindly using a spotlight for somewhere suitable to pitch camp, and so we never really knew where we were until morning. It added a nice element of surprise – though sometimes we ended up directly over a termite nest or in a village dung heap. One morning we were awoken by the quaking of the ground beneath us and, looking out the tent flap, saw a cargo train hurtling between our tents on tracks that we hadn't noticed in the darkness.

On two occasions we had awoken to find we were camped on dry riverbeds. If a flash flood had come, we might all have drowned. It was Suzi who had warned us that sudden torrential floods after a downpour in the highlands were one of the biggest killers in Africa.

We finally confronted her about the campsite issue the morning we were woken by a pilot, politely asking could we remove our tents from his runway as he had an aeroplane with forty passengers ready for take-off. The nurses had been fuming all day about it, and it had all come to the boil at that evening's meeting.

"What do you think this is," Suzi had scoffed when they pleaded with her that we stop driving an hour before sunset, "a fucking democracy?"

A few days later, driving through the scrubland of northern Algeria, we were shown precisely how far Suzi was willing to take things into her own hands. A sound of human voices came rippling on the air across the desert at us as we were driving one afternoon: rhythmic and incessant; somewhat like the call to prayer but less monotone, more insistent. At first, all we could discern was a grey blur on the road ahead. It was hard in the wilderness to distinguish sizes or distances, when there was nothing to compare things to. Eventually we made out a solid mass of people clustered around some trucks. The sound broke into many voices, angry and impassioned, and we realised it was a mob of some kind, with arms waving and a determined expression on their faces. They were blocking the road ahead.

Suzi had no choice but to pull up in front of them. Four of them jumped on to the cab, clinging on to the wing mirrors and telling us they were organising a protest and weren't letting anyone through. They advised us to find another route south. Unfortunately, that wasn't really possible; there were few roads in the desert, and the nearest one would have meant a hundred-mile detour. We were about to lower the steps and hop off to discuss the matter further, when Suzi's voice came through on the intercom, ordering us to bolt the tailgate shut and strap down the canvas.

"Why?" one of us buzzed back, but she had already switched off the intercom.

We had just finished stretching the canvas over the roof bars and lashing it down to the side cleats when suddenly the engine gunned to life and we jerked forward straight into the crowd. The mob panicked at first and ran back, amazed that a crowd of tourists would dare do such a thing. They soon recovered, knitting back together and forcing Suzi to slow to a crawl. They brought her to a virtual halt, but she continued making threatening noises with the engine, firing the pistons like an angry bull elephant. The crowd's chanting took on a menacing air, and I began to realise that we were in deep over our heads. Suddenly a rock was thrown, ripping through the canvas and landing directly in on top of us. More stones followed, dozens of them, mostly just pebbles that bounced straight back off the canvas, but some larger ones pierced it and came raining in on us. A few men began banging the body of the truck with sticks and shovels, and two of them pulled themselves up on to the tailgate to try and undo it. Henry unclasped the axe and began waving it over their heads. His cheeks were fiery, his eyes wide with adrenaline, and looking into his bulging pupils I realised he was capable of anything at that moment.

"Get down on the floor!" Suzi shouted at us through the intercom, and we all did.

I didn't get to see what happened next but felt the engine straining under us and heard the crash of stones smashing against the cab until eventually Suzi crunched the gears into reverse and retreated. She drove about a hundred metres back and pulled in off the road. The crowd didn't make any effort to follow us. They meant us no real harm; they just didn't want us passing their picket. We got up slowly from the floor, looking around us, assessing the damage. The engine was still idling menacingly, and I wondered whether Suzi might be planning a fresh assault, but eventually she turned the key off and got out. She was smiling broadly, seemingly having enjoyed the whole thing. The rest of us were really shook up. The initial energy rush had drained away, and we were beginning to feel queasy. The most alarming element was not seeing what might lie ahead on this trip for us, but seeing what Suzi was capable of, if pushed.

Rita was looking around her, punch drunk with adrenaline and determined to confront Suzi.

"Come on, Vinnie," she said to her husband, "you're not going to let that bitch get away with that, are you? She almost killed us back there."

"You reckon?" Vinnie said, reluctantly, his hard eyes angry but resigned. His family could trace their lineage on the Isle of Man for seven generations. They had grown accustomed to being bossed around by outside powers.

"I'm serious!" she said, pushing Vinnie towards Suzi, who was lounging nonchalantly against the truck with her shades pulled down, arms crossed, coolly chewing gum – daring anyone to approach her.

Vinnie meandered up to her, nervously clearing his throat. Suzi pulled her shades off, fixing him with a frigid stare.

He looked anxiously back at his wife, then at Suzi, just as Mustafa's friend had when he offered us the herbs.

"Vinnie?" Suzi said coldly. "A problem, *peut–être?*"

Vinnie hummed and hawed. In truth, there was little he could say. Suzi alone knew the relative risk of any situation. Maybe she had been right to react as she had. If she hadn't, the protestors might have sensed our weakness and commandeered the truck or, possibly worse, done something we could never imagine. We simply didn't know. The fact was that we knew nothing, and being on the back of the truck for most of the day meant we were learning very little as we went along. We were like lab rats with the cage door left open. Our little army truck with its ridiculous intercom and sand-ladders bolted to either side as fortification was our cage. If Africa wanted to experiment on us, all it had to do was pick us out one by one.

Rather than driving the hundred-mile detour to the other road, we decided to cut loose from the tarmac and head overland to the next oasis south of us, relying on the compass to steer us clear of the mini war zone we had created. It felt good at first to be bounding our way across the open landscape, driving along dry riverbeds and rutted camel tracks – striking out into the heart of Africa, but it made the journey a bit more uncertain. Looking around me, I soon realised there were two principle forms of desert: the slinky, sandy one of my imagination and the flat, stone-swept terrain that spread out as far as the horizon all around us – plains of sandstone shards, strewn here and there with large boulders and quartzite rocks that shimmered blindingly in the sunlight.

Every now and then we came upon a tiny oasis with blue-tiled colonnades sheltering stalls and a precast overhang that cantilevered out so far it masked the sun completely, making the room so dark that fluorescent strips were needed to reveal the stocks of shampoo, safety pins, dry biscuits and yoghurts on sale. The yoghurt must have been some incredible mutant form to withstand the kiln-like ambient temperature, as I never once saw a fridge.

The buildings in these oases were made of mud and sandy concrete, and thus they tended to blend in with their surroundings so that one was hardly aware of them until the smell of fresh baguettes wafting on the air announced their presence. The bread was a legacy of the French. Each oasis village, no matter how small, had at least one *boulangerie* producing fresh bread three times a day. There was no way that the villagers could get through this amount, and most of it was dumped. It was the French who were to blame for this ridiculous squandering. They had instilled an addiction to fresh baguettes in their subjects which was impossible to satiate as the bread went stale immediately in the arid air, and so new batches had to be baked every few hours. It was a terrible waste of materials and energy, and the government ended up footing the bill. If they didn't, prices would soar and there would be a revolt.

Each oasis was a cause of wonder. The very fact that it managed to exist out there in the oceans of gravel, the shifting sands and outcrops of soaring rock that stretched as far as the Red Sea, left me dumbfounded. After driving for days, I would feel certain we had reached the furthest extent of civilisation, and yet a day or two later the smell of baking would come drifting across the plain. The cartographers who had drawn the maps felt the same amazement, and they displayed each village, no matter how small, with inordinate zeal – paroxysms of cartographic glee. Yet these were as nothing compared with their response to the presence of a well or a spring, which elicited the equivalent of cartographic cartwheels.

Fortunately, the dreams diminished in the desert. Perhaps it was too dry, too dead for them – or perhaps the days themselves were so like one long waking dream that I simply couldn't recall my night wanderings. I was rather disorientated during most of my time in the Sahara. The intense heat and endless burnt-out vista of muted nothingness left my mind sluggish and my body enervated. The lack of activity meant that I wasn't tired at the end of the day and so didn't sleep much. I'd lay awake beside Wayne, listening. The few audible sounds were heightened by the lack of any other noise – no leaves rustling or wind blowing or other signs of life. I found myself tuning into the conversations of the group.

"Please, no . . . not again," I would hear one of the women say.

"Come on, love."

"No!"

"Look, we've . . ."

"Please!"

"What am I supposed . . . ?"

She would emit a sigh and it was always this that seemed to provoke him the most.

"For fuck sake!"

"I swear, it's just . . . !" she would plead, but she knew she had already lost. There would be a barely stifled cry and the sounds of a struggle and she would give in. She always gave in.

It was hard next morning to have breakfast with them and pretend I had heard nothing.

There were other sounds too. Lucy and Natasha were almost always chattering away until late into the night in their iggle-wiggle language. I began to make out some of the words, or at least I could spot names easily enough. Can-iggle-dun was Duncan's. His name cropped up a lot, often accompanied by nervous giggles from Natasha. I grew anxious about what might happen to Natasha when Duncan inevitably made his move. I asked Stella, my cooking partner, whether we should do something about it.

"What do you mean – do something?" she said.

"You know, intervene," I said.

"You sound like you've stepped from the Victorian age. Do you want them to ask your permission?"

"It's just that she's so young."

"She's eighteen, for god's sake," Stella said. "She's no child."

"But he's luring her in."

"He's flirting. Can't they flirt?"

"So you think they're a good match?" I said.

She sighed. "Look, he's a *bad* boy. Girls her age like bad boys. It's just the way it is. And anyway, he is quite cute."

It was my turn to sigh. I noticed all the women found him attractive. Although he was a bit chubby, he had wonderfully sallow skin, a scraggy shock of blond hair and large bovine, blue eyes.

"Are you jealous or something?" Stella said.

"I don't want to see her get hurt."

Stella laughed. "We're heading into the heart of Africa," she said, "one way or another we're all going to get hurt. That's for sure."

I looked up at her, about to say something, but all of a sudden I was distracted by the sight, far off in the distance, of three figures coming through the haze towards us. We had been driving for six hours straight through a particularly desolate expanse of granulated, lead-coloured stone without seeing anything, any person, animal, insect or even rock, except a sole cirrus cloud that had accompanied us since breakfast, and yet suddenly here were three figures silhouetted on the skyline. It was like a waking dream, a scene of apparitions and half-baked mirages.

As they approached, I realised they were children. The eldest was a girl of about twelve in a torn dress the colour of lush grass. She was holding the bony hands of her two brothers, who were both naked except for an empty jerry can which shielded the genitals of one.

We were all – them and us – dazed by the heat and simply stared at one another, mesmerised with incomprehension. Neither of us had a clue what the other was doing there. Their slow, ponderous movements, minimised in an effort to conserve every spare kilojoule of energy, added to the sense of otherworldliness.

The youngest boy suddenly began to cry, which broke the spell, and the girl held up the jerry-can beseechingly towards us. We suddenly realised that she wanted water and began to rush around unlocking water tanks to fill the can and whatever extra bottles we had available. In a vain attempt to bridge the chasm between us, Mildred threw down a pack of *Juicy Fruits*, which the girl picked up and turned over quizzically, while her brothers rolled in the moist patch where our water tanks had dribbled. The wetness dried instantly into their shellac skin, and they turned back into the wilderness once again. Dudley and Stevi began clicking their cameras, as though they felt some reaction was called for and this was the only thing they could think of. They had the grace at least to look embarrassed, possibly knowing how inappropriate their behaviour was, but conceiving of no better alternative. Luke and Holly were uttering those unintelligible sounds you resort to when no intelligible ones will do.

Episodes like these burned themselves on to my mind, sparking a hundred questions that there was never time to answer. On another occasion, we came upon a caravan of mangy camels led by an outrider on a white horse. They too had wanted water from us, and we siphoned out as much as we could spare for them before they turned back into the expanse. I wanted to know more about these people, what they were doing here, where they were going, but Suzi insisted there was no time. Our trip was like a trashy movie: a rapid series of superficial images with a minimum of interpretation.

At least in the oases we had time to wander around on our own. People there were open and outward-looking, having dealt with travellers and traders for thousands of years. Yet, I noticed, they were careful not to reveal too much about themselves – they realised that we were just more new faces in an endless line that had been passing through for ever. Other foreign travellers, on the other hand, were more amenable. They tended to be an eclectic bunch: a Canadian couple on a tandem, a French bodybuilder pulling a bus to Burkina Faso, ten members of the Devon Young Farmers' Association driving a Massey Ferguson to Ethiopia. They were all following the same route as we were, and we kept bumping into each other from oasis to oasis. The sense of wilderness that was so prevalent in the desert was completely absent in these pit stops. One was liable to meet anyone from anywhere – one could feel oneself part of a timeless cavalcade that had been winding its way across the desert since the Roman era. I was keen to meet the three one-legged Vietnam vets who we were told were crossing the desert on Harley Davidsons. It seemed that they were on the lookout for us too, as someone had told them that Joe was a phenomenal mechanic and they needed him to check out a faulty fuel pump.

We pulled into the oasis town of In Salah just as a sandstorm was about to hit, and the first person I met as I jumped off the truck, eager as ever to escape temporarily from the group, was Salade, a middle-aged English woman who was sitting on a flour sack sheltering from the storm behind a low wall outside a café. She looked up into the flying sand and grimaced. These frequent storms had been exciting at first – each stinging grain pricking one's pores like a Lilliputian dart – but soon they grew wearying. I began to feel sure that the sand must be embedded beneath my epidermis like the African timber that glistens when sawn with the crystals of long ago sandstorms. Salade was ill-dressed for the weather in a tiny blue dress made of a crepe-like material. I could see the grains needling into her bare arms and legs. Her long brown hair, brittle and dusty, was pulled in tight under an embroidered cap. Curls of hair peaked out from her armpits – it was as dry and dusty as the rest of her. She had evidently been on the road a long time. I wondered whether she had hiked here, or at least hitch-hiked. I could see no sign of a vehicle, and certainly if she were a Land Rover driver, would most likely have already been dragging me over to it, to take me through its specs and modifications.

"Hi," she said in a flat northern English accent, smiling blissfully and revealing a missing front tooth.

"You off that truck?" she asked.

I nodded.

"You silly sausage," she said. "You silly, silly sausage."

I couldn't think of a suitable reply.

"Are you buying me a drink?" she asked.

I made for the bar, thinking that any company was better than the ones I had. I had hoped that Luke and Holly and I could be friends, but they seemed to be spending more time together now. I felt a bit in the way.

"The name's Salade," she said when I returned with two cold beers. "My friends add the preface 'mixed' when they're feeling unkind."

I told her my own name, and quite unexpectedly she got up off her hunkers and hugged me, squeezing me tightly against her droopy fried egg breasts, letting me go and then reaching in again to kiss me wetly on both cheeks. The dryness of her hair and skin was more than made up for by the wetness of her mouth. I hoped the others hadn't been watching. They would tease me unmercifully.

I asked her the first question travellers always ask, and she was outraged.

"You're asking me where I'm from!" she screamed. "What a fucking
question! Who cares? Maybe I'm a gypsy, a rambler, a karmic gambler."

"I was just asking," I said.

"Maybe I'm from the East, or the West – the womb of my mammy.
Who cares? Let's just say from Daddy's dick and Mammy's box. From
whatever divine movie mogul set up this whole surreal light charade in
the first place. Why does it have to be one particular place? You going to
ask about my health now? Or the weather? Do we have to swap photos of
loved ones?"

I heard my name, followed by a catcall coming from the truck, and
looked around. It appeared the others had been watching. Rodney was on
guard duty. I could see him pointing at me and whispering to Dorothy.

"I'm actually on the look out for a man," Salade said. "Are you staying long?"

I told her I wasn't.

"Well, have you come across any suitable suspects?"

I told her about the French bodybuilder and the Vietnam vets that I
had heard about.

"Sounds promising. I never mind a bit of baggage – which of us has-
n't got at least some? Just no kids or pets, that's my rule. I draw the line;
had my fill of kids and pets. I've been the mummy, been the guru, been the
pimp for others and even the gimp. I don't need all that ego stroking any
more, just the stroking. I'm a lady who needs a lot of stroking . . . And stok-
ing too, get it . . . ? I *enjoys* all that stuff. I want a boy who can see beyond
these sagging chicken wings and laugh the cosmic giggle with me."

She looked at her empty beer bottle.

"Do you believe in ascension?" she asked forlornly.

I shrugged.

"Tell me you believe in another round of beer at least," she said, calling out to the waiter, asking for the same again. "Ascension – you know?
The way that all thoughts and feelings we release are vibrations sent
through us as sort of spell-weaving . . ."

She looked at me, expecting an answer.

"I'm really not sure," I said.

"You should be," she said disappointedly.

She wetted her finger and ran it around the mouth of the beer bottle until it sang. It suddenly struck me that it was people like her that I was hoping the truck would be full of. Oddballs, eccentrics.

"Are you present?" she asked, straightening up and staring at me.

"Sorry?"

"Present?" she said again. "You know, in the here and now?"

"Oh," I said doubtfully.

"Well, are you?"

"I suppose," I said.

"Good," she said, visibly relaxing. The focus with which she had asked the question and then the relief following my reply reminded me of someone holding their breath under water and shooting to the surface. "Keep asking me the same, OK? It's important. I need to stay present. Sometimes, I . . ."

She fell quiet and drank her beer distractedly. The storm had abated and the street sweepers were out cleaning up already. It was the neatness of oasis towns that struck me most; particularly El Golea with its elegant palm-lined, colonial boulevards and pretty *patisseries* with delicacies laid out on pastel paper in the windows.

After a while, Salade raised her eyes to me expectantly.

"Well?" she said when I didn't react. "Ask me!"

I stared at her for a moment. Then I remembered and asked her was she present, and she nodded that indeed she was.

"Actually, even if you *were* staying around, which you're not, you're no good to me," she said emphatically. "I need someone substantial. Meat in their mind and on their bones. Ideally, a bit Goth around the edges. Someone who's done the whole processing thing, you know? Cut the ties and come out the other side."

She slugged from the bottle, and I watched as a dribble of beer slipped down her clavicle. It seemed to awaken the smell of her skin, which had all the sweetness and intensity I remembered from the markets in Morocco: the dried figs and dates, olives and fresh almonds. There was something alluring about her despite the flat English accent. An element of exoticness. It was as if she had become part of the desiccated desert – a little solitary oasis in it fighting for life.

"Can you read runes?" she asked without much hope in her voice.

I shook my head.

"Guessed as much. Well, you'll have to give it a go, 'cause I'm not going to find anyone better around here."

"I don't know how," I said.

"Course you do," she insisted. "You're Irish, aren't you – it's instinctive."

Weren't they Nordic? I wanted to say, but kept it to myself. She dug out a small black pouch from her pocket and threw it in front of me, undoing the drawstring and pouring out the tiny figures.

I stared at her questioningly.

"Do you dream?" she asked. "That's the only skill you need. If you can dream you can read runes – any pillock can read runes."

I didn't tell her I happened to have an A+ in dreaming, but it gave me a bit of confidence, and I picked up the pouch and decided to give it a go. She unrolled a few sheets of lavatory paper from a roll she had in her bag and laid them out on the step as a sort of altar mat.

"This'll mark the boundaries of the casting," she said. Then she got me to put all the tiny symbols back in the bag and juggle them about. "Now, just follow your heart."

I closed my eyes and pawed around until I found the pouch and stuck my hand in, pulling out a few symbols and laying them on the altar. They meant nothing to me, but I could see that I was expected to interpret them. I closed my eyes again and tried to think. Nothing came. I opened one eye and she was staring at me, her face wide with expectation. I shut my eyes tighter and forced myself to come up with something.

"I see an antelope," I said, eventually.

She rounded her eyes wide in amazement.

"You do?" she said.

"Well . . . kind of," I said hesitantly.

"Really?" she said breathlessly. "Tell me truthfully."

"It wasn't very clear or anything, but . . ."

"Did it have horns?" she asked.

"I think so."

"Jesus," she said, brushing a cricket from her shoulder. "Who would have thought? You're a right little warlock, aren't you!"

"What?" I said.

"Well, you're pretty spot on. You know about this place, yeah? In Salah – why it's here?"

"The hot springs?" I said.

Suzi had been telling us about the springs and the mineral baths of In Salah since we'd left England. They were the perfect antidote to weeks of sandblasting by Sirocco storms.

"Yeah, the springs," she said impatiently, "but not just that; the springs are what's left of the swamps that used to be here. Archeologists found remains of elephants and hippos. And antelopes! Most of all antelopes. This was the main gathering point for them. You didn't know?"

"No."

"Do you find yourself aware of stuff like that often?"

"I wasn't aware of anything," I said.

"Have you been dreaming of antelopes?"

"No!" I snapped. "I haven't been dreaming at all."

"Of course you have," she said knowingly.

"No, not since coming here," I said, "to the desert."

"But you were dreaming about antelopes before?"

"No," I said.

"About sex?"

"No!"

"Loss?"

"No," I said. "Well, sort of – about death."

"That figures," she said sadly. "Me too. Actually, my dreams are about men, but they are all dead, in their hearts or minds or dicks. I think it comes with this place. Everything is dead here. You can't have a desert without death. I just wish I could find a man – a living one."

"These dreams I'm having . . ." I began.

"Tell me, Mocha, do you not get lonely on that truck of yours," she ploughed right over me, "with all those nerds and retards? Just look at them, like nasty little ants beavering away in their metal nest. That's what I said to myself when I saw you guys pull in: primordial, knuckle-dragging scum. No offence, of course."

"Right," I said.

"Don't you ever want to just *be*," she said. "To be with someone, to

88

share that gasp of beauty as you look around you. Remember what Winnie-the-Pooh says: you're the bee of the invisible madly gathering the honey of the visible to . . ."

"Why are you talking about Winnie-the-Pooh?" I interrupted, rather more curtly than I intended.

"I'm not," she insisted.

"Yes, you were," I said. "Why Winnie-the-Pooh?"

"I never mentioned him."

"All that stuff about the bee of the invisible," I said.

"Oh that," she said, "that's Benjamin Hoff, his book about Tao. How does it go again? Something about gathering the honey of the visible to build invisible hives. I don't remember exactly. What do you have against Pooh bear, anyway?"

"Nothing," I said.

She huffed dismissively, and then said, "Don't you find you get terribly thirsty here? I certainly do. Maybe you should go up and stand us another round. I'd get it myself, but . . ."

She opened up a pinched leather purse to show its empty innards. The storm had abated and the sun was pounding down angrily again. I felt a bit dizzy, but I ignored it and went up to the bar to get us more beer. I was feeling frazzled by her mentioning Pooh like that, as if she was trying to hint about Lucy. She had all the philosophy and spark that I wanted Lucy to have. I wanted to meld the two of them, to create a Lucy salad.

"Sure, I feel a bit stifled sometimes," I said when I got back. "We all do . . ."

"Who are you telling? Believe me, you can't know how homeless I feel on this planet sometimes," she said, "or how I want to cry with loneliness. I get this desperation to belong, to beeee-long. I'll tell you this much: when my heart is hurting most, that's when I'm really alive. Do you understand? They say never show a poem to a non-poet. Are you a poet, Mocha? Are you?"

I shrugged.

"Kiss me!" she said.

Suddenly I found myself kissing her, this woman almost three times my age. Feeling her tongue sliding deeper and yet not pulling back. I think I was just so grateful to her for showing me what I was missing, for showing me how wrong my decision had been to come on this trip, to strap myself on this truck. I knew now that I would never make the same mistake again. Hopefully there would be other opportunities for travel in my life, but never again would I condemn myself to a group. In that moment of clarity, with her tongue riding around my mouth, I made myself that solemn promise, and in doing so, pulled away from Salade. Part of me was reluctant to. Beyond her sun-cracked lips was a place of such wetness and tenderness that it was a drag to leave it. It was strange to think of it existing contemporaneously with this arid land. It was only when I heard the laughter coming from the truck that I came fully back to reality. I noticed Salade was crying – large, sun-glistening tears streaming down her cheeks. I ignored the laughter and bent forward to kiss them, and to my surprise they didn't feel wet. They were arid and salty and vanished beneath my lips like the ghost of the ocean that had once covered this whole desert.

"Silly me," she said. "I'm the silly sausage now, crying tears of sand in this uncaring place. Sometimes my tears turn to pearls, but not often, I admit. It doesn't stop me shedding them, casting them with fecundity before lovers and swine. I figure this place needs all the moisture it can get. Now, buy me another beer and I'll blow your dick."

"Sorry?"

"When was the last time you were offered that?" she said with a laugh.

I didn't know what to say, but my mind was intensely conscious of the sweetness of her mouth.

"Come over here with me and I'll sort you out," she said, "I'm serious. You look like you could do with it."

Without thinking I got up and followed her around to the lavatory block at the back of the café. I tried to block out the series of squalid drop-holes in the ground, but the smell of faeces and the swarms of flies brought me back to my senses and before she had even unzipped my trousers I pulled away from her and went reeling back into the harsh sun, bewildered.

"Sorry," I heard her calling after me. "My fault, Mocha. All my fault."

Chapter 8

THE MINERAL BATHS were one of the things we were most eagerly anticipating since reaching the desert. Suzi had been telling us about the exquisite sensation of soaking away weeks of sand and dust in deep concrete baths filled to the brim with mineral water. We planned to spend a whole afternoon there, but when we arrived a skeletal woman in a radish-coloured *djellaba* explained that we could only have an hour and that each bath had to be shared by two people. Without any further discussion she pushed Norman and me towards the first one and closed the door on us.

"I'm not getting into the water with that queer," Norman tried to say to her. "I want Duncan. He's my brother."

But she had no English, and had already moved on to the next cubicle. We were left standing there staring at each other.

"Well, this is an odd one, Norman," I said, my words echoing back down off the dripping walls and calcified pipes. We both looked at the intimate pit filled to the brim with mineral-rich water. It was so inviting. All I could think of was how desperately I wanted to soak myself in this last vestige of the Saharan swamps and seas that preceded them. I could smell the iodine in the air, taste the saline on my lips – proof that this water had indeed once been ocean. It had the same saltiness that always took me aback when I tasted it on the grains of sands that flew at us during sandstorms.

The situation Norman and I now found ourselves in was complicated by an incident that had occurred the previous week. We had reached El Golea, a town in Algeria that will always be associated for me with the best *pain au chocolat* in northern Africa, and on driving into the main campsite, we noticed that the rich overland group whose tent the boys had urinated on in Fez was parked beside us. At first we feared that they might seek revenge, but we soon gathered that they weren't the sort of people to descend to such behaviour, unless indirectly through their solicitors. The fear in their eyes when they saw us made it clear where the balance of power lay. But, just to be on the safe side, we decided to be extra vigilant during our stay and intensified the guarding rota for the truck. Wayne offered to spend the night on board in case they tried tampering with our belongings while we were asleep, and this left me with the tent all to myself. I thought about Lucy, about inviting her over, but I chickened out for all the reasons I have tried explaining earlier. In the end, I went to bed soon after dinner and was just falling asleep when the front cord of my fly-sheet was twanged from outside – someone had tripped over it accidentally. Next I heard Norman make some caustic remark about the state of my tent, and he gave the poles a quick shake. I made no comment and turned over to try and sleep again, but before I realised what was happening, he had unzipped the outside flap and was poking his big head through.

"You're not lonely are you?" he said with a big sheepish grin. "Without Wayne and all?"

"No, Norman, I'm fine. Thanks," I said.

"You're alright, you know that?"

"Thanks," I said.

"Yeah," he said, "you're not thick, like some of them. Know what I mean? You're open to stuff. New stuff."

"Am I?" I said anxiously.

"Yeah," he said, sticking his torso in further and kneading my shoulder chummily.

By this stage both his arms were inside the tent, and he seemed to be about to leverage the rest of his vast girth in. I began to get concerned, but suddenly from behind I heard his brother calling him. Norman smiled weakly, a sort of *these things are sent to try us* smile, and began the awkward process of extracting himself from the tent. I had no idea what had been on his mind and preferred not to think too much about it. He was very drunk at the time, and I hoped he wouldn't remember it in the morning.

It's fair to say that this incident definitely added a certain frisson to the situation we now found ourselves in with the bath. Norman was looking back and forth between me and the water like a rat in an experiment. He too desperately wanted to soak himself in the revivifying waters, but nothing in his life thus far had prepared him for having to share a bath with another man.

Finally he said, "We're both getting into the water, Mocha, right? But neither of us is taking our clothes off."

"For Christ's sake!" I said.

"I'm bloody serious, mate," he said, "you can take your top off, but that's it."

We had a stand-off for a moment, but in the end I realised he wasn't going to back down. Reluctantly I stepped into the water with my trousers on, then squeezed myself as far as I could to one side as he pulled off his football top and manoeuvred his flabby body in beside me, displacing half the water in the process. We sat there staring at each other like two ruminating cows, until finally the skeleton woman returned and signalled for one of us to follow her. I leapt out and she led me into a central room with a grand dome that soared upwards. It was embedded with tiles of coloured glass from which shards of sun shot across the stone floor. The woman told me to lie down, and she began to pummel me with a stiff brush, rubbing me now and then with a bar of carbolic soap. She grabbed my limbs and began to stretch and twist them like toffee. It was hard to reconcile such brute strength with such a tiny woman. I felt helpless, but cared for – like a side of beef in the hands of a good butcher. Before I knew it, I was on my feet again and she was pointing at me to stand against the wall facing her. She pulled out a long rubber hose and sent water shooting out at me at tennis-serve velocity. I felt the lash of its jet hard as willow against my stomach and thanked God that Norman had made me keep my trousers on. The hose seemed to be bucking wildly, and I didn't believe she could possibly maintain complete control over it. Just to be safe, I turned to face the wall so she could play riot police on my back instead. Finally she turned the tap off, and sent me away as clean and red as a boiled lobster.

When I got back to my cubicle, there was a beautiful tattooed woman in a ragged lilac night-gown sitting on the side of the bath talking to Norman. She was teaching him Arabic curses, which as far as I could gather were all based around the sexual proclivities with camels of the mother of the person concerned. Norman had got the hang of it in no time and was already extemporising wildly.

"Go screw your mother while she rims my camel . . . Why don't you help your mammy sucking my camel's balls."

The various subgroups that were beginning to delineate themselves in the group became most apparent a few days later when we pitched camp in the shadow of some sand dunes south of In Salah. These were the first genuine dunes we had come across, and half of us wanted to get up and play on them as soon as our tents were pitched. We grabbed whatever we could find – plastic bags, fly sheets, floorboards – to use as toboggans and spent the whole evening running up the slopes and sliding back down again. It was like a massive playground. You could throw yourself off the top and land on the bottom having tumbled head over heels the whole way.

The increased exertion brought added thirst, which in turn put increased pressure on our water supply. Suzi had been cutting back the amount of water we could each have since we'd arrived in the desert. We were forbidden from using any for cooking and so had to eat tinned chicken stew for four nights in a row and wash our dishes in the sand. Each of us was permitted three litres a day. It was meant to be strictly for drinking, although some of the more hygiene-obsessed used their ration for a sponge bath.

The group who had gone tobogganing had by necessity drunk a bit more than their allotted share of water for the day, but not all that much. Nevertheless, after dinner Felicity gathered us all together and said, "I can't believe how irresponsible you guys are. You put all of us at risk."

"How?" I said.

She looked at me indignantly, refusing to dignify my question with a reply. Turning to the rest of the group, she said, "What happens if the next well is dry or, God forbid, something happens to the truck? What then? I don't want to die of thirst just so that you monkeys can have your playtime."

"For God's sake," Luke said.

"Nothing is going to happen to the truck," Joe, the mechanic, said defensively.

"No, she's right," Henry, the retired surveyor, said. "What if one of you had got lost? If you had taken the wrong slope down you could easily lose your bearings and not find your way back. Do you expect us to risk our lives looking for you? Even a few hours out there without water could kill you."

We looked to Suzi in the hope that she would mediate. It was she after all who had suggested we use the floorboards and sacks as sleds in the first place. But she just looked around wearily and grimaced. She couldn't summon the energy to care any more about our minor bickering. Of course, the tobogganing was a little bit risky, but it was fun; something to alleviate the monotony. Suzi had spent the day before teaching us how to sand-surf by dragging the bonnet of an abandoned car behind the truck with a few of us clinging on to it. That game had had to be abandoned too after the two prickly nurses pointed out the dangers. Suzi now got up and wandered off, leaving us bickering back and forth for most of the night.

When she finally did come back, we were still squabbling.

"For Christ's sake," she screamed, throwing her hands to her head. "You guys got to get your shit together."

She spoke slowly, each word falling like snow without wind. We didn't say anything, just stared at the sand. I think we all understood what she was feeling.

"What the hell are you like?" she whispered. "Are you all completely insane?"

If there had been any nascent leader amongst us, that would have been the moment for him or her to come forward. We needed to be guided or at least to find someone who could help us to air our frustrations and resentments properly. Instead we all remained silent, just chewed bitterly over the others' intransigence. I think that was the moment I realised that the marriage was over; relations between the various factions had become irreconcilable. From here on in, things would inevitably get sourer. At its core it was a split between those who wanted to have a bit of fun occasionally and those who were so frightened of the uncertainty of everything they had signed up for that they just hoped to get the whole thing over with as quickly as possible.

Oddly enough, the ones who objected to us using extra water for needless exertion had no problem giving it away to people we met along the way or using extra water themselves while straining to help others. As we got deeper into the desert, we came across trucks and cars stuck in sand, and we occasionally would have to use our sand ladders to dig them out. Our truck with its huge bulbous tyres and powerful engine could winch almost anything out, even the massive old twenty-tonne Mercedes trucks from post-war Germany which students drove across to sell on the other side. The extra exertion always meant we drank more than our allotted rations that evening, but no one ever complained. As long as there was no fun or frivolity involved, it was OK.

As we got deeper and deeper into the desert, the obsession with water heightened, especially as we approached the dead zone in the centre. If anything went wrong here, we would be in real trouble. No one would find us, and if they did, it was unlikely they would be able to rescue the whole lot of us. Once our truck stopped moving, it turned into an oven with only the canopy to provide some shelter from the sun. We had eight forty-gallon water drums on board, but were down to our last two by the time we reached the "graveyard stretch", an area of notoriously soft sand in the centre, where the skeletons of long-abandoned trucks and Mercedes 200s, Peugeot 305s and 2CVs were scattered far and wide. I wondered whether the owners of these vehicles could possibly have escaped alive. In theory, everyone who crosses the desert has to register with the police beforehand, and if you don't report back on the far side, a search party is sent out, but by then it is almost always too late.

After 5,400 kilometres of driving south, we reached Tamanrasset – the driest, deadest point in the journey so far. From here on in, the land would become gradually more fertile until we reached the Equator, another 5,600 kilometres south. Pulling up outside a jumble of dried-blood coloured buildings in the centre of town, Suzi got out and told us to wait while she sorted something out. She returned shortly after, telling us to grab jumpers and sleeping bags and follow her. We got into four battered old Land Cruisers and began driving out of town again.

"Where are we going?" one of us asked.

"Up," she said pointing towards the black outcrop of volcanic boulders,

lava flows, burnt quartzite and grotesquely twisted spires that had gradually arisen before us over the last two days like some long-forgotten citadel
swallowed in the wilderness. I had never known there were mountains in
the Sahara, especially not gruesome black ones that soared 3,000 metres into
the sky.

"You'd think someone would have thought to mention them," said
Luke. "Even just once, in a book or a movie – Tintin or those old Foreign
Legion movies, for example."

These were the Hoggar Mountains, a dust-blown skeleton of rock
grown brittle through the ages, mostly buried in layers of lava dust and
scree. Our convoy of jeeps attacked them as one, skidding and sliding up
over the bare rock for bone-juddering hours on end. It was dark by the
time we finally stopped driving.

"What now?" we asked.

Suzi led us across a gravel-strewn ledge to a bare room, saying we
should try and get some sleep as she would be waking us again before
dawn. It was freezing up there, and the sudden change in altitude was disorientating. No one slept well. (Cold was something I hadn't expected in
the desert: the fact that at night you longed for heat as passionately as you
did for cold during the day.)

At around 4 a.m. Suzi got us up, and we grumbled about the discomfort and wanted to know what the hell we were doing here anyway. All Suzi
would say was that the view would make it all worthwhile. She led us up
the last stretch of mountain along a narrow, winding trail to the summit.
It was still pitch dark as we made our way across the rocks using our hands
as antennae. Finally at about 5 a.m. the sun appeared way off in the distance, out towards Egypt. We wrapped blankets around us and watched as
it began to climb its way through the blackened spires and gnarled
columns, carving around the monstrous needles and illuminating bits of
quartzite as it went, making the world look like a monstrous neon sea
urchin. We were perched on the only high point for hundreds of kilometres around – 3000 metres above the rest of the world – watching as it was
slowly set alight. We looked around at it awakening, all of us realising the
same thing, that as long as we lived we would probably never again see a
sunrise like this. It was something we all shared in common. No matter
what other differences there were between us, we would have this as a

shared memory. We may all have had different reasons for being here, and we would be bringing very different things back with us, but the one spectacle all of us would surely hold in common was this, burnt into our memories for ever. If we met in fifty years' time, this is what we would talk about.

Afterwards Suzi led us into a bare stone oratory where a hermit was saying mass. He looked up at us in surprise and then smiled, recognising us for what we were, another batch of travellers who had just had their hearts blown open by the ethereal light show – stray lambs ripe for holy intervention. We sat there on a simple plank bench, smiling blissfully as he finished his mass. Afterwards, he came over to us to explain about Charles de Foucauld, the original hermit who had built this place a hundred years before – a debauched French playboy who, after experiencing an epiphany, had turned towards religion with the same passion with which he had previously caroused. The charm and vivacity with which he espoused his new beliefs attracted so many followers that he was forced to run away, and he ended up here. From a life of sumptuousness, gorging on the finest food, he found himself surviving on the few boiled dates and grain kernels that he managed to barter with passing Tuareg nomads. His idea was to formulate a new interpretation of Catholicism that was free of all the hypocrisy, guilt and evil-fixation which had turned him against it in the first place. But in the end he never got to put his plans in place. He was beaten to death by an errant tribe of Tuareg herders who were suspicious of his motives.

The first person I saw when I got down from the mountains was Salade. She was in the campsite helping some English people repack their Land Rover.

"Sorry about the other day . . ." she said to me bashfully. "I may have been a bit drunk."

"No, no, I'm sorry," I said, unsure of what I was apologising for.

She smiled wanly.

"What are you doing here, anyway?" I said. "I didn't think you were an overlander."

"I'm not!" she said. "These nice people gave me a lift."

I nodded at the Land Rover owner and her husband.

"Is that your truck?" the husband asked.

"I'm just a passenger," I said.

"Wouldn't mind getting myself a set of those tyres," he said, pointing admiringly at our vast sand tyres. "I could turn my old Rover into Herbie the beach buggy!"

I made my excuses and escaped before he could trap me in an endless discussion about his jeep. I had learnt from experience that there was no limit to the extent to which Land Rover drivers were capable of talking about the specifications of their particular model. Many of them had been preparing their whole lives for the trip and presumed that the rest of us were as devoted as they were. It was impossible for them to imagine that I had just signed up for the trip a few weeks before leaving, basically because I couldn't think of anything better to do with £1,000.

"So what are you doing here?" I asked Salade, who had followed me back towards the truck.

"Research," she said, "with the Tuaregs."

"Research!" I exclaimed.

"Yeah," she said defensively, evidently hurt by my surprise.

"I'm sorry," I said, "I just didn't . . ."

"I went back to college as a mature student. Now I'm doing my thesis. I got a grant and all; studying the influence of enforced settlement on . . . something or other. In fact, I'm not meant to be here at all, I'm heading further south. I have to meet a man in In Guezzam. I presume you're heading that way? You all do."

Stella, my cooking partner, waved across the campsite at me. We were on cooking duty that night, and we had arranged to go to the market to see what was on offer. It would be our first meal that hadn't come from a tin in five days.

"Sorry, but I have to go now," I said to Salade. "Maybe I'll see you around."

"Were you up on the mountain?" she asked, ignoring my comment. "Did they tell you what the Tuaregs did for de Foucauld?"

"Yeah," I said, "they murdered him."

"No, not that!" she said impatiently. "Did the priest tell you about how they saved his life? Bet you he didn't. They never tell you that."

Stella came over and glanced suspiciously at Salade, who ignored her, being too caught up in her own story.

"You should have asked him about the time de Foucauld got bitten by a snake," Salade went on. "It was a fatal bite – a horned viper – incurable according to every doctor in the world. But not the Tuaregs; they knew different. They burnt the venom out with red hot irons and tied a tourniquet on his arm to stop it spreading. It saved his life, but it didn't cure him. He was in a coma for days until they branded his soles with irons. Did the priesty-man happen to mention that? Like hell he did! It wasn't Jesus Christ who came to his rescue, it was the pagan Tuaregs."

"I really have to go," I said.

"When is your truck leaving, anyway?" she asked. "I need a lift."

I hesitated. "You want to travel with us?"

"Just as far as In Guezzam," she said. "It would save me a bone-rattling journey in the back of a pickup."

"I'll see what I can do," I said.

"Who's she?" Stella asked when we were out of earshot. I tried to explain.

"And you want to give her a lift?" she exclaimed derisively.

"It can't hurt to ask," I said.

"Fat chance!" she said.

Stella's scepticism proved correct. The usual dissenters ruled it out straight away, saying it was an unnecessary risk. She would only be a burden, using up our precious food and water supplies.

"Fine," I said, somewhat irritated. "I just thought I'd ask."

"Yeah, well, it's not happening," Vinnie said.

"Maybe if she pays well above the odds we can bring her," Felicity suggested. "The kitty could do with the extra money – we're going to need more alcohol at some point."

"I don't think she was planning on paying," I said. "She just wanted a lift. We're heading her way."

"No, it's not on," Vinnie insisted.

Chapter 9

A S IT HAPPENED, we didn't leave Tamanrasset for another week. Sorting out visas and restocking supplies took longer than expected. I kept on bumping into Salade. She introduced me to some of the Tuareg men she had been interviewing. One morning she brought me to the edge of town to meet Fahlatwan, a widower who was dressed head to toe in heavy swathes of deep blue cloth. He was walking with his camel on the outskirts of town, and I was struck by how his gait was in perfect rhythm with the thin, heavy-jointed legs of his rather gristly looking camel. Salade offered him a bundle of sticks, which he accepted gladly – it seemed to be a recognised gift. After leading us towards the shade of a tamarisk tree and mumbling some words into his camel's ear to get it to crash down on to its knobbly knees, he began to prepare a fire on the sand. He spoke very little French and we had no Berber, so communication was quite stilted, but he seemed to be on good terms with Salade and was happy enough to have us sitting there with him.

"I've been coming out here every morning to have breakfast with Fahlatwan," she said, settling herself on the sand. "I met him in the market a few days ago selling a camel calf, and we've become firm friends. Haven't we, Fahlatwan?"

He nodded jovially, though it was unlikely he understood what she was saying.

"See that twinkle in his eye?" Salade said with a laugh. "He's quite the old codger, you know? Sex is pretty big for the Tuareg. They don't even have a word for virginity. That was the first thing I knew about them, that and the fact that they can go their whole lives without washing. I was sold on them after that!"

She laughed again and Fahlatwan mimicked her, all the time gazing implacably at us through the open band of his headdress, which acted like the metal hatch on a knight's visor. Even though his eyes were laid bare, they were largely inscrutable, having been narrowed by years of sunlight to the thinnest of slits. It struck me that this headdress, rather than masking him, actually funnelled one's attention completely to his core, to the windows of the soul, the place a doctor looks for signs of life. Its purpose was the exact opposite to Suzi's ever-present sunglasses.

Once the fire was blazing, he revealed from a fold in his robes a narrow-spouted teapot whose base had had its enamel chipped away. Into this he crammed dried twigs, the consistency of shag tobacco, and water which he drained from a goatskin *guerba* around his neck. He placed the pot on the fire and sat back.

"D'you happen to know County Kerry at all?" she asked me out of the blue.

"Yeah," I said. "A bit."

"Yeah?" she said. "Really? Do you know Dingle? Dick Mack's?"

"Of course," I said. Anyone who visits Dingle has a drink at Dick Mack's.

Fahlatwan swirled the tea around the pot, looking at us from the side of his eye now and again, seemingly happy enough to just listen to us chattering away.

"Is it still the same?" she said. "The long counter, the snug, the leather shop on one side?"

I nodded and she laughed delightedly.

"I had my first beer there," she said. "And my first whiskey, and gin, and vodka. Had my first Guinness there too, of course, lots of it. I was only fifteen."

She turned sombre.

More to fill the silence than anything else, I said, "The owner, old Dick Mack himself, is quite sick now. He's not the man he was."

"Poor love," she said sadly. "He was so good to us, gave us sandwiches and all."

At this she began to cry.

"What's wrong?" I said. "His son is still running the place."

Fahlatwan had dug out what looked like a collection of scrimshaws from his pocket and was holding them out to me. He was pointing at the sand around him, I think trying to convey that he had found them here. They were old bits of pottery and what looked like the remains of ancient fish hooks.

"It just brings me back, that's all," Salade said, taking no notice of Fahlatwan. "I'm sorry . . . My mum had just been put away and Dad for some reason thought it would be good to bring us all to Ireland. All five of us – my two brothers and two sisters and me. We took one of those horse wagon things for a week. You know, like the gypsies? What was he thinking? We couldn't stand being around each other at home, so what chance was there all cooped up in a hoop cart? My two brothers smoked pot the whole time and laughed at how ugly the locals were. My little sisters stayed under blankets inside all day moping. It pissed rain from morning to night, and Dad took to drinking again. I was the only one left to steer the damned horse. Every evening I'd have to unharness him and feed him oats in the pouring rain. When we reached Dingle I said, 'No fucking more!' We abandoned the wagon at the quayside and ran to Dick Mack's. Spent the next four days there. I've never laughed so much in all my life. Everything my brothers and sisters said seemed so damn funny. I had my first drink within a minute of stepping up to that great whiskey-stained counter, and we didn't stop drinking for three days – except once or twice to vomit out the back. God, the toilets in that place were basic. Are there new ones yet?"

I shrugged.

Fahlatwan had laid his bits of pottery down beside him and was now holding the pot up to the sun, peering inside examining the movement of the water, judging its heat. With elaborate dexterity he poured the tea in three foot waterfalls from pot to glass and back again, before setting it back to heat some more.

"I suppose old Mr Mack knew there was more important stuff to be doing in a day than cleaning the shit house," Salade said. "What was the word again – tayack an assol?"

"*Teach an asal*," I said. "Shit house?"

"That's it!" she said delightedly, repeating it for Fahlatwan and getting him to do likewise.

"Tayack an assol," Fahlatwan said.

"Well done, boy!" she said. "You're probably the only Irish-speaking Tuareg in the world."

"Tayack an assol," he said again.

"He made us ham sandwiches, old Mr Mack," she went on, "three times a day and wouldn't take a penny for them . . . I guess he felt sorry for us. He knew about our mum, you see? Everyone did. We never shut up about her. He even added tomato to Chrissie's, 'cause she claimed she was a vegetarian. Chrissie ate the whole thing – ham and all! She didn't have the heart to tell him what being a veggie really meant."

"He probably knew," I said. "He was just trying to make sure she got something into her to soak up the alcohol."

"You think?" she said dreamily. "Some of the regulars wondered if we weren't a bit young to be drinking, but someone would always pipe up, 'Sure hasn't their Mammy been put away and don't they need something to steady the nerves.' I loved that, *Steady the nerves!*"

Fahlatwan pulled out three shot glasses from a saddle bag and poured the tea, handing a glass first to me, then Salade.

"Tayack an assol," he said by way of a toast.

"That's right," Salade laughed. "What does it mean exactly?"

"Donkey house," I said.

"Yeah?" she said, shaking her head wistfully. "Poor old Mr Mack. He had even sent someone down to the quay to fetch the horse and bring it to a paddock. It's a shame he's poorly. Be sure to tell him I say hi if you ever see him. He used to call us the rainbow kids 'cause me and my sisters had these sleeveless puffer jackets like on Mork and Mindy."

I sipped some tea. It tasted ghastly – like camel urine.

"Good, eh?" Salade joked. "Got a certain kick to it."

"Tell him it's excellent," I said.

"*Efulki behara*," she said to Fahlatwan in Tachelhait. He bowed graciously.

"It's hard to imagine these people were invincible once," she said, nodding at him. "Controlled trade routes from Tripoli to Gibraltar."

Fahlatwan nodded back at her, recognising the place names, and she smiled at him.

"They're my sort of people. The women didn't do any household duties, did you know that? They were poets and writers. And they never covered their faces. When I heard that, I was smitten! All the menial work was done by slaves – black slaves from further south."

She noticed me struggling to drink the tea.

"It's a bit like nicotine soaked in urine, isn't it?" she said. "Definitely got a tang to it."

I grimaced.

"Now's a good time to ask me," she said.

"Huh?" I said.

She frowned. "You know! The question."

"What?"

"You know," she said impatiently: "am I present?"

"Oh, right," I said. "Well, are you?"

"Yeah, I guess I am," she said.

I looked at Fahlatwan, this representative of a ferocious warrior tribe who had once inspired fear throughout all of Africa and southern Europe, sharing tea with us on the edge of Tamanrasset, and realised that I too was very much present. Salade was definitely a good influence on me. She drew my focus away from the internal bickering on the truck.

"What's happening to Fahlatwan's people now?" I said. "How are they doing?"

"They're screwed," she said. "The government is trying to corral them in weird houses with no roofs, so they can put their tents up inside. It'll kill them, of course. The only reason they exist here at all is because they took over the land after it had been destroyed by others. Remember, this place was once covered in grain fields and saltwater lakes, but when the Romans finally exhausted the last of it and it began turning to desert, everyone left. It was only fit for nomads. Did Fahlatwan show you the stuff he finds?"

"No," I said.

"Yeah, he did," she said, pointing at his collection of crockery bits and metal fragments.

"Those metal lumps are fishing hooks!" Salade exclaimed. "Can you believe it? Imagine a fisherman here now. Only nomads will ever be able to live here – it's too fragile. The place depends on a few remaining wells and springs. If they get polluted, what hope is there?"

"*Non, merci,*" I said to Fahlatwan, who was offering me dates from a cone of waxed paper. They looked interesting, but the goat hairs and sand grains mixed in was a turn off.

"We need to learn from them," Salade went on, picking out a date and wiping it on her skirt, "instead of forcing them to follow our screwed-up ways. Maybe they can tell us how to survive in these places."

Chapter 10

TAMANRASSET WAS THE first mail-stop on route, and although I didn't get anything, those who did found it strangely disorientating. Our lives had become so subsumed in this bizarre subworld aboard the truck that they found it hard to relate to news from home. Everything appeared inconsequential compared to our new lives. Henry got a refund cheque from Tesco's, while Duncan got a poll-tax demand. News about a cousin's sore hip or progress on the new patio seemed outlandish when read in these monochrome Martian surroundings. For a thousand kilometres in each direction, there was nothing but sand and stone, and after a while it became hard to conceive of anything else. I tried to imagine the snow and ice that the World Service said was closing motorways in Britain, which was said to be experiencing its worst winter in forty years, but couldn't.

After our week of relative safety in town, we were reluctant to head back out into the burnt sands again – this endless shore that never reached the ocean. We knew that from here on in the trail became a lot trickier, with softer sand, less traffic and a less defined route to follow. Suzi cut our water ration to two litres a day, and a sense of heightened anxiety took hold of all of us for the duration of the days it took to reach In Guezzam, the next oasis. None of us talked much, each mulling over our own private anxieties. The sun beating back up off the dirty beige earth made my eyes bleary, as though I had just regained consciousness, and in fact it was only after sundown that my senses would return to normal.

One evening, as we were camped around a heap of burning tyres that we had picked up along the route and set alight, an old Peugeot came hurtling out of the darkness towards us with two Tuareg men and a woman inside. The men wore the same indigo-dyed robes as Fahlatwan and carried swords around their waists, but there was no trace of the former nobility that he managed to convey, nor any sign of his spark in their eye. These men were now little more than hawkers, leading a transient, gypsy existence selling wares they had made themselves or more likely bought in from others.

Without saying a word, the men got out and spread a grey flannel cloth on the sand and began languorously laying out various bracelets, daggers and Coptic-looking crosses from Agadez. They had copper pots too, but they knew we would have no use for these. Some of the girls showed an interest in the jewellery, and the woman began to pull agate eggs out of a pouch below her cleavage. Stevi was excited by these.

"Oh, yeah, now these are the babies," he said. "She's pullin' out the good stuff now. Look at the strata – flawless! And a whiff of Tuareg boob to boot! I'm such a sucker for it!"

He bought three eggs, and some of the others bought jewellery. Norman tried out a few of the daggers for size, but in the end decided he was looking for something longer, a full-length sword.

"No problem," said one of the hawkers, opening the boot of the Peugeot and pulling out swords and scabbards from beneath two live goats which were bound on the floor. "Take your pick."

We all jumped back when we saw the goats. I had heard something from inside the car earlier but decided it was just the metal creaking in the heat.

"Jesus!" Rodney cried. "What are they?"

"Swords," the hawker replied. "You like?"

"No, not them, the goats!" Rodney yelled.

"Food."

They had given up their traditional life of roaming with camels, which had always provided a constant supply of milk, and had come up with a means of still managing to keep a fresh supply of milk with them wherever they went. It was inspired. The man explained that after a few days of travelling and milking the goats each morning, they would then kill one when they got hungry, and a few days later they would kill the second one. The meat was kept absolutely fresh until it was needed, and it meant that they had no need to carry much water with them except some for the radiator and the goats. The rest of the roof space could be filled with tanks of diesel.

Once we had bought a few items, they wrapped up their wares again and pulled a tyre of their own out from the backseat and threw it on the fire and began to make tea. These noxious petroleum rings had become the new timber in the region. They gave out such heat that the sand beneath them turned orange as plumes of black smoke rose into the dazzlingly crystalline sky. In the morning the sand would have turned to glass, and a heap of tangled black wire would be all that remained. This was what we left behind us at every camping place.

At In Guezzam, the Harley Davidsons were the first thing we spotted. They were parked in a line, listing on their shiny chrome stands like yachts at low tide. Two of them had Confederate flags painted on their tanks, with sparkles of sunlight shooting off the handlebars. The riders were seated on the porch drinking Cokes, looking out admiringly at their mounts. When they saw us, one of them got up and waved, yelling at us to come join them for a drink.

"You're the guys with the mechanic, right?" he shouted over the truck's engine. "Joe, isn't it?"

He was waving so eagerly it was like he was doing the breast stroke or guiding in a Boeing.

"The one and only," Joe shouted down amiably from the cab.

We parked up, locked down the hatches, arranged a guard schedule and went over to the bar. It was hard to imagine these bikers, unkempt and overweight looking now, as having ever been soldiers. It was Rodney whom they turned to first, as if there were some type of grunt radar that could sniff out a former service man straight off. His neat carrot-coloured military moustache was a giveaway.

"How's it been?" they asked us.

"Great," Rodney said. "We're soaring along."

"Know what you mean," the waving man said. "How have the borders been? Are they fleecing ya?"

We went through the usual ritual of comparing notes about each stop along the way and finding out about others we'd met. We learnt that the Canadian tandem riders had packed it in and were now hitching a ride in the tractor trailer with the Devon farmers. The French man was still pulling his bus, but making slow progress.

We drank a few colas with them, and as evening fell we moved on to beer.

"Any chance one of you guys sent a chick after us?" one of the veterans asked. He had the words "2 wheels and a diaper bag" studded to the back of his jacket. "A British chick with a weird name – Lettuce or something. She came on real strong, said you guys had told her about us. Said she got off on cripples!"

I said nothing. I had forgotten about their disability until then. I looked down and saw the grey-ivory sheen of a prosthetic shin above one of their leather boots. The man caught me looking, and I turned away too quickly.

"It won't bite," he said quietly.

Rodney was already into stories from his army days. It seemed he had no problem telling them about it though he had barely told us anything. Whatever we found out came from his wife Marsha – she often talked about life on the bases in Germany and Cyprus. Stella looked across at her now in amazement at Rodney's loquaciousness, and she shot an equally surprised look back. He was halfway through a story that he had mentioned briefly to me already one night when he was very drunk.

"What got to me in the end was all the extra shit on the side?" he said. "You know? Just ask Marsha. It's why I had to get out; it was doing my nerves in. On my second tour in Ulster, they had me carrying an unmarked handgun when I was out on patrol. That was when I thought, screw this for a game of soldiers! Anyway, that was my second tour; they say you never come back from your third."

"What was with the handgun?" Holly asked.

The Americans just sighed knowingly.

"What?" Holly said.

"It was *just in case*," Rodney spat, rubbing the prominent veins of his forearms.

"Huh?" Luke said.

"Just in case you shot a civvie," Rodney said. "They were the orders: leave the gun by his side and walk away. That was when I knew it had all gone to shit. I said so to Marsha. I said, 'If I mess up and kill someone – a fuckin' non-threatening target – I'll take the rap. I'm not messing around with any unmarked pistols.' Bollix to that!"

It was late at night by this stage and we were all quite drunk. One of the Americans got up with difficulty and hugged Rodney, who to my surprise didn't pull away or squirm. They stayed in each other's arms for quite a while.

I felt bad now about my earlier feelings about Rodney. I had taken a dislike to him early on because of a story he told about his time guarding Bobby Sands, the IRA prisoner who had died after sixty-six days on hunger strike. He had boasted how, as a practical joke, he and his mates had arranged for a chip van to be parked beneath the air vent leading to Sands' cell. Everyone had laughed when he told us, and to be honest so had I. It was only afterwards that I began to see how sad it really was. It clarified for me why as a group we would never come to connect with Africa. We just didn't have the compassion. We had been told a story about a man being tortured and we all laughed. I realise there was a war going on and the British had genuine cause to resent the IRA, but all I could think of was Bobby Sands lying there in his shit-smeared cell, his body slowly consuming itself from the inside, his gut toxic with excess bile, his mind still working on the poems that he wrote until the end. What must have gone through his head when he smelt the chips and heard the squaddies laughing?

"It's just good you got out alive," the American said, squeezing his shoulder. "The way I see it, every day's a celebration for the others, the guys we left behind. The greatest honour we can show them is to regard our own lives as sacred."

"Yeah," said Rodney quietly.

"I'll drink to that," one of the Americans said.

"To the fallen!" the third man said, and we raised our bottles.

"Try and forget the bad stuff," the first man said to Rodney, "but not your buddies. Don't ever forget them. That's our duty now . . . That fat bastard over there, Joshie, him and I were together only three months. Am I right, Joshua? But it might as well have been since childhood. I hated

him too, a real pain-in-the-ass Born Again weirdo. But you look back and
. . . some days it's like a lifetime away, others . . . At therapy they get us to
talk it out, do mock funerals and stuff, you know? Maybe you should look
into some of that."

Marsha nodded keenly at them and reached out to take her husband's
hand. He was staring at the sand with that haunted look that came over
him at times – shadows tunnelling into each eye socket. They were a well-
suited couple physically, both carrot-haired and wispy like larches in winter. When I first met them, I presumed they were siblings, and
occasionally the thought still crossed my mind. I wondered was that why
they hadn't had children. This trip was the beginning of a whole new life
for them. They were having to reassess all their old assumptions. I had
seen them wavering occasionally between their old mindset and the new
one. They hadn't been sure who to support at the sand dunes. Rodney had
been tobogganing with us, but when the others started pointing out about
the dangers, he had taken their side.

Chapter 11

IT WAS A relief to come upon the first scattering of stunted, sinewy trees in southern Algeria, and as the days passed more and more brave bits of flora dared to defy the furnace. We entered the Sahel, the semi-desert, a slightly less bleak expanse, carpeted in threadbare walnut-coloured vegetation. We were approaching Niger, a place few of us had ever heard of before, and although at first we welcomed the new vitality of its landscape, we soon realised that it had its own risks attached: snakes, spiders and scorpions became more prevalent, particularly a tiny, lumi-nous-eyed insect which hammered on the earth at night to attract its prey. Suzi reassured us that its bite wouldn't kill us, although the pain was so bad that it might seem that way for the first hour after being bitten. Sitting out by the fire at night didn't feel so good after that, seeing the sapphire blue eyes glowing up at you. We had to keep constantly shaking out our clothes and checking our shoes for creepy crawlies. Joe was keen for one of us to get bitten so that he could test a new cure he had devised – a series of sixteen electric shocks from the truck batteries, said to neutralise any poison.

As we were driving across the Sahel one afternoon, we saw what looked like a mile-long, pulsating car-wash roller coming towards us, a dense brown cloud. We tried to warn Suzi about it through the intercom, but she just laughed. When it reached us, we realised it was composed of thousands of tiny parts – too fast and too numerous to make out what they were at first, until someone shouted "locusts!" – a sea of ramming armoured maggots battering into our faces, tangling themselves in our hair.

Holly had come up to me just before they attacked to say she wanted my advice about Luke. She had got as far as saying, "Did you ever brush your fingers against a piece of old chewing gum under the seat in the cinema and have the urge to touch it again, to make sure it really was what you thought it was?"

We dived to the ground. I had thought the sandstorms were bad, but these hurt far worse, like thousands of crab claws and wishbones being pelted from airguns.

"What are you talking about?" I shouted to Holly, still cowering low to the ground.

"Luke," she said.

"Are you two getting on well?" I said.

"I suppose," she said shrugging. "He saved me the other day. Dudley came into my tent with a cucumber, rubbing it as though it were something else, and Luke came along just at the right moment and pulled him out by the ear."

I tried to reply, but as I did a locust landed directly in my mouth and I had to spit out violently. We kept quiet after that. There was nothing one could do but cower down until they moved on, leaving behind an even more denuded wasteland and countless tiny corpses, like crashed Airfixes, which had been stunned or killed by head-on collision. Fortunately, this area hadn't all that much vegetation for them to destroy, but as we drove south we came upon hand-irrigated fields of sorghum and wheat that had been instantly stripped to the root, and palm trees robbed, not only of their dates which the goats and camels depended on, but of leaves too so that they might never recover.

The locusts were our first sign we had entered Black Africa – a different world in which all the iconic images of the continent awaited us. It was here that Stevi had been looking forward to most.

"These aren't real Africs," he had said when we first entered Morocco. "Not even true A-rabs when you get down to it. Wait till we get down a bit further. That's when we see the real ones. A whole different kettle of fish."

And now here we were, seeing them all around us: herding scrawny goats, lugging water on their heads, washing clothes in rivers, asleep beneath hedges, or just waiting by the roadside. Stevi was delighted.

"See what I mean?" he said. "Real Africa. Look at them, happy as can be."

Superficially at least, the cliché did seem true: no matter what they were involved in – milling grain, mending thatch, mucking out barns – they would stop and wave at us. And it was no half-hearted wave; their clothes would ripple with the passion of their greeting. In the villages, the truck attracted a shoal of followers, as did we as soon as we stepped away from it. The sense of reserve of northern Africa was replaced by a frenetic chaos in which we were caught up and swept along, being jostled and whistled at wherever we went. Within three feet of us at any moment there were people offering every conceivable product and service: food (oranges, fried bread, kebabs, peanuts, boiled chickpeas and Coke in cold boxes), cigarettes, letter-writing, portage, message running, sex. Yet, we weren't just seen as customers; we were objects of entertainment. The children stared bug-eyed at us, chanting for "*un bic*" or "*un cadeau*". It wasn't so much begging as just a form of interaction. They marvelled at our oddness, laughed at just about anything we said and did.

"Oh yeah, this is it now," Stevi said, rubbing his hands. "You can smell it, can't you? Different kettle of fish."

Although Stevi had been a bit at sea until now, he was really looking forward to Niger. He had family here, as he kept reminding us. A cousin of his had married a girl from a village outside Niamey, and while it had caused outrage in the family at the time, they had by and large got over it, and in fact they now rather liked her. I never knew how much of what Stevi said was true – he had a tendency to embellish the past. It was impossible to be certain he actually had a cousin who had married a girl from Niger, but there was no reason to doubt it, I suppose. Normally his embellishments were plain enough. He didn't go in for subtlety. Although there was one story about his childhood that I could never decide if it was true or not. It was about his fondness for killing the hen for the Sunday roast on his family's farm in northern Germany. He claimed he had devised a way of catching the hen's neck in the barnyard door so that its sphincter contracted at the moment of strangulation, giving Stevi an instant orgasm as he would have inserted himself into the hen beforehand. I never wanted to ask for more details to corroborate the story. Even his story about accepting a place on the trip in lieu of a friend's gambling debt might not have been entirely true, although there was definitely some basis for it as he had demanded, and received, a tent for himself at the beginning of the trip. Also, he was given seconds at dinner whenever he felt like it because of having paid for two places. Suzi also took account of his insistence that we didn't drive too fast first thing in the morning as the wind irritated his eyes, causing a milky syrup to leak from behind the eyelids. This, combined with his pale, almost translucent skin, made him look unsettlingly like a formaldehyde-preserved alien in the early morning.

"So are we going to make things all Christmassy or what?" asked one of the nurses at the weekly meeting in the middle of December. My heart dropped. I thought Christmas would be one thing we would escape from here. I pointed this out, but Mildred, the middle-aged divorcee from Glasgow, said it wasn't about us; it was about the little baby Jesus. I could think of no reply to that, so I decided to just keep my head down and my mouth shut. They could do whatever they wanted for all I cared. I certainly would take no part in it. Suzi had promised that she would get us to Niamey, the capital of Niger, in time for Christmas Eve, and true to her word, we pulled into the car park of the Score supermarket in Niamey mid morning on 24 December. Joe was sent under the truck to get the kitty money out of the safe.

The sight of traffic lights, illuminated bubble-lettering on the roof and two-for-one deals in the plate-glass windows took us all aback. After weeks in the desert and Sahel, such things seemed genuinely shocking. How had the world ever developed them? And why? Stacked along the fluorescent aisles were processed foods from France and Germany at prices no local could afford. It was a moment of culture shock, and yet it didn't take us long to get over it and begin filling baskets with as much Yoplait yoghurts, Philadelphia cream cheese and Mars Bars as we could afford, appeasing a homesickness that hadn't been apparent until then. We filled three trolleys with rubbishy processed food which was all paid for by the kitty.

At the campsite, we selected a pitch for ourselves, and the others set about making it look festive once they had introduced themselves to the other campers and established a place in the pecking order. This working out of our position in the hierarchy of any camp was always a tiresome routine involving sniffing around each other like wary dogs, seeing who could boast of having experienced the greatest dangers, the fastest times between towns and the riskiest border crossings. There was something therapeutic about such predictable venting of our achievements and setbacks.

No matter how much effort the others put into tarting up the campsite, it was never going to look like anything other than a patch of barren wasteland surrounded by rusting barbed-wire and pock-marked with oil slicks from old trucks, yet they diligently spent the whole afternoon cutting out paper Santas and hanging tinsel on the barbed wire. Wayne found a cylindrical brush from a road-sweeping truck, and after routing a nest of chameleons from its bristles, he dragged it back to the campsite and stood it upright as a Christmas tree. It was blue and spiky and stank of detergent, but the others were delighted with it. They set about festooning it with golden baubles they had been given by a Polish couple who were returning home after just a few weeks of their trip – their marriage already in shreds from the strain of it. Natasha pulled out a can of snow spray she had brought from London and smeared white foam over the bristles as though she were about to shave it. I said nothing, just focused on doing the job I had been assigned, cutting out reindeer from coloured paper and sticking them to the truck. I did it because it was either that or make a snowman out of the insides of tampons, and that would have been a step too far. Meanwhile, the men busied themselves digging a huge pit in the sand which was to be filled with ice and beer so that, in the best of Christmas traditions, it could be a drunken one.

All the time I was thinking to myself: *What sort of a person brings snow spray to Africa?*

"Perfect, eh?" Stevi said to me, looking around. He started into a verse of "Feed the World". "Do-they-know-it's-Christmas-time-again . . . ? Fucking-A we do!"

He laughed merrily.

"Look, mate, I've of a bit of a favour to ask actually," he said. "I wanna go see the cousins, but I'm worried 'bout not speakin' the lingo and I was thinking maybe you'd come along. 'Cause you've got your French and all."

I was looking for any excuse to get away and agreed immediately.

"Yeah?" he said. "Sound!"

We left the camp straight away, waving down a number of taxis until we found one who had heard of Stevi's village and wasn't quoting an exorbitant fare. The village was only about an hour away from Niamey, but it was out in bushland, a world away from neon signs and traffic lights. We turned off the main road on to a dusty, rust-coloured track leading to a collection of mud huts that rose like dough from their surroundings. The walls were made of manure, peanut shells and straw held together with mud. The roofs were millet stalk. It seemed like half the villagers came out and surrounded the taxi as soon as we pulled in.

"Are you sure this is the place?" I asked the driver.

He nodded confidently, and we stepped out into a sea of tie-dyed wrap skirts and brightly printed head wraps. I began to say the name Hadiara over and over again with a questioning gesture and then asking in French if anyone knew of them. This was the family name of Stevi's cousin-in-law, or at least what he thought it was, and it did seem to spark some hint of recognition all right, but little more than that. A young girl who was drawing water from a well stopped and came over to us, nodding encouragingly. She pulled her rough-sewn blouse away from her skin as she walked and wiped beads of sweat from her eyes. I said the name again, and she smiled at me, gripping my hand in hers, which was dry and earthy, and stroking the blond tangle of hair near my wrists. A green parakeet swooped down towards us and then onwards to the south. I noticed her eyes were unnaturally bright and realised she might be mentally deficient and began to extract myself from her. I looked around at the others, asking if any of them had French, but none of them seemed to, and we were left staring awkwardly at each other for a while. I asked the taxi man to translate for us, but he wasn't keen to get out of the car. The children looked awe-struck by our gangly, ghost-like appearance.

"What's the matter?" Stevi said.

I told him they didn't seem to understand French.

"Well, that's a bit shit," he said.

He started explaining to them in English that Tanya Hadiara was married to his cousin in England and that he was very glad to meet them all. There was a sudden commotion behind us as an old woman with a shock of white hair came out of her hut and screamed at the sight of us. She stopped suddenly and froze where she was, staring at me as though I were a monster. I smiled and said hello, but she screamed again and went running off, her large candyfloss hair bobbing behind her.

Stevi shrugged and went back to explaining the situation in boisterous pidgin English, but then he stopped suddenly, turning to me to say that it had just dawned on him that Tanya wasn't really his cousin's wife's name, just something the family had thought was easier on the ear. Her name sounded like Tanya, or at least a bit like it, he thought. He mimed this fact with one hand cupped around his ear like in charades and the other hand outstretched and tilting from side to side. This seemed to go down well with the villagers, and they asked us to come and sit down with them. I was hesitant and told Stevi we should probably keep the taxi on standby.

"No need, mate," he said, "This is it. We're home now."

He passed some francs in to the driver, who sped off with a look of relief, and then settled himself on the ground under a mango tree that provided some shelter. Stevi looked wonderfully at ease sitting there on the ground, smiling beneficently and surveying the scene around him. He had absolute confidence in the rightness of his being there; Tanya had been to his mum's house often enough after all.

"A cup of tea wouldn't go amiss," he said cheerily to me, miming the action of drinking to the others, and straight away they sent a young girl to fetch some pottery bowls. After that we just sat there, Stevi confident that everything would work out in time.

"To be honest," he said, "it was a bit like this when Tanya came around the first few times too. Lots of silent looks, long stares, but now we hardly notice at all. She could be any colour."

He was clearly delighted with himself and unaware of the looks of concern passing through the others. Someone handed us a pan of blackened peanuts which had been roasted on a fire, and I sat back and tried to relax, chewing the freshly dug up nuts and watching life go by. A boy came along leading the old woman who had been so frightened earlier back to her home. He encouraged her to wave at us, but she blanched again and turned away. The boy shrugged and squatted down beside us, laying the tyre-wide bowl he had been carrying on his head on the ground. It was full of unwashed rice and two bright-yellow Maggi stock cubes.

"Smell that!" Stevi said, inhaling extravagantly. "It brings me right back."

There was a vague smell of smoked fish and chilli peppers, although the sweet and piquant peanuts masked a lot.

"Smells just like Tanya," he said approvingly.

After a long period of silent staring, some of the women got bored and wandered back to their chores of pounding millet with heavy wooden clubs.

"I could watch them for hours," Stevi said. "They're so happy. Tanya says they use the same word for stranger and guest here. Imagine! It really makes you think."

A group of women approached along the path carrying basins, which sparked a sudden heightened interest in us again. The others pointed determinedly at them, and a gang of children ran out towards them, pointing back at us as they went. It seemed these were the elders arriving home, and a minute later one of them, a small stout woman in a chrysanthemum-flowered dress and matching headdress, was standing over us looking confused and a bit agitated. She put down her pail of yams and introduced herself in French as Mama Hadiara. She had an angular face and the most lustrous skin I had ever seen, like petrol on a sunny day. She didn't seem happy to see us, but nevertheless greeted us formally and asked the obligatory questions about our health and the nature of our journey and offered the wish that Allah would guide our path from here on in. I tried replying, but she didn't seem to want to know what I had to say. She became gradually more het up as she went on talking, eventually turning away and explaining indignantly to the others something in the Hausa language. Whatever she said seemed to intrigue them, and they looked at us in a whole new way. I began to feel a little nervous. What was she saying? I looked to Stevi, wondering whether there was something he hadn't told me about his cousin-in-law. I could feel a definite sense of menace in the air.

I tried explaining to Mama Hadiara about Stevi and his cousin in Birmingham who had married Tanya, but this just upset her more.

"Liar," she said, getting up and walking over to a nearby hut covered completely by a gourd bush.

She came back a few moments later with an old newspaper, handled many times, and threw it at our feet. It was in English and folded open at a page which read "My Sin: being born a woman". She grabbed it back off me before I could have a proper look.

"My own family," Mama Hadiara said, "making shame! Telling lies."

The other women crowded around us. Before she managed to fold the paper away under her arm again, I made out most of the top line which was in larger italics. It said something along the lines of, "They left me with dead wood between my legs." I glanced at Stevi and whispered what it said to him, but he just shrugged. He had no idea what was going on.

"Is Tanya a journalist?" I asked him anxiously.

"Our Tanya? No way!" he said. "She works in the co-op – on the check-out. Sometimes she stacks shelves if things are quiet."

"Well, what's going on?" I said, pointing towards Mama Hadiara.

Stevi thought for a while and said, "She is doing something in night school all right."

"What?" I said. "Journalism?"

He shook his head. "Pottery, I think."

"Could she have written this?" I asked.

He shrugged.

"All we did was to protect her," Mama Hadiara said, tapping at the paper. "This is how we care for all our girls. It is just saving her from the boys in heat who sniff around. We want our daughters clean and healthy, if not their milk turns to poison."

"What's she saying?" Stevi asked me.

"I'm not sure," I said. "I think she thinks your cousin shamed them in some way . . . maybe writing something about them."

"*Our* Tanya wouldn't do that, mate," he said, shaking his head determinedly. "Tell her!"

Mama Hadiara paused while I conferred with Stevi, but not for long.

"It's important for the women," she went on. "We have no hospitals here. The children and grandchildren, they need us. We are the lifeline. It is not like Paris here. We cannot be fooling around, playing with ourselves and women with women . . ."

She broke off to translate for the others, who murmured respectfully. One or two giggled, but she silenced them with a stare. She seemed to be one of the matriarchs of the village; certainly she was treated with deference.

"I've seen in the big towns," she said, "the way women prepare food and water when they are unclean – it's disgusting," she said. "They kill our men with diseases, and our babies."

"I think you have us mixed up," I said. "We don't know anything about this."

She was too distressed to hear me and instead beckoned one of the younger girls over. The girl collapsed down diligently into her lap, and Mama began combing through her hair, separating out strands to braid while she talked.

"It is a part of growing up. *Un grand fête.*"

She paused and looked down at the girl, who seemed to understand French, but was staring shyly at the ground, saying nothing. Madame Hadiara bent over and patted her, making scornful clucking noises as she did so. The girl got up and began rinsing out clothes in a colourful dye-stained basin. She seemed paralysed with shyness.

Suddenly the girl looked up and in beautiful fluent French she said, "We get a new dress, yes, Mama? And five whole chickens for the feast."

"Yes!" Mama laughed. "Days of hectic preparing – buying in herbs and linen and towels and fruit too. Buying more chickens than even for *Eid Ul-Fitr!*"

"Is she still going on about the same thing?" Stevi asked.

I nodded.

"She's like a broken record player," he said. "Does she have an off button?"

Mama looked at me to see what he was saying, but I just smiled wanly and she went on . . . "Such a happy day, throwing rice and millet on the river . . ."

"Look, just ask her if she knows Tanya or not?" Stevi said. "Does she want me to send her a message?"

"She's really bothered by the article," I said.

"Jesus H! Tell her we don't give a monkeys about her bloody article," he said.

I ignored him.

"This is not how I imagined it at all," he said with a sigh.

Behind him I noticed five men shuffling along the path towards us, walking listlessly, their rusted, orange-handled machetes dangling by their sides, looking exhausted. One of them, walking a few feet ahead, had a frown and tribal tattoos cut deep through his curly stubble like the rubber loops on a tennis ball. I pointed him out to Stevi, indicating that it might be better if we left.

"No problem," he agreed. "I'm bored anyway. If I had wanted bitching and moaning, I could've stayed at the campsite. At least we did our best, mate. I can tell Tanya that I tried, but they went all Zulu on me."

He stood up and started walking towards the main road. Mama Hadiara stopped for a second and stared. I tried to explain that we didn't have much time and would have to get back to town. She didn't make any response except uttering a few huffy clucks to herself and then went on complaining to the others. I turned and made my way through the men, who had all stopped in their tracks and were staring at Stevi. His spiky hair, gangly figure and, most especially, the traces of sticky, white gunge seeping from his eyelids made him look barely human. We walked out towards the road hoping to find a pickup heading into town.

About two kilometres along the road, a jeep pulled up for us and the driver allowed us to jump in the rear. We got back to the campsite just after dark; in plenty of time for the Christmas Eve celebrations, unfortunately. I spent the journey mulling over what exactly had happened in the village. It was hard to be sure of anything. Perhaps we hadn't got the right Mama Hadiara at all. Niger villages tend to share one or two common surnames between them, and Suzi told us later that Tanya's real name was more likely to be Tani or Tanisha, meaning born on a Monday. There might have been a few Tanisha's in the village. Stevi said he'd write home to check with Tanya if she knew about the article, but I'm not sure he ever got an answer back; at least he never told me about it. I wondered why Mama Hadiara had been so upset. Possibly some foreign NGOs or missionaries had visited recently and were needling her about the circumcision customs; making it a condition of future aid that such things be stamped out. Maybe it was they who had given her the article and she had confused us with them, or regarded all white men as somehow related. I don't know. Perhaps it was weighing on her mind because the young girls were preparing for their own initiation. She may have been trying to justify to herself the frightened cries she would soon be hearing.

"Jesus H," Stevi said when I mentioned this to him. "It wouldn't be like just having your foreskin lopped off, but the entire head, and then the shaft shoved up between your balls and stitched so you couldn't get at it."

I had come back from the village more determined than ever not to take part in Christmas. The village had highlighted for me more clearly than ever how inappropriate our customs and outlooks were in this place. I had no wish to stuff myself with turkey and sing stupid carols. Yet somehow by midnight I was as drunk as everyone else. I think the whole spectacle became so depressing that I had to do something to block it out. I pulled up a floorboard and rooted around until I found a bottle of some kind. It was Baileys, which I've always hated, but I drank it back nonetheless. I figured no one would notice it was missing. I was mistaken. It turned out to be Henry's prized possession. Mildred had brought it for him specially from Glasgow and was saving it for the last few days in Nairobi. When he saw me tipping back the last of it, he grabbed it and pointed to a big H scrawled on the side.

"What does that say?" he roared.

"Goalpost?" I slurred. "More or less the international sign for goalposts, I would say. Also used to indicate helicopter landing pads on roofs and on road signs to point to the nearest hospital – though in that case it is usually surrounded by a circle."

Henry was as drunk as I was.

"I'd been saving that," he spat. "What are you going to do about it? Huh, Paddy?"

I waved my hands nonchalantly.

"There's not much I can do," I said. "Sorry."

"Don't sorry me, you smart-ass prick!" he shouted. "I said I was *saving* it."

"And I said I'm sorry," I pointed out merrily.

He lunged at me. I managed to dodge him, and he fell to the ground. The others laughed. I did too. It was too much for poor Henry. Suddenly the forty years he had diligently spent buckled under the leash of convention, obligingly plying his career as a quantity surveyor, became too much to bear. The tranquillisers which had fought so valiantly to keep him together tried to hold the flood back a while longer, but it was no use. I could see the cracks beginning to appear, a storm tide surging up through his eyes. No amount of beta-blockers could contend with the pent-up frustration he was now trying to contain. I walked away, hoping that if I gave him time to compose himself he might manage it. But he came lunging at me from behind, grabbing hold of my neck so tightly that I began to choke. I was far too drunk to consider his age or state of mind. All I could think of was breathing again, and I twisted violently around, hurling him to the ground. Then I began to kick him. I was taken aback by my ferocity. I didn't have the excuse of a life of weary toil, or any other mitigating factor. It just felt good, and I didn't seem able to stop myself. Finally, someone punched me and I fell to the ground, relieved at having been stopped. I was just getting to my feet again when I saw Henry charging towards me. He looked even angrier now. He grabbed my throat again and managed to clench it so tight that the windpipe squeezed shut. I tried freeing myself, but my brain was becoming starved of oxygen, and I almost conked out before my fist finally made contact with his cheek and sent us both hurtling backwards together into the ice pit.

The shock of the cold water sobered us immediately, and we felt the shards of broken bottle sticking into our backs. Suzi and Rodney came and hauled us out, and the nurses went to fetch the first-aid kit. For me, it was a moment of pure shame. I went straight to bed.

As if as punishment, I woke the next day with not just diarrhoea, but acute dysentery. And shame too, of course; more shame. What had I done? While everyone else had been happily celebrating our biggest feast day, I stole an old man's drink and then beat him up. Apart from Vinnie and Rita's minor domestic in the first week, it was the first incidence of violence amongst us.

It made for a particularly grim Christmas Day for me, but everyone else was miserable too. The dysentery was of a particularly virulent nature and had spread through most of the camp. We lay sprawled at various points between our tents and the bucket lavatory on the far side of the campsite for most of the day. By mid afternoon, some of the group had recovered enough to think about cooking a meal. They were still too sick to be hungry, but nonetheless they wanted to cook a big dinner so that they could tell their friends about it later on, how we had enjoyed a wonderful Christmas feast in the African sun.

Vinnie and Rita set to lighting a fire and preparing all the food we had bought in the supermarket. They hung two chickens on a spit while Duncan and his brother grated carrots and cabbage for coleslaw. This was all done between numerous trips back and forth to the lavatory, between bowel spasms as their bellies fought off the invading parasites. Of course it was obvious that our food would be re-infected with their germs, but such was the desire to celebrate that this was overlooked.

When the meal was finally ready, we all got up out of our tents and gathered round the camp table, singing obligatory carols before tucking into the birds. It was late afternoon, but the heat was still stifling. Everyone was feeling too sick to think much about where we actually were or what day it was, but it didn't matter. We took good photos. At least we would be able to look back and boast about it later on. We could reminisce in our dotage on this wonderful moment – this highlight of our lives.

Chapter 12

CHRISTMAS DAY WAS the beginning of a hellish fortnight for me. While everyone else recovered from the dysentery, I just kept getting worse. I got a soaring fever which kept me flat on my roll-mat for three days with barely enough energy to carry my somersaulting intestine back and forth to the dung pit every hour. Everyone was a bit worried about me, but they kept away because I smelt so terrible.

"I can't think of a more deserving person," Mildred said to me as I was tip-toeing gingerly towards the latrine, cradling my belly, one morning. She had got Henry to write out an invoice for the Baileys and leave it in my locker.

Lucy was more sympathetic. She brought me bottles of water and said, "This is probably a good experience for you, Mocha. In some way. My dad always says that whatever he can't teach me, I would definitely be able to pick up from the road – that's what you're doing, learning what you need to know."

"Thanks," I managed.

We stayed on in the campsite for three days and I had a chance to rest, but then Suzi insisted we get going again. I was lifted on to the truck and dumped on the floor, which is where I spent the next week, intermittently dozing and crying out from time to time in delirium – storms of feverish wind and weather raging through me. I remember little, except the conviction that I was teetering on the threshold of life and would probably end my days there in a cesspool of my own fluids. But Suzi had enough experience of tropical fevers to know that I was in no real danger. It must have been awful for the others to have me there, spitting and whining.

Holly came to see me one day and said she thought I really ought to hook up with Lucy.

"Why?" I said.

"Luke and I have been thinking," she said: "it's like you're on this determined crusade to go it alone. Sometimes we all need a little help, you know? You won't get through it otherwise."

"I'm sick," I said.

"I know," she said soothingly. "All I'm saying is, Lucy seems to like you. . . . She means well."

"She's young," I said. "So frail."

"That's OK."

I said nothing. It was hard to put into words what I wanted to say. Basically, I was confused – sad, scared, angry. I didn't want to inflict that on anyone. I knew I'd end up resenting her before long.

"You can take care of her," Holly said. "She needs that. We all need it. It's why I'm with Luke. You don't think we'd be together in the real world, do you? Here it's different. Here we need someone. I'm happy to be there for Luke, to share myself."

"I know," I muttered reluctantly.

"Look, I shouldn't tell you this, but Luke and I, we're not sure you're going to make it through," she said to me.

"Oh, come on!" I said.

"Seriously," she said. "You look really bad. We tried to ask Suzi to stop for a few days to let you rest, but . . ."

She was called away to fill the water tanks, and I fell back to sleep. The dreams had returned as soon as I got the bug. They weren't as repetitive, but possibly even more intense. Something my father had said the year before he died came back to me, and it helped make sense of Johan's constant presence hanging in the boathouse. My father and I were walking in the hills together the Easter before he got sick, when he suddenly turned to me and asked had I ever wondered why Johan committed suicide. I hadn't. It was just another horror story from my childhood, and I had accepted it as that. My father fell quiet for a while and then said that he found that strange. His tone was not rebuking, just interested. He told me it was the first thing he had wanted to know when he had heard the story all those years ago. A shepherd somewhere outside Innsbruck had pointed him towards a trail and told him about the refuge and boathouse about a day's hiking away, and recounted the story of where and how Johan had hanged himself. My dad had walked on and found the refuge and spent the night there, and sure enough, he thought, or at least imagined, that he saw something in the night, a figure swinging. Next morning he trekked back down to the nearest village to find out anything he could.

"So?" I said to my father. "What did you find out?"

"Well, that's not really the issue, is it?" he said brightly. "The issue is you never asked."

"I thought it was just a story," I said.

"Even a story has a reason behind it," he said.

"Well? Why did he do it?"

My dad smiled enigmatically.

"Come on!" I said.

But he wouldn't tell me.

The revelation that suddenly struck me now was that just as I had never questioned the reasons behind Johan's death, nor had I questioned my father's. I just accepted it. Was that why I was dreaming of Johan the whole time? Was I, or he, on some subconscious level, trying to make a point? My dad had gone into hospital for a minor cataract operation, and in an unprecedented chain of events managed to contract an infection that spread through his neural system to his brain, killing him in a few weeks. On the surface it looked like simple bad luck, but the strange thing was that he had told us beforehand that he wouldn't be coming out alive. We hadn't taken him seriously, of course, as no one dies of cataracts, but he had been right. The question was how? Had he actually wanted to die? That was what suddenly came into my mind and kept echoing around the whole time I was sick. The answer was clear, but it was just hard to accept.

From my position on the floor, I saw little of Burkina Faso, considered one of the poorest and most tragic countries in Africa. Its people were still being used as slaves by the French long after the Russians had sent a man into space. The northern part was barren, and regular droughts were killing off the cattle. The further south we went, the thicker the vegetation became, but only as we approached the southern border did it get really lush. In Ouagadougou, the capital, I found myself giving money to every beggar I met, hoping that my few francs might somehow delay their setting out on that same journey as the boy I stumbled upon in the port in Ceuta.

Any account of my own illness would seem crass when compared with the suffering around me. Such descriptions in travel literature always put me off. I read once of a man with the same illness as mine having to re-introduce a length of his lower intestine back inside him, and I swore I would never inflict such things on a reader, although now having experienced something similar I realise how tempting it is. It's enough to say that it was a nasty period of sweating, shivering and starving, but by the time we reached Togo nine days after Christmas, my fever had lessened somewhat, although my stomach was still churning. The land was becoming ever more fertile. I should have been able to put aside my minor discomfort and appreciate the increasing lushness and fecundity of the landscape, the massive ribbon-like rivers that slashed through the forest, swaggering along in bright ochre colours that perfectly matched the dirt-roads, but in truth I resented it all. It conspired against me, turning my frequent trips into the bush at night to squat alone into terrifying affairs in which I imagined cobras, mambas, puff adders and leopards lurking in the dense thicket, ready to attack. There was the constant squawking of monkeys and furtive rummaging of monitor lizards and whooping of tropical birds through the undergrowth. Praying mantises would creep up on me from surrounding branches like malevolent matchstick men. Ants regarded me as a sweet, salty totem pole that they felt compelled to climb, often waiting until they had reached my groin before sinking their pincers in. The whirring and thrumming of toads and cicadas and slowly shifting contralto noises of nervous birds set me on edge, tormented me. I hated it, just as I hated the whole trip and everyone on board. I spewed with bitterness from every end, blistering with self-pity. I could neither eat nor sleep, but spent the nights cursing my sick body and my misfortune for ever having signed up to this moronic ordeal.

In the central highlands, things improved a bit. We hadn't yet reached the full-on equatorial rainforest with its daily downpours, and so the land was liable to burst into flames whenever the scrub became too dry. We came across whole mountainsides under flame, cauterised of everything except the toughest trees, left covered with an angry black scab. We drove for days through the smoke without any sign of life except for the vultures that patrolled the fire line, searching out animals fleeing the flames.

Two weeks into the new year, when I was going to the lavatory one night, I tripped in the forest and sprained my ankle. I landed in a heap on the ground, screaming out in pain. It was so severe that I was convinced I had broken a bone. I tried pulling myself to my feet, but my body wouldn't allow it. It kept shooting waves of stabbing pain through me and then going into shock so that I passed out for a second and fell back to the ground again. I felt certain that if I called out for help someone would come for me, but no matter how loud I shouted no one heard. Or at least they didn't come. I was determined to get myself back to camp somehow and began pulling myself up against a tree trunk using the vines that hung from it and then trying to propel myself forward from vine to vine like an elderly person using the straps on a tube train, or Tarzan with a fear of heights. But each time I put any pressure on the ankle it felt like the tendons were being hacked at with a rough-serrated knife. I realised I had no option but to settle down and wait it out, hoping that someone would find me in the morning.

For the first hour I managed not to think about the insects that were beginning to colonise various parts of me. I knew that if I stayed still they were unlikely to harm me very much. It was more efficient for them to wait until I was no longer breathing and the decomposing bacteria had set in. But I soon became convinced that the insects weren't the only thing aware of me. I was being observed by an animal somewhere in the undergrowth. It might have seen me fall and knew that I was injured. It was biding its time, waiting to make sure I was totally alone. If it decided to attack, I realised there was no way I could defend myself. I had no option but to get out of there. Once I had realised this, I resolved to get up one way or another. Only one leg was injured; it ought to be possible to hop. I stuck a branch in between my teeth to dull the pain and tried again to put pressure on my legs, but the knee on my good leg was bruised and kept quaking and buckling. The weeks without proper food had left me weak. I found there was no way I could maintain my balance on the uneven forest floor. The pain would stab through me and my mind would go numb, making me dizzy, and I'd fall over, crashing down on to the sprained ankle. In the end I got down on my belly and crawled and rolled inch by inch back to camp, using my knee as a lever to propel myself along, pulling at roots and low-hanging vines wherever I found them, dragging the other leg out behind me. It took seemingly for ever, and I kept on getting bitten and stung by nocturnal lowlife in the leaf mould. But somehow I made it back to my tent and crawled inside. I lay flat out across both beds (Wayne had taken to sleeping outside under a mosquito net to escape my fever and dysentery), and I began to whimper to myself. This was the end; I had no reserves left. I just felt so sick, so weak and sore. I was trapped on a truck in the wilderness with no friends or family. At that moment, I would have given anything to escape home, but the nearest airport was hundreds of kilometres away, and anyway even if I had the money for a flight, there was no way of getting there.

It was at that point that I gave in. I stopped trying to be strong any more and just let go. I started to cry and continued for most of the night. I was twenty years old; I shouldn't have been here. Somehow I had made a wrong decision along the way. I needed to go back and start over. I let the poisonous cocktail of irritants and anti-coagulants which the midges, ants and spiders had been shooting into me for weeks take control and admitted defeat, begging God, or anyone, to take over and save me from myself. Around dawn, with every muscle, every tendon, every cell exhausted, I fell asleep. A deep sleep like I hadn't known in weeks. My dad appeared out of nowhere and began poking at my sore leg.

"Is that really you?" I said.

"I was wondering who that distinguished-looking boy was," he said.

"My leg is really sore," I said.

He frowned a bit, looking down at it uncertainly.

"I'm not sure I can go on," I said.

"We make our lives so difficult," he said wistfully. "Tell me, did I do this to you?"

"Bring me here?" I said.

He nodded.

"I don't know," I said. "Maybe."

"I didn't mean to make things difficult," he said. "I just couldn't go on."

"Is that really you?" I asked. "Is this just another dream?"

"Huh?" he said distractedly.

"Dream," I said. "I've been having terrible dreams."

"No idea, love," he said hesitantly.

"Is it really you?"

"No, I shouldn't think so."

I said nothing. I was holding back tears.

"You'll be fine," he said.

He paused and looked at me in an equivocating, pensive manner. It was as if we were both trying to understand each other. It reminded me of when we first started reading poetry together, both nervous about suggesting the idea. Was it too odd, too intimate a thing for a father and his teenage son to do?

I woke at lunchtime with the sun scorching through the filaments of my tent. I was sprawled in the habitual pool of sweat on my roll mat, but all I could think of was the delectable eight hours of sleep I had just been granted. Eight hours reprieve. My mind, though still somewhat addled, could sense something had changed. An unmistakable shift had occurred, and with it came a powerful sense of optimism the likes of which I hadn't felt in months. It thrilled through me like lightning. I crawled out from the tent, ready for the jolt of pain that would stab up from the swollen ankle as soon as I put any pressure on it. I was sure I could cope with it now no matter how bad it was. But when I tried to move the ankle there was no pain, nothing. I looked down and the swelling had completely disappeared. Cautiously, I poked a bit at the bone, which I was sure would cause me to grimace, but there was no soreness at all. I looked at it for a long time, going through the facts, wondering whether I might have dreamt the whole thing, but I knew I hadn't. There was a trail of dirt and leaf mould in the tent that I must have dragged in the night before. My hands and knees were still scratched and filthy. I unzipped the tent and got up on to one knee, which didn't even cause a twinge of discomfort. Carefully, I put both feet on the ground and pushed myself out of the tent, lifting one foot and wiggling the ankle. It was fine.

My attention was suddenly drawn to my stomach, where the rumblings and stabbing pains were now absent. I squeezed and prodded my stomach to provoke some discomfort, but there was none. I strode over to the food table triumphantly on my healed leg and helped myself to food. Suddenly I was hungry again. Thick tranches of corn bread were laid out on the trestle table with a pot of pineapple jam, and I devoured slice after slice.

I cannot explain it. It didn't seem possible that a sprained ankle and infected stomach could cure themselves overnight, and yet the one thing I was beginning to realise was that Africa could do what it wanted with you when it wanted. Impossible things happened here all the time. Any semblance of control we had over our lives was absent, and the sooner I took this on board the better.

The world was bright and good, and there were a hundred things I wanted to experience right away: eat a full meal, wash myself, apologise to the others, continue exploring Africa. I could still feel the afterglow of having talked to my father, of having finally shared a few words with him.

I went straight over to Stella and told her to take a rest. She had had to manage the cooking and washing on her own while I was sick. I told her not to lift a finger today, and she smiled with relief. I told Wayne that I'd take down the tent on my own too. It was something he had been doing for me every day, despite not sleeping in it himself. I was so full of energy I thought I would never get tired again. I gambolled around the camp, joking and gossiping with the others, telling them how great it was to be with them all. They seemed relieved to see me up again, and I realised that they had been concerned. There were stories of a mysterious fever attacking travellers in the area – elephantine swelling, internal haemorrhaging, the slow breakdown of the nervous system. The victims had all died within weeks; they thought I might be next.

We broke camp around mid afternoon and headed south once more. I sat up on the safari bench over the cab with the wind rushing into my face, clearing the remaining toxins from my body. The rolling carpet of rainforest around me suddenly seemed achingly beautiful. Thrilling. This massive undulating organism of deepest olive. So sumptuous, with its white wispy clouds strung from the tallest boughs and glimmering sequins of light falling through the leaves. I felt such love in my heart for the group sitting below me on the benches. We were all in this together. We were family. Everything was suddenly clear to me: Africa was a training ground in which the potency of everything – good and bad – was

heightened, and I was here to learn. I had survived the first major chal-
lenge. Maybe Africa would be kinder from now on.

As if to signal her consent, the continent gave us a little present later
that day. Another minor miracle. A slight distortion of time and space
which allowed us to reach the coast sooner than we had anticipated.

We were driving along a high plateau when suddenly upon rounding
a bend we saw the ocean spread out before us. It shouldn't have been there.
By Suzi's calculations, which were invariably accurate, we wouldn't reach
the sea until the following night. She was an excellent map reader and had
been able to predict the distances perfectly so far. It was simply not possible that she could have got this wrong now. We pulled up at the side of
the road, and she double-checked her maps and logbook of previous journeys. Her calculations were all correct. We definitely shouldn't have been
here, and yet we were.

The Atlantic looked beautiful, five times warmer than the same ocean
we had left behind in Casablanca, and with a seam of cream sand and
coconut palms stretching out both ways and fishermen in dugout boats
casting nets. Suzi gunned the engine, and within an hour we were parked
up on the beach, pulling off our clothes and diving head first into the
waves. We swam and surfed and splashed like children all afternoon. It
was heaven. I swam out as far as I could go and stayed there treading water
for maybe an hour, just revelling in the isolation. When I finally made it
back to shore, I got Lucy to shave off all my hair as a sort of final cleans-
ing. I wanted to start anew. Everything would be different now – I plunged
my shaved skull back into the surf by way of baptism; feeling the tingling
thrill of every newly exposed nerve ending.

We spent a week on the beach, and every morning after my swim I'd
call by the ice-cream stall along the coast road into town and buy a coconut
ice cream from Mossallu, a Coca-Cola vendor who mixed up coconut
milk, cane sugar, shredded coconut and cream every evening and froze it
on sticks for the next day. I was addicted to them. Mossallu liked to practise his English on me, and often we spent the whole morning chatting. It
always felt good to talk to someone beyond the confines of our snow globe.
He brought me to meet his father, who ran a stall in the local market, a
fetish market that sold items for rituals and cures. They had pots full of
small grindings of the copper that the *fikh* in Morocco had been looking

for and trestle tables with every sort of skull laid out on them, from elongated feline ones like weaving shuttles to tiny frail bat skulls with lozenge eyes. The most eerie were the chimpanzees', with their broad eye-sockets screaming in wide-eyed alarm. When I told Mossallu's dad about the *fikh*, he was fascinated. He considered her far more foreign than me, as she came from the faraway world beyond the desert, whereas I was just another white boy like all the other missionaries and NGO workers he saw passing through. He wanted to know all about her, but I couldn't remember that much except that she was kept pretty busy and had an impatient streak about her.

"No need for impatience," he said in French, with a warm smile. "If she is busy, she should be happy. Here, our problem is too many priests. All these shop owners here practise fetishism. There is too much competition. It is hard to make money. The doctors and Christians try and take people away too. And now also the diviners, and the herbalists, and the bonesetters and bush devils and brain healers. All wanting the same work."

Mossallu told me that his father used to be a brain healer, carving out sections of brain with a hacksaw to remove evil spirits, but then his powers went and he had to set up the stall. Now he just did simple rituals. He offered me my choice of whatever I wanted from his stall, but it all looked rather gruesome: a collection of wizened body parts, dried skins, baskets of incisors, horns, eggs, claws and dried phalli laid out like in a greengrocer's. Hanging from the awnings were scalps, pelts, tails and feathers and buckets piled with powders and poisons. In the end I chose a leathery, lumpy thing like a large dried apricot which had a yeasty smell and a nasty hint of ammonia. Mossallu said it was an ape foetus and would bring me luck.

Chapter 13

LIFE ON THE beach was paradise. We became children again, messing and playing in the sea. One afternoon we were chasing each other through the waves, splashing great arcs of water up skittishly with our arms.

"Let's get Dorothy's cozi," Rodney called out, and we all went racing off after her while she shrieked deliriously and dived beneath us. Rodney managed to catch her ankle as she went by, but she was nimble and able to slip away from him easily. She went pounding off in a powerful front crawl. Vinnie, the Manx man who had fought with his wife in the first week, came at her from the other side, lunging towards her when she surfaced, but she whipped around and came up the other side of him. She was by far the best swimmer amongst us and she clearly had the advantage, but we kept after her until she began to tire. Eventually Norman was able to catch her and rip the swimming costume straight off her. We all laughed gleefully.

"Who's next?" he screamed.

With the sun glistening on the water and the palms swaying in the breeze, it felt like we were on some tropical movie set.

"Lucy!" Rodney shouted, and the girls all shrieked and laughed and leapt out of the way so we could chase her. She was also an excellent swimmer and went soaring off under the water, but she hadn't the stamina or the strength of the men, and Stevi was soon on top of her, pulling her bikini off, revealing her little breasts, pale and pert in the warm water. She lowered her eyes and slunk down, wrapping her arms across herself.

I had read about idyllic beaches in books and seen them in films, but somehow I never thought places like this really existed; like the way New York is hard to countenance the first time you see it. I definitely never thought that by the age of twenty I'd actually be on a palm-lined, paradise strand.

"Get her bottoms," Norman shouted, and Stevi dived under again.

I watched them, my interest increasingly turning to concern. Stevi was tugging at Lucy's bikini bottoms, but he wasn't a good enough swimmer to stay under for long and he called for Rodney to help.

"Hold her down, mate," Stevi said. "I'll rip at 'em from this side."

Rodney doggy-paddled across to help, his bright orange head bobbing like a safety beacon. He gripped her shoulders tightly and Stevi was easily able to finish the job. A few people roared laughing, in fact most of us did, except Lucy. Looking frightened, she skulked off as soon as she could, her thin arms failing to cover herself. Stevi was still laughing and making his way towards the shallows waving her costume over his head triumphantly.

"Come and get it!" he was shouting. I noticed an erection straining against the fabric of his togs.

"Who's next?" Rodney was saying in a leery Jack Nicholson voice.

"Eanie, meanie, minie, mo," Duncan said, pointing to each of the girls. They said nothing, just looked anxiously around them, like the zebras we would see in a few months watching a hyena at a watering hole. Lucy's shoulders were hunched up tightly to her neck and one hand was still covering her groin. Her torso was wonderfully toned, like the underbelly of a lobster or a marble sculpture. There were tears in her eyes.

"Are you OK?" I shouted over, but she turned away and began walking up towards the camp. Dorothy was approaching her, practically naked too, her costume ripped and sagging.

Duncan's rotating finger settled on Stella and he shouted, "Mo!"

"Run for your life, girlie!" Vinnie said, and the chase was on again.

Stella was a poor swimmer and wasn't taking any chances. She made straight for the shoreline towards Lucy and Dorothy, thinking she would be safe there. Some of the men were tiring of the game, but Rodney's military training gave him extra reserves; he managed to reach Stella and whip her bikini off just before she reached the sand. She screamed and ran away, a tragic figure with her hands holding on to her bikini bottoms and her large breasts swinging ponderously from elbow to elbow. It was only then that I fully realised that this was no game. It never had been, really. Most of the others realised this too and stopped chasing. Only Stevi and Duncan were left. They followed Stella off down the beach, with Luke shouting at them to stop and them pretending not to hear.

"They're only having a laugh," Norman said breathlessly.

"Yeah, you homo," Stevi shouted back.

Stella looked like she was close to tears.

"Just stop!" I shouted.

"Faggot!" Stevi said, but he did slow down a bit, and when Duncan caught up with him, they both collapsed to the ground panting and laughing. Stella loped off to her tent embarrassed. Nobody said anything more about it. We went our separate ways, but there was an awkward feeling in the camp for the rest of the day, as if we had witnessed something we would rather not have. In the evening, Rodney's wife, Marsha, said she wanted to discuss it at the weekly meeting and she asked Suzi was it OK.

"Do whatever you want," Suzi said. "Who do you think I am, your headmistress?"

So, the next evening after dinner, Marsha and Rita, the two wives who hadn't been chased, stood up and said they felt very uncomfortable with what had happened.

"Yeah, only because we didn't pick you," Stevi said.

Suzi laughed out loud. She found the whole thing risible. She found everything about us risible. We were pathetic. Duncan said the whole thing had been just a bit of harmless fun. He pointed out that everyone had laughed and joined in.

Luke came up to me afterwards in low spirits.

"I came looking for a sense of wonder and I get this," he said. "We've just recreated the world back home, have you noticed? It's a perfect microcosm – all the same shit."

He pointed out that the wives, schoolgirls and nurses all had less of a say in the day-to-day matters than we did. We had created a mini patriarchy, presided over by the most testosteronal of us all, Suzi.

"So what do you want to do about it?" I said.

"Mount an insurrection?" he said, laughing.

A few weeks before, Luke and I had proposed a traffic management system for the back of the truck as a way of lampooning the endless rules, ordinances and by-laws that were being passed at each weekly meeting. We suggested that people could only travel clockwise and had to keep to the left at all times. If they intended turning in towards their locker, they had to indicate by clicking their fingers. People thought we were serious. They debated the idea and were even about to implement it when we pleaded with them that it was all just a joke. After that we realised we were better off staying quiet.

With all of us living on top of each other and scarcely any privacy, there was bound to be some bullying and manipulation, but it was the sexual stuff that bothered Luke most. Holly had been complaining to him about Dudley, the Welshman who had become our personal punch bag after annoying everyone in the first few weeks. Most of the time I hardly noticed him. He tended to keep to himself, but occasionally he would single out one of the women for special attention; playing his "little tricks" on them, as he called it: spying on them as they showered, slipping naked into their tents, streaking, whispering lecherous asides. He was too harmless to be considered a genuine threat, and he knew enough to realise that the men were just waiting for an excuse to teach him a lesson if he ever overstepped the mark.

In a way Dudley's easily visible lecherousness was a handy smokescreen for the rest of us. We all got away with things. After Dudley, the second most obvious offender was Duncan, who was slowly making good his promise to bed every woman on the truck. He was astute enough to pick his moments carefully, biding his time until a woman was feeling weak or vulnerable and then coming to her full of sympathy and comfort. A surprising number of them relented. It even got to the point later on in the trip that he had women turning up at his tent in the middle of the night begging for his attentions; their urges and isolation overcame them. He was always at hand, although as time wore on he became more discerning, and sometimes he would turn them away; but most he invited in, sending Norman off to sleep outside for the night.

Neither Luke nor I should have been surprised, I suppose, that there was no sense of wonder, that our mini-world would reflect the issues of the greater one so accurately. The notions I had had of a harmonious, nurturing community that would be a haven for everyone was farfetched, I realised now. The truth was that as a community we were normal, even down to an alpha male who regarded the women as his personal harem and a lonely pervert who fondled himself in public if he could get away with it. At some level, I think, it was comforting to find the real world mirrored here. It provided a bearing in the strangeness around us.

Oddly enough, it was possibly Dudley, of all people, who most hoped to find a different type of society amongst us. He had recently divorced his wife and in doing so had alienated his family and friends. He needed to find comradeship. That was why he had made such an effort in those initial weeks, and it had made us all turn against him. He took on the role of whipping-boy that I had been so careful to avoid. It wasn't his fault. He was just the sort of person who rubbed people up the wrong way. His need for validation, or at least attention, was so great that he was willing to go to any lengths for it. He knew how to annoy each of us individually – by complaining, boasting, lying, being lewd. He was incredibly pernickety – the sort of man who closed the tiny buttons on his boxer shorts. In fact, his irritating habits proved useful to us; they provided a focus for our frustration and anger. You could say anything, or do anything to him, and no one minded. If you made a mistake and blamed it on Dudley, no one questioned you. He was your get-out-of-jail-free card. In fact, we all welcomed the opportunity to dump more opprobrium his way. He united us in our dislike of him, made us feel more connected, and in some way better than him, for in comparison to him we all shone. Most of the overland trucks we came across had their own pariah figure, and they delighted in swapping stories about the idiocy and awfulness of theirs.

By the time we reached Togo, Dudley was so worn down by our constant harassment that he was spending most of his time on his own. He would wander around aimlessly, looking morose and introverted. It was on our second day at the strand that he went into town and found himself a prostitute. She was a pleasant, chubby woman who lived with her mother and brothers in a nearby village, but was happy to move into the tent with him for the period we were there. (He had been forced to buy a tent in northern France when we all refused to share ours with him.) She seemed like an intelligent woman: bright-eyed and encouraging, and with a smattering of pidgin English. They got on well together. Her presence lifted him, and for the first time in weeks I saw him smile, but she made the rest of the group uneasy. Some of the women were reluctant to share their meals with her.

"I didn't pay into the kitty to feed the likes of her," Rita muttered to her husband at a level she knew we could all hear.

Dudley said nothing, but from then on he made sure to eat his meals in the village and spent most of the day there, only returning at night. This eased things for a few days, but then some of the men began revealing a new moralistic streak and claimed that the whole situation offended them. The guy whom I used to overhear forcing himself on to his partner at night was particularly vociferous. It simmered for a few days until it was inevitable something would happen, and sure enough, one night when everyone was very drunk, they decided to take matters in hand. They formed a little posse at the bar, toasting their resolve with rounds of rum and self-righteous talk, and set off into the night. I saw them go and feared for what they might do, but I didn't do anything to stop them. I was still conscious that Dudley's whipping-boy mantle could so easily have landed on me.

In the end their plan was no more than a variation on the old school staple of dunking a boy's head in the lavatory. They crept along the sand to Dudley's tent, sneaking as stealthily as they could in their drunken state. They lifted the ground pins out, one by one, then picked up the tent in one go and carried it to the sea with Dudley and the prostitute still inside. The gang tried their best to stay quiet, to stifle their laughter so that the couple wouldn't know what was happening, but as it hit the water they couldn't help themselves and burst into hoots of cheering. We all watched as Dudley and the woman struggled to unzip the flap and pull themselves out. They were naked and wet and the woman was in tears. Stella was stirred by the sight of her and went to help, but Dudley wouldn't let her come near them. He gripped the woman to him and shepherded her past us and out on to the road towards the village. We all went back to the bar, and Stevi stood us a celebratory round.

When I went for my ice-cream next morning after my swim, Mossallu had heard all about it. His dad had been woken in the night by the woman's mother and asked to do a late-night ritual to clear Dudley's spirits. The news in the village was that they were in love and that Dudley was planning to bring her back to Wales and marry her, but first they wanted to clear him of any spirits that might cause the relationship harm.

"What do you mean?" I asked. I had become fascinated by his father's profession. He often tried to explain elements of it to me, but I found it hard to grasp.

"Do you remember I was telling you about the chicken?" he said. "How he kills and then . . . ?"

I nodded.

"It was like that," he said. "He sent the bad spirits into a skull, and when he was sure they were all inside he smashed it for ever."

"So now he's fine?" I asked.

"Hopefully," Mossallu said vaguely.

I had told Mossallu how strange all this seemed compared to the beliefs I had been brought up with.

"But we are Catholic too," he said. "We pray with the same beads on a string and smelly smoke powder. It is all one. Same spirits."

According to Mossallu, everything in Africa was based on spirits. Every person, every living thing, every action, had a spirit that existed for ever. At any point, one of these could decide to start meddling in your life, and it was their interference that was usually at the root of the events that we experienced; almost nothing ever happened by chance. The fact that you were at their mercy was handy in a way. It meant that you were never fully responsible for anything. You were a puppet on a string, and the only way you could be sure of having any influence over your life was by constantly paying fetish priests to intercede with the spirits on your behalf. Mossallu advised me that I should search one out in every village if I wanted to keep safe. At any point, a spirit could decide to take a grudge against me and lead me into any type of danger. Terrible, terrible danger. It was vital that I consult with priests as often as I could. But it was even more important that they were reputable. If I went to the wrong sort, they could just as easily set more evil spirits on me. Another thing I ought to watch out for was sterile charlatans with no power at all, pseudo bush devils, fake seers. With them I would just be wasting my money and encouraging them in their deception.

I asked him how I would know the difference, and he looked at me aghast, his mouth opening and closing, trying to formulate the answer, but realising that the very fact that I had to ask meant there was no way I could understand the answer. The only guide he could finally come up with was to steer clear of the ones who used little boxes in their ceremonies.

"Why?" I asked.

"These are ones you cannot trust," he said.

"Why?" I said again.

"They trick you," he said. "If you see the little wooden box, just say goodbye and go somewhere else."

He wouldn't say any more.

"Are all the spirits bad?" I said. "Are there no good ones? Ones who want to help us?"

"Spirits aren't good or bad," he said. "They are just spirits. Some can do good things, but most often they like to cause trouble."

He explained that it was pointless getting too worked up over anything at all – drought, a broken light bulb, impotency, a bad fish stew – because it was all down to the spirits either way. You just had to accept it.

I suggested that this was a bit fatalistic.

"Do you really believe you are in control?" Mossallu asked me. "That the spirits are not influencing everything you do?"

I thought about my dad and the dreams and my uncertain reasons for ending up in Africa and found it hard to reply. It was difficult to get my head around the things he was telling me, but he insisted it was simple logic. It was the only way the world made sense. Everything was a form of energy, constantly moving, causing positive and negative repercussions. You just dived into the middle and tried to keep afloat. The idea reminded me a bit of elements of chaos theory or quantum physics. It made the world richer and more resonant to think that everything had echoes and repercussions creeping out in all directions through time and space, and it possibly made life easier to believe that you were at the mercy of invisible powers. Everything could be blamed on begrudging ancestors and mischievous plotting by others. Ever since the Age of Reason, we've wanted to escape such chaotic thinking. We had hoped we could nail down reality to the black and white rules of classic Newtonian physics, but then Einstein came along and began to undermine all our certainties. It would be odd if eventually we were forced back to the African outlook. One of the reasons white people found the place so unsettling was its insistence on harbouring the ghosts of our own long-discarded beliefs.

Mossallu's non-rational worldview brought to mind some of the odd occurrences that had taken place in the preceding days: the overnight healing of my body and the sudden appearance of the ocean in a place it shouldn't have been. When I told Mossallu about it, he just laughed, saying that it was like his father always said: Western minds were so wedded to a logical reality that we constantly papered over the cracks that made up most of it. To clarify his point, he showed me the bottom of his cup in which the glaze was shattered into a thousand shards.

Rough palm-distilled alcohol was cheap and plentiful on the beach, and we ended up getting drunk most nights and having loud beach parties. I tended to fall asleep around midnight when the party was still in full swing, and I'd only hear rumours in the morning of what had gone on. Duncan managed to cross Stella off his list one night after they had all gone skinny dipping and she had been too drunk to resist him. She was a bit disappointed with herself in the morning, but overall didn't regret it. He was a surprisingly considerate lover, as far as she could remember, and the bright, moon-tinged surf had made a truly romantic setting. He hadn't by this stage become blasé about notching up another score on his tent-post, and so we all got to hear about it as he preened around the camp next morning. There were claims that Rodney had led Lucy off into one of the lavatory cubicles and they had been seen cuddling and possibly more, but no one was exactly sure what had happened, except that his wife was refusing to speak to him the following morning.

So much for my grand notions of protecting Lucy. I got increasingly angry over the following days whenever I thought about it. It melded together in my mind with Rodney's torture of Bobby Sands and the taunt-ing of the rich overlanders in Fez and all the other little things that annoyed me. I told Lucy that I was determined to have it out with him, but I wanted her to tell me her side beforehand.

"Poor Rodney," she said, shrugging lightly, "he has a lot on his mind."

"Is that all you have to say?" I said.

"Oh, Mocha . . ." she said sadly.

The following morning was our last day on the beach, and I woke early to get a swim in before packing up. On the sand just above the retreating shoreline, I came across two massive banners made of wet stucco-work, surrounded by an intricate curlicue border made of drier sand. It was beautiful, like something you'd find on the walls of a Venetian palazzo. It must have taken most of the night to make. Inside each border in brown stone lettering underlined with bleached razor shells were two different messages. One of them said, I'M SORRY LUCY, the other I'M SO, SO SORRY MARSHA.

When I had my gear packed up, Suzi asked me to go into the village to tell Dudley we were about to leave. She thought my French might be required to diffuse any unpleasantness that might arise with the girl's family. I had heard from Mossallu that they were outraged by our treatment of her. They believed we had dishonoured her, and her brothers had threatened to seek revenge. Suzi offered to send a posse consisting of Wayne, Rodney and Norman with me as backup but I refused, thinking they were bound to be more trouble than they were worth. In the end, things worked out fine in the village. There was a certain degree of tension when I turned up first, but Dudley managed to ease things. He stood proudly beneath a palm-leafed shelter and shook my hand formally, as if we were two colonial adventurers meeting at an official rendezvous. This seemed to put the locals at their ease. He stood between me and them, saying he was sick of all the fighting and just wanted peace now.

"Sure," I said, relieved. "Well said! Now we better get going, the truck is leaving in an hour."

"I'm not coming," Dudley replied.

"What do you mean?" I said.

"I'm staying. I've had it with you lot. I'm going to teach Ana to read and write, and, if she'll have me, I'm going to ask her to marry me."

I was staggered. I had presumed Mossallu had been joking when he talked of marriage.

"We'll set up home back in my mother's village in Wales and have kiddies," Dudley continued. "Lots of them!"

"You're kidding?" I said.

"I love her, Mocha," he said.

"Right," I said, looking over at the woman. "She seems really nice. Strong, healthy."

They seemed like such inappropriate words, but I didn't know what else to say. I looked down at my feet and shook the sand off my sandals.

"You know nothing about love, do you?" he said, smiling sadly.

I shrugged, still not able to make eye contact.

"When you're older, maybe," he said and patted me on the back. "Tell the others I'm sorry for pulling out on them. I didn't mean to let you down, it's just that I find you all . . . I don't know. I don't want to be rude and I don't want to be too harsh, but the word that comes to mind is, reprehensible. Yeah, that's it. Childish, cruel, vulgar, etc. Not just to me, but to everyone. And you don't seem to like the people here, the Africans. I can't understand that. I can forgive anything, but not that. You're racist, all of you. You too Mocha, I'm afraid."

I didn't know what to say.

"We're not that bad, really," I said half-heartedly. "Maybe you should give us another chance, see the thing through. You know, show a bit of spit 'n vinegar."

Pep talks never came easily to me, and I resorted to Wayne's line for want of anything better.

"I'm not coming," Dudley said confidently. It was the first time I had seen him behaving decisively in all these months. His arm was draped affectionately around Ana's shoulder. "I'm sick of all the sneering. I hate it. You're so cruel. All of you, Mocha."

I said nothing; there was nothing I could say. He was looking me straight in the eye, and I thought about apologising but knew it was too late for that. I realised with shame that he was the only one of us to have changed for the better since we had left England.

"Anyway," he said wearily, getting to his feet and putting his hand around his lover, "maybe I'll see you around sometime. If you ever do get that diary of yours written up and published, send me a copy . . . Or actually, don't bother. I probably don't want to know."

"What about your stuff?" I said at last.

"I don't care," he said; "keep it, or leave it there. Maybe I'll come by later and pick up anything you've left."

That was it. He walked off deeper into the village, and I turned around, wondering how the hell I was ever going to explain it to the others. I stopped in at Mossallu's for a quick final ice cream on the way back and I told him what had happened.

"You see," he said delightedly. "My father's spells are still so strong. Maybe he is not good at cutting into the brain now, but he can make people's spirits bold like a lion, and he doesn't need to use anything from a little box. He gave Dudley his courage back. Now he is strong."

Logically I knew that his explanation didn't make any sense, and yet . . .

Mossallu told me that his father insisted he do a ceremony on me too before I left. He was worried about what could happen to me in the deep Zaire jungle. I told him to thank his father for his concern, but I had to get back to the truck as we were about to leave. Mossallu wouldn't listen and practically dragged me to the fetish market, where his father served me tea and outlined the various ceremonies he could perform: either dancing, or the decapitating of a chicken and reading auguries in its blood-spatter pattern. I told him I wanted whatever was quickest, and that if I didn't get back soon, Suzi might leave without me. Reluctantly he agreed on a few simple prayers and the scattering of some seeds on the ground. The whole thing took only a few minutes, and without warning at the end, he pulled out a lizard and sacrificed it, and from this was able to tell me that I had been going through a lot of trouble at night and that I needed to get some more spells done to counter the bad spirits.

I presumed he was referring to my dreams again and said, "Yeah, my nightmares, the *fikh* mentioned those too – thanks very much, I've got to go now."

"No, not that," he said as I was getting up to leave. "Diarrhoea. Your stomach needs help to get the spirits out."

He told me to find a doctor and get myself checked out as soon as I could. I promised I would as I ran out of the market and back to the camp.

In the end, the others were still packing up their stuff, and they had no problem accepting the news about Dudley. The girls seemed relieved – it would definitely be easier for them not to have him around, not to have to keep such a sharp eye out when they were undressing or showering or going to the loo. Straight away people began fighting over who got his books and sleeping bag. Suzi somehow managed to bag his Walkman for herself before anyone else could, and Norman tried to take his tent, but I insisted that we at least leave him that.

By midday we were all packed up and loaded back on to the cattle truck ready to be shunted further along the route towards Benin, leaving only Dudley's tent and a few bits of his cutlery behind. I had never once felt any guilt about our treatment of him until the moment he looked me in the eye and condemned me. Suddenly I was overcome with a sense of shame, and I don't think I was the only one. We all felt a bit put out once he had gone. We needed him. He played a vital role in the group dynamic, and it would be difficult to replace him. Writing this now I find it hard to remember what was so annoying about him; I suppose it was our treatment of him more than anything that brought out his irritating side. His increasingly pathetic attempts to befriend us just made him all the easier to dislike.

The moment he had gone, I became aware of a core shift in balance among the group and made an effort to keep a low profile for a while in case I ended up becoming the new Dudley.

Chapter 14

THE ONLY RADICAL change of direction during the entire journey was in Togo. Since leaving England we had headed straight south, first 2,500 kilometres to the Mediterranean and then 6,000 kilometres onwards down to the southern Atlantic coast of West Africa. Now, after pulling out of the campsite on the beach in Togo, we made a momentous 90° turn east towards the Indian Ocean, which we would be driving towards for the next three months. There was 7,000 kilometres of track and occasional stretches of road ahead, which would bring us across the entire breadth of Africa to Nairobi, more or less following in reverse the path of H. M. Stanley's famous 999-day exploratory expedition a century earlier. We were approaching the true heart of Africa, the core of the equatorial forests of Cameroon, the Central African Republic and, most especially, Zaire (which went on to become the Democratic Republic of the Congo in 1997). Here, among the bottle-thick vines, sepulchral trees, cathedralesque canopies and coiling waterways, was the energy centre from which human life had first emerged. Some of the most awesome regions on the planet lay ahead, but also some of the most isolated. If Africa was to make a stand against us, it would most likely be here – the furthest point from our safe, predictable world. There would be no forewarning, that much was certain. Guerrilla tactics were the methods Africa had been employing since white men first arrived in the nineteenth century, ambushing them when they least expected it. That was the one certainty you could depend on. Ambush was always the favoured technique of both the tribes and animals of the region.

Benin, the first country we hit after Togo, was another undistinguished sliver of land cut haphazardly from the cake of nineteenth-century imperialism. It was barely 100 kilometres wide. I had never heard of it before and learnt little more as we sped through it, but the next country, Nigeria, made a far greater impression. The landscape was similar to Togo's and Benin's — forest on the hills, scrub on the plains and palms along the coast — but its wealth set it apart. In the Fifties, Nigeria had struck oil and now, instead of the tiny mud villages set in scrub land, there were factories and refineries and industrial estates and cities of rundown apartment blocks and shanty towns for the workers. Decades earlier, millions of people had been enticed from their villages to work in the new industries until the oil fields dried up and the companies pulled out. The workers were left stranded in blocks that soon became dilapidated ghettos. Many had sold their ancestral land or burnt their homes to discourage squatters or were simply too old now to return to farming and had never thought to pass the old methods on to their city-bred children. It made Nigeria feel like no other country we had seen so far. Angry, bitter, hopeless. The people knew they had been conned and had become cynical. They had believed that the world of the Kung Fu movies shown to them by the petrochemical companies on mobile cinemas that toured the villages to entice them to the cities actually represented the life that was waiting for them in Lagos and Benin City. They were promised they would never have to fetch water again or cook over an open fire. What they were not told was that the piped water would be filthy and undependable and that the price of gas for their stoves could soar, often leaving them unable to afford to cook a meal. They had been cheated, and they seemed determined now to take revenge on any white man they came across with bribes and scams and harassment.

The roads were maintained better than any on the trip so far, built by the foreign companies to get the oil out as quickly as possible and to make it easy for them to pull out completely when things went bad. We were able to drive faster than ever before, but it was pointless; we lost more time at the makeshift roadblocks that appeared every few kilometres, where soldiers would delay us for up to an hour, harassing us for bribes. A plank of

nails would be thrown across the road, and on either side would be soldiers slouched against their AK-47s like spiders waiting for something to
stick to their thread. Suzi, on principle, refused to pay bribes, which
meant a long drawn-out argument every time. Sometimes, if she was feeling impatient, she would swerve around the plank and accelerate off, hoping that they didn't open fire. It took real skill to tell the ones who were
likely to shoot from the ones who would just laugh it off.

There were churches everywhere. When the oil industry collapsed,
American evangelical churches moved in *en masse* to save the souls of the
newly desperate people. They were seen as easy pickings for small-time
churches in places like Michigan, Montana and Wyoming. By simply
handing out a few bales of old clothes or building a school or clinic, they
could muster up an impressive congregation. Since the locals spoke
English, there was no need for the missionaries to learn a new language or
translate Bibles – it made the whole business of chalking up converts very
efficient. Streamlined. They were able to report impressive growth figures
to their donors back home at the end of each year. Most of the roadside
chapels, which were almost as common as the roadblocks, had names that
sounded like those kooky desserts you see on diner menus in the Deep
South (Double-Hershey, fondue-fountained, chocolate-sprinkled cheese-
cake): Celestial Stars Church of the Immaculate Vision, or the Deeper
Meaning Bible Loving Society. Guesthouses and restaurants had similar
names: Jesus First Happy Hotel, The Heaven of Goodness Hygienic
Restaurant.

Nigeria was the first country we visited which had something the
West had recently coveted, and it was sobering to see the ruthlessness with
which we had gone about acquiring it. It seemed the oil had been taken
with the same impunity as slaves and diamonds and ebony a century
before. Although officially Nigeria was the richest country we had visited,
it felt by far the poorest – and the angriest and most frightening. I pointed this out to a local school teacher when she asked me what I thought of
her country, and she said I had it all wrong.

"We are the lucky ones," she said. "Africa has been asleep for hundreds of years. It has to wake up. It is good that you came and woke us
early because now we are ahead of the rest. I am not saying it was nice. No
one likes being woken from a deep sleep and nice dreaming, but it had to

be. At least now it's all behind us. Before oil, we were just human bodies for you – a scar you would open when you needed fresh blood. Now we are a nation. The world knows about us."

We were in a market one day in southern Nigeria, enjoying the rich assault on the senses that increasingly accompanied such places as we drove deeper into the continent – crocodiles being gutted in concrete gutters, knives being sharpened, baboons being butchered on massive, purple-stained chopping boards bent convex from years of chopping – when all of a sudden Norman collapsed to the ground and began to shake convulsively. An old man with grey hair tight against his skull, like lamb's wool, came forward and splashed water over him from a powdered-milk can which he had been using to wash a child. Norman was muttering incoherently and trying to get to his feet, clawing at a rickety trestle table, threatening to knock the whole thing over. I went to help him, while Wayne helped the stall owner rearrange the little piles of thread, fishhooks, gobstoppers and tweezers that had been shaken about by the fall. Norman seemed to have recovered himself. He was able to stand up on his own, but was covered in a dusty mush of diesel, fish slime and congealed blood which he didn't seem to notice.

"That was messy," I said, brushing him down.

"Was it?" he said. His tone reminded me of my father's in the months before he died, conscious but not fully present.

Dorothy felt his brow.

"You've got a fever," she said. "We should get you sitting down."

He stared hard at her as though he weren't really sure who she was. It was as if he were sleepwalking and not fully conscious of anything. He kept pointing at things and going over to examine them – caterpillars fried in palm oil, a baboon hide being singed with a blow torch. He smelt everything deeply as though he were in a rose garden and everything had been placed there for his personal wonderment. I found it a bit eerie the way he remained so quiet, just pointing and making gentle sighing sounds now and again.

We had lunch in a restaurant a little later, and that seemed to perk him up a bit. The owner told us afterwards that the stew we had eaten was made with clawless otter, and while the nurses found this horrifying, Felicity even gagging like a sick cat, Norman licked his lips appreciatively.

This wasn't really out of character, however; he had an intensely carnivorous streak and was always the first to try anything new – crickets, catfish, white-nose monkey.

The afternoon's drive was made easy by a petrochemical-built road and an absence of roadblocks. Norman seemed to have recovered, and he dozed happily for most of the journey; his pulpy eyelids opening languorously now and then to glance around him contentedly, his long, heavy tongue slurping around his chapped lips. In the evening he said he was feeling very hot and insisted on parading around in his Y-fronts. It was malaria tablet night, which always made people act a bit strange. The drugs made some grow elated, others moody and emotional. The group meeting used to be held on the same night until we realised this was a recipe for trouble.

The following morning I was awoken by Suzi shouting outside my tent.

"Lock and load, right now," she growled as I stuck my head out of the flap. It was barely dawn. "Group meeting in the truck at seven sharp."

This was worrying. An emergency group meeting was never good, especially so early in the morning. We had only once before had a dawn meeting. It was after someone had been found not digging a hole for themselves when they went to the lavatory at night and we had had to sit in silence for four hours until one of us owned up. We had sat there under a blinding sun without breakfast or lunch until finally I realised that Suzi would keep us there all night if she had to, and I admitted to the crime just to get the thing over with. We never found out who was actually responsible. The previous (nighttime) emergency meeting had been in Burkina Faso when Suzi found the butt of a joint in the embers, but on that occasion Luke had owned up straight away and as punishment was made to scrub the truck clean every night for a week.

Now, while Suzi was making her way around the camp waking everyone, I shook Wayne, who had taken to sleeping in the tent with me again, and told him what was happening. I got out before he stirred, wishing to avoid the sight of his hairy back and too-tight jockeys shoved in my face first thing in the morning. Suzi took one look at me and growled. She clearly was in bad form. She was wearing her signature bandana, bra and ski pants. After spitting in my direction, she turned and began kicking

Rodney's tent and shouting at his wife to get up if she knew what was good for her.

By a quarter to seven, we were all huddled around the back steps of the truck waiting anxiously. We just wanted to find out what was wrong and get it over with as quickly as possible.

"The shit shovel," she began, "where is it?"

Her words were said with such harshness that there was no need to even look around and check if it was still bolted to the back of the truck where it should have been. We looked nonetheless, in hope and idle expectation, and an anxious inhalation ran through us as we saw it was missing. This was bad. Of all her endless rules, putting the shovel back in its correct bracket and locking it was almost as important as not taking drugs. We glanced desperately around, hoping for someone to speak up and offer a viable explanation, but none was forthcoming. Putting the shovel back where it was supposed to go was so deeply ingrained in us that someone must either have mislaid it on purpose or else the padlock that secured it to the truck had snapped and one of the locals had taken it.

"Where's the fuckin' shovel!" she roared again.

We kept our heads bent and our eyes low. We knew it was vital not to show even a trace of defiance or she was likely to explode. At this stage, it was best to just stay quiet and take the brunt of it.

"I am not your bloody nanny, am I?" she screamed. "I've had it up to my tits with you, you're fucking morons. My job here is to drive the truck, that's it, get it? I don't need this extra grief."

She went on at length about how none of us were leaving that spot until she found out who was responsible. I grimaced. This was bad. I didn't dare own up a second time in case she suspected that I was covering for someone and we would all be in even more trouble. People rarely ever owned up to things they did in the group; it was a repercussion of Suzi's autocratic leadership. We had been infantilised, and infants aren't expected to take responsibility for themselves. We had long ago adopted the no-snitch code of all non-sophisticated inmates and so invariably kept our counsel, unless we thought we could blame Dudley for it. Now that he was gone, there was no natural patsy left.

"We're not eating, we're not driving, we're not moving from this spot," Suzi said, "until I find out. Is that clear?"

We nodded.

"And believe me," she went on, heady with moral fury, "when I start getting hungry, that's when I get really angry."

It was at times like this I suspected she might have introduced a system of corporal punishment if she could get away with it. She was a slightly built woman among a group of twenty, but none of us had ever dared stand up to her; at least not until that moment . . .

I was startled by a voice behind me – midway between a growl and a cry. Looking up, I saw Norman lifting his great mass up off the ground and standing stoically, facing Suzi head on. He reminded me of Obelix having just swallowed back the magic elixir. He was staring dimly at her, licking his lips defiantly. He must have weighed at least double, possibly three times what she did, but she didn't flinch, just stared at him, slowly allowing the side of her mouth creep up into a sneer.

"Yes, Norman?" she said icily. "Do you have something to say?"

I pictured her claws readying to snap out and tear him limb from limb. He licked his lips again, moistening the scabs in preparation for what he had to say.

"Guaagh!" he began with a grunt. "Just . . ."

His words were barely audible. He seemed to be mumbling to himself more than anything and was having difficulty balancing, rocking back and forth and gripping the hams of his forearms with his podgy fingers for balance. It seemed as if the fever or illness might still be affecting him. As he continued his words grew louder, but they were still mostly incomprehensible, being too choked and full of emotion.

Finally he screamed, "Fuck off! Yeah? Just fuck off! I've had it with people shouting at me. All my life people have been shouting, and I've had it. I didn't come to Africa for this. Maybe the others are frightened of you, but I'm not . . . Who are you? You're just a big sick bag of hot air! A Hitler-bitch. No better than the nig-nogs. You think you're the only one who's been places, who's seen things. You're not. I've been *places*."

There was a shocked silence from the rest of us. We already feared the repercussions. I hadn't noticed at first the emphasis Norman laid on the word *places*, but it must have alerted his brother to what was coming.

"Don't!" Duncan said warningly. "Don't!"

His voice was weary as though he knew it was already too late.

Norman glanced over at his brother, pausing for a moment, considering his warning, but dismissing it.

"When I was nine we were coming back from my aunt's and I was taken on board from my Dad's Ford Cortina . . ."

"For God's sake," Duncan interjected pleadingly.

". . . a tractor-beam whooshed me straight up," Norman ploughed on regardless, "and next thing I was lying on the floor and there were three bodies standing over me and a metal cap on my head with holes in it and wires. So! They were from Betelgeuse. They said if I wanted I could come with them; anywhere, to galaxies and all. So, tough tits, what makes you so important?"

Everyone looked to Suzi. She was staring at him in bewilderment. She had taken her shades off and her eyes were scrunched up like walnuts; her nipples stood out through her bra, firm with fury.

"Maybe I don't speak French or Swahili like you," Norman went on, with a rasp in his throat like he was crying, "but I understood what they said. They don't need languages. So, don't go thinking I'm a yokel who's never been out of Cornwall. I've travelled, I have – on a beam of light with all my atoms separated apart and sucked through space, you silly girl, you silly, silly bitch in a bandana."

Norman seemed oblivious to the rest of us, but after a time he paused a moment and turned towards his brother.

"Huh, Duncan? Amn't I right?" he said, looking eagerly at him.

Duncan had his face buried in his hands. We were all staring dumbfounded. I was marvelling at the genius of the phrase, "bitch in a bandana", wishing I had thought of it myself. I wanted to cheer him on, but he looked so manic that I thought it would be unfair to goad him any further. It was still early morning, but the sun was blazing hot, the glare so bright it hurt your eyes. Norman's T-shirt was drenched in sweat across his belly. He was visibly shaken and seemed to lose confidence when Duncan didn't back him up.

"They said . . ." he continued with a sadness in his voice, and then paused to breathe a while, before struggling on, "they said I could go to any of the 80 trillion other galaxies – that's how I know it was true, because I checked later in the *Encyclopedia Britannica* and there really are

80 trillion others – and they had no wrinkles because they didn't experience gravity and that's just physics, and . . ."

Norman fell quiet, immersed in his own memory for a few moments, then all of a sudden he stood up and wandered off. We all maintained our silence, staring at the ground, until finally Suzi turned to Duncan and said, "Is he OK?"

"It's why I didn't want him here," Duncan muttered wearily. "I knew this stuff would come up."

"You better go check on him," Suzi said.

"It's always the same whenever he gets sick," Duncan said before heading off after his brother.

We all looked to Suzi, who was staring around her disconsolately, her thunder truly stolen.

"OK," she said, "meeting over. We'll find a clinic in the next town and get him taken care of."

Before we disbanded, Duncan ran back over to us and said, "Look, don't mention any of this to him when he gets better, OK? I mean it. It'll just make it worse. Just leave him alone and he'll be fine."

"Did he really get taken up?" Natasha asked.

"What did I just say?" Duncan shot back threateningly.

There was such ferocity in his voice that no one dared say another word. We went our separate ways. Henry and Mildred, who were on shopping and cooking duty, bought a new shovel and padlock in the market, and the matter was never raised again. We found a clinic near by, where a Mexican doctor checked Norman out and insisted on keeping him in over night. Following Mossallu's dad's advice, I took the opportunity to get some tests done myself to make sure that my stomach infection had fully cleared up, and sure enough the tests came back with traces of amoebic dysentery still in my gut. I told the doctor that a witch doctor in Togo had told me the same thing by slitting a lizard from throat to belly and he didn't seem at all surprised. He prescribed a course of Flagyll, telling me that if I had taken it when I had first got sick it would have been cured in a few days, and I could have avoided all those weeks of pain. He was concerned about the long-term damage I might have done to my stomach.

We stayed overnight while Norman had his tests done, but they showed up no abnormalities except for the presence of a mild fever which the doctor said would clear up on its own. He had wanted to prescribe some cortisone cream for his lips, but Norman refused, saying he liked their crustiness.

We drove on eastwards all day, and as evening fell, Suzi turned off the road and headed down a track into a region of remote jungle. When we buzzed through to her to find out where she was going, she refused to answer. We looked at each other worriedly, but knew there was nothing we could do about it. Finally, after about an hour on the track, we arrived at a massive, rundown concrete building in the middle of nowhere. It looked like a disused asylum, and for a moment I feared for what she might be planning to do to Norman. She buzzed through to us to say we would be staying here for the night. We looked around us searching for any sign of where we might be, but the building gave no clues of what it was, or what it had been. Suzi came around from the cab and told us to stay where we were for a few minutes.

"Where are we?" Luke asked.

"Just wait here until I come back," she said, wandering off towards the anonymous crumbling building.

The jungle was growing right up against the walls, so that it looked like it was in danger of being swallowed up completely by its surroundings. She pushed her way through a large weathered teak and glass door set into the grim façade of peeling paintwork and disappeared inside. We grew increasingly anxious about what she was up to.

Finally Luke jumped down, saying, "This is crazy. We can't just sit here and wait . . ."

He walked around the yard looking for something or someone that might tell him where we were, and finally, on the far side of the clearing, about as far from where Suzi had parked the truck as possible, he spotted the edges of a mottled marble and brass plaque covered in foliage. He pulled back the bushes and found the name of a hotel written on it. He ran back to the truck, reaching it just before Suzi came swinging out through the door again to tell us that it was indeed a hotel, a five-star hotel, and that she had just negotiated twelve rooms for us at £10 each, which the kitty would pay for.

We weren't foolish enough to believe her. There was no way this could be a five-star hotel – not now anyway; perhaps long, long ago.

"What do you think we are?" Felicity said. "Imbeciles?"

"Sorry?" Suzi said.

"It's not a hotel," Felicity said. "It's a ruin."

"I told you, it's a five-star hotel," Suzi said. "If you don't want to stay here, that's fine. We can go camp somewhere."

"Are you messing with us?" I said. "Playing with our minds?"

"I told you, it's a luxury hotel!" she said. "I just thought you'd like a treat."

She seemed hurt by the fact that we didn't believe her.

"Granted, it doesn't look so great on the outside," she said, "but you'll just have to trust me."

We didn't know what to do. We looked around wondering whether or not we could put our faith in her. If it really was a five-star hotel, we didn't want to miss out on such a unique opportunity. Yet, at the same time, we didn't want to be made fools of. I feared we would get our bags out and head through those doors only to find an asylum or a barracks or an abandoned empty shell. I could imagine her cackling with laughter. I didn't want to risk having my hopes trampled.

"Damn it, I just wanted to give you a treat," she said. "You make everything so bloody difficult."

"Will you promise?" Lucy said. "Cross your heart and hope to die?"

"For Christ's sake, forget it, OK?" Suzi snapped. "We'll find somewhere to camp instead. I just thought you'd like a bit of pampering, that's all."

We looked at each other, weighing up the situation. None of us wanted to be the first to be caught out.

"I'll go check," I said at last.

Suzi huffed indignantly, but she didn't try and stop me. I walked towards the big door and stuck my head in. It was dimly lit, but sure enough I saw a vast marble floor stretching out ahead and a brass-lined reception desk. I came back with an enormous beam spread across my face.

"You see!" Suzi said smugly.

"It has a reception desk anyway," I said. "A really fancy one."

I smiled at Suzi in gratitude, and I noticed the trace of a smile of appreciation flash back. It was a humble, wordless moment, but I definitely noticed softness in her eyes. It was broken almost immediately as everyone began rushing madly around, pulling out sleeping bags, towels, soap, and then suddenly stopping, as the realisation dawned on us that if this really was a genuine five-star hotel, then none of this would be needed. As soon as we walked through those doors, our every possible desire would be taken care of.

As I stepped away from the truck, I looked back at Suzi, wondering how far she was prepared to go to torture us. Could all this be a set up? I was reminded of the mind games that Rodney had told us were used in Northern Ireland: blindfolding prisoners and bringing them to the roof of a building, letting them think they were standing at the very edge before pushing them off a low step. Or else, bringing them up in a helicopter and pushing them out while hovering just a few feet off the ground. It didn't cause them any physical harm, just messed with their minds. Even the fact that I would think such a thing in relation to Suzi showed how skewed things were on the truck. In theory, she was only there to help us – and most of the time that's what she did. We had paid for a service and she provided it. It was mostly our ineptitude that made her appear unreasonable. It was inevitable that she would lose patience with us. We were almost always at fault. At least, that's how I saw it at the time; looking back now, I wonder was I suffering from Stockholm syndrome – sympathising with my jailer.

The hotel turned out to be a genuine five-star hotel, or at least it had been one time. It was set up by a petrochemical firm as a sweetener to the local government for securing a mining license in the region. The mine had never materialised, but some contractual obligation forced them to keep the hotel open, offering accommodation to anyone who bothered to turn up. My room had a king-sized, orthopaedic bed, linen sheets, a trouser press and feather-soft cotton towels. The contrast with my nasty rubber roll-mat and fetid sleeping bag was too great to countenance. I went into the bathroom and filled the huge bath with bubbles, grabbing the contents of the minibar and lining them up on the tiled edge. I downed a few Black Label whiskies as the water was filling and then lay back into the frothy water. I had almost dozed off before I remembered the antibiotics I was taking and the fact that I had been warned not to mix them with alcohol. My mind suddenly began tail-spinning into a dizzy blur, and it took all my wits to keep reminding myself not to let go and to keep my nose and face above the water.

When I finally got out of the bath, I collapsed on the bed and turned on the huge television to find out what was happening in the wider world. Squadrons of tanks were moving across the desert – the same scenes on every channel, interspersed occasionally with tracer shells lighting up the night sky in spangled reds and turquoises. It looked like scenes from Space Invaders shooting across the screen. I had never seen anything like it before and it chilled me. I wasn't sure whether it was the drugs playing tricks on me, but I felt suddenly so scared for the world, knowing something terrible was happening somewhere and having no idea what. I rang Luke's room to see what he knew.

"Did you see the TV?" I asked.

"Yeah, isn't it great!"

"Sorry?" I said.

"It's huge," he said.

"What is?" I said. "What's happening?"

"What do you mean?" he said.

"The scenes – the war," I said.

He hadn't turned on his television yet. I rang around until I found Stella was watching.

"There was an American flag on one of the tanks," she said, but that was all she could tell me. I hurried down to reception to find out what the hell was going on in the world. The porter looked puzzled, and I pointed at a television.

"Oh, Kuwait," he said. "Much bombing. Saddam Hussein."

Chapter 15

WE LEFT NIGERIA (the only non-French-speaking country we had come across so far and the last one until East Africa) and crossed into Cameroon, driving high up into jungle-clad mountains on narrow winding tracks with precarious crumbling edges that threatened to fall away under the slightest pressure. Norman had recovered from his fever and made no more reference to the abduction, but it turned out he was desperately afraid of heights and would cry out any time the road swung out over a gorge. He was right to be anxious. The road had collapsed in places, and looking down we could see the skeletons of tumbled trucks caught in the trees. If we fell down there, it was unlikely we would ever make our way back. Even if the trees cushioned the fall and we survived, we'd never find our way out, getting lost in the jungle, or bitten, or poisoned, or attacked, or contracting malaria before anyone could find us. Hunger would be the least of our problems: there was fruit growing everywhere: pawpaws, date palms, pineapples and bananas. All wild. Here and there along the roadside, we came across small homesteads hacked from the forest: metal-roofed huts with children staring wanly out and scrawny pullets picking at the coffee and cocoa beans that were scattered drying in the front yard.

We judged our progress by the tin-metal restaurants we would pass along the way, each painted either the red and white of Coca-Cola, or the black and orange of Benson and Hedges, or some other brand colours –

all had the logo replicated perfectly by hand. The jungle clawed its way right up against the corrugated sheet walls, which were riveted together with nails and Coke bottle tops as washers. We normally stopped in for a cold drink or a bowl of rice and beans; often just to eavesdrop on the soap opera of local life inside: farmers haggling over yucca prices, women practising for the Sunday choir, children tumbling among the sacks of beans and rice and onions.

Lucy offered to buy me a Fanta one afternoon at a place painted the black and ochre of malt Guinness. Normally we didn't buy things for each other; everyone paid for themselves, even if it was just a bowl of rice costing five cents. (Even at night when people were feeling drunk and magnanimous, they still bought drinks individually.) I suspected that Lucy must want something from me.

"Pity Dudley wasn't there for the hotel," she said, handing me my lukewarm Fanta. "He would have loved it."

"Dudley?" I said.

"Yeah," she said.

"You're joking?" I said, signalling to the owner for some ice.

"No." She seemed taken aback. "Me and Natasha are dying to know how he's getting on. Natie thinks they're a good match – him and Ana – but I don't know. He's so sensitive, he needs someone with a soft heart."

"Sensitive!" I said. "Didn't you find him irritating?"

"Dudley?" she exclaimed. "He reminded me of my uncle Jake. He was a Catholic too. Well, he converted so that he could become a monk, but he wasn't happy and he left. He's a sweetheart – a little bit lonely like Dudley, but a real sweetie. He finds it hard to shop and cook and clean for himself now."

"I thought all you girls were relieved to be rid of him," I said.

"Why?" Lucy said.

"I dunno," I said awkwardly. "I just thought he was always hassling you."

She looked at me amazed.

"We used to sing Bette Midler songs together," she said. "And you know that song 'He's So Vain'? He taught me all the words! Have you heard who it's really about? Dudley says it's that bloke in Dick Tracy."

"When I went to see him in the village, Dudley told me he hated all of us," I said, wanting to prick the balloon of her complacency. I wondered sometimes was I even on the same trip as she and Natasha were. They seemed to occupy a beautiful alternate existence.

"Maybe he was just feeling bad about the tent thing," she said after some consideration. "The boys were very naughty."

"Naughty!" I said. "That's putting it mildly. Brutal and mob-like, more like."

"They should have been nicer," she agreed. "Actually I wanted to ask you something."

"Yeah?" I said warily.

Before she could continue, the restaurant owner came over with a block of ice wrapped in hessian and shaved off some slivers for our drinks. There was a freezer in the corner, just as in all the shack restaurants, but as usual there was no electricity. Most of the freezers didn't even have motors; they were salvaged from dumps in Europe and brought here as iceboxes. Through a paisley sheet marking off the kitchen, I saw the owner's wife bent over a brazier stirring a blackened pot. She looked up at me and smiled, then unbent herself and came waddling out.

"*Ça va, mon chéri?*" she said.

"Yeah," I said, "and you?"

"*Pas mal,*" she said, planting her tree trunk legs and leaning back to stretch her spine. "Are you not having casserole? It is excellent today."

"I'm sure," I said, "but I'm not hungry."

"He is *sure,*" she said mimicking me with a laugh. "Is this your wife?" She glanced at Lucy.

"Just a friend," I said.

"Your wife must be very trusting. Do you like to dance?" she said. "If so, come along to Café Basso tonight. There is great music."

I told her we were just passing through.

"Always the same with the *muzungu,* always just passing through," she said. "You're going east?"

"Yeah," I said.

"To the waterfall?" she said.

"Waterfall?" I said.

"Yes, you know?" she said. "The Chutes d'Ekom. It is in all your Hollywood movies. As big as the Eiffel Tower. Bigger. It is . . ."

She stopped to look outside where a young boy was fixing a three-wheeled bike. He had two stumps for legs, and the bike was his wheelchair. She shrugged and turned back to us, trying to remember what she had been saying. The boy called in for a screwdriver, and she sighed theatrically and hurried off to fetch one, stopping first to adjust the crimson wrap around her waist, tucking the ends tight and blowing us both kisses before disappearing into the steamy kitchen.

"What was it you wanted?" I asked Lucy when we were alone again.

"It's not just me, it's Natasha too," she said eagerly. "We want to learn to smoke."

"To smoke?" I said. I often needed clarification for things Lucy said. I could never guess where her mind was heading.

"Yeah, exactly," she said. "We figure because we're in Africa and everyone is smoking cannabis, we should learn too."

"But, you know what Suzi says?"

"Yeah," she said, "that's why we'll have to do it stealthily."

"Stealthily?" I said.

"Yeah."

"I see," I said.

"So, if I come to your tent some day will you teach me? Then later I can show Natasha."

It sounded unmistakably like a chat-up line, but knowing Lucy I sensed it probably wasn't.

I was about to refuse but Dorothy came along at just that moment.

"What are you guys up to?" she asked.

"We're talking about the waterfall," I said, telling her what the woman had said. The news went around the others quickly, and it seemed everyone was keen to go check it out. We wondered how amenable Suzi would be to the idea. A week before I would have said there was no chance. She had even refused to allow us to camp an extra night when the nurses had advised that Rita might have malaria and needed to rest. Yet now after the hotel incident I wasn't so sure. Norman's outburst may have marked the beginning of a turning tide.

When we told Suzi about the Chutes d'Ekom she said she knew all about it and she had intended bringing us there all along, but she wanted it to be a surprise again. We cheered.

"Well now, you've ruined it, haven't you?" she said glumly.

She looked genuinely put out, as though she really wanted to surprise us again. It was hard to fathom her.

The restaurant owner told her he knew a shortcut to the waterfall and that he'd get his cousin to show us if we liked.

"Sure," Suzi shrugged. "Thanks."

We chatted excitedly about this new adventure while the restaurant owner went off to fetch his cousin and his wife got us to bring in our cooking pots so she could fill them with casserole as there was no food at the waterfall. Half an hour later, we were heading off down a dirt track with the owner's cousin, Ami Ata, up in the cab giving directions. Ami was a trainee teacher and spoke good English as she had been brought up in Kenya. I liked her straight away. She had the shiniest chocolate skin and a beautiful, tightly cropped head. She was bright and giggly, with a shamrock nose twisted a few degrees to the right and a puncture wound in her left cheek. She told us with great pride that she came from a family of singers and that at night she sang in a local bar, the Café Basso. It was fourteen kilometres away, but she cycled there happily three nights a week after school just for the joy of using her voice. I was surprised that she had moved from one African country to another. I thought that tribal affinity was too strong for people to move around like they do in the United States or Europe.

"Perhaps," she said, raising her winged-eyebrows. "But for me the tribe is not so strong any more. I am African more than Kenyan or Cameroonian."

She was probably an exception in this. She had been forced to leave her people when her family were chased from their village. Her father was a respected marimba player who had played with all the big names in Nairobi, but when his village was struck by an outbreak of cholera, he was accused of being somehow responsible. They said he had learnt sorcery in the big city and had now brought evil to the village. He was forced to flee. The village paid some mercenaries to make sure he never came back. Ami was ten at the time, and she still remembered every day of the nine months it took them to travel across the continent. They kept running because someone told them a lion-man was after them and if it caught them they were sure to die. They didn't really know what a lion-man was, but they knew enough to be scared. They never stayed more than a few days in the same spot, just in case the lion-man really was after them. They ran until people could no longer understand their Bantu tongue; that was how they ended up here amongst the Sudanic-speaking people of northern Cameroon. As soon as they had reached this region they felt safe. It was the first place they had been that was free of even the merest drop of Swahili blood. No one here had ever heard of their tribe or their language, and this reassured them. They were able to start their lives again. Ami's mother had got work at the restaurant, and in the years since the two families had grown as close as cousins.

I asked her what a lion-man was, but she just shook her head and said, "Just a figment – nothing really."

The waterfall was spectacular, a vertical ocean crashing into a bubbling tempest below, with deep, clear rock pools all around and a dozen or so locals playing and washing their hair. They all knew Ami; many of them were her pupils. We swam in the pools, letting the water hammer down on our backs and climbing up the rock face behind the waterfall, hollering out like Tarzan through the glistening blue curtain and thrilling as our echoes spun back upwards at us from the roaring water. Suzi told us some of the Tarzan movies were actually filmed there, and it gave us a thrill to think that we were somehow connected with that icon of virtue, virility and self-sacrifice, who each week would join together with his animal friends to battle manipulative, evil-hearted white men trying to invade or exploit his paradise. It struck me that we probably had more in common with the original Tarzan of the Apes, from the Edgar Rice Burroughs novel, than the schmaltzy Hollywood recreation. The young Tarzan in the book went on to become Lord Greystoke, but was brought up among the "anthropoid apes" and "black savages". He boasted that he was "the killer of many beasts and savages" and spent his days knifing animals, murdering cannibals and teaching himself to read and write by means of the hereditary genius that all English noblemen acquired at birth. That Tarzan of the Apes went on to become the "terrible god of the jungle".

As the sun set, we lit a fire and heated up the casserole, and Ami began to sing for us. Her spontaneous burst into song was something I had been getting used to since arriving in black Africa. At home it only happened in pubs late at night, or on football terraces, but here it was like a musical;

people often started singing for no reason, in the market or while walking along the road. It was as natural as birdsong or as whistling used to be.

Ami's voice was beautiful: sensuous, honey-dipped, and accompanied by a booming bass note that was totally different from the circuitous *soukous* rhythms we had heard in West Africa. Her appearance changed noticeably when she sang, shape-shifting from a modest trainee teacher to a playful, passionate diva, her eyes radiating fire.

When she finished the first song, we were all smiling, glowing inside in spite of ourselves.

"That one I am teaching to the children," she said. "It is about all the things I want for them. All my hopes."

She launched straight into another one – a simple chant and chorus which she repeated until we all got it and joined in.

Something like *"Ama-baraka-uh Ama-ara rapa . . ."*

It was amazing how it energised us all. Made us feel one. People who only ever moved their bodies functionally began swaying their arms and shaking their hips almost in spite of themselves. Ami kept it up for a long time. She knew she was riding a wave now, and I don't think she could have stopped even if she wanted to. Her small body seemed to grow as she sang, oozing dynamism and certainty. Luke pulled out one of the water tanks from the truck and began beating out a rhythm on it. An infectious smile took hold of the group, and I felt closer to them than I had in a long time. Ami's voice bound us together. We were surfing on it, carried along in it, following it from its sweet soaring highs through to its gritty lows. And when it came around to the chorus again, we all belted it out as though our lives depended on it. Her face cracked into a beaming smile.

She asked if anyone else knew any songs, and to my surprise a few of the group came forward and sang different things: a sea shanty, a piece of an aria, a pop song. I sang something in Irish, and then Ami said, "This next one is African, but I think you all know it, everyone does . . .

"Malaika, nakupenda Malaika . . ."

She paused and looked around, nodding encouragingly, certain that we would recognise it and join in, but we stared blankly back.

"You don't know it?" she cried, shaking her head incredulously. "It's '*Malaika*'!

"Malaika, nakupenda Malaika.

> *Nami nifanyeje, kijana mwenzio,*
> *Nashindwa . . ."*

None of us had ever heard it.

"It was written by Fadhili," she said incredulously. "My father actually knew him in Nairobi. *Malaika* means angel. When Fadhili was a boy he fell in love and he called the girl Malaika because she was so beautiful. They were going to get married, but Fadhili couldn't afford the bride price, and so she married someone else. He knew the only way he could be sure she would never forget him was if he wrote the best song in the world, which would be played for ever on radios and in dance halls and whenever she would hear the song she would remember. Her husband would not know, so she would be safe. Every time we sing it, we are thinking of Fadhili's girlfriend, hoping that she might be listening and reminding her that he still loves her."

The air was rich and warm, and the moon shone brightly down through the trees. The sound of water gushing along the rock face into the pools below took on a more intense and subtle rhythm in the darkness. The more we listened to it, the more multi-layered it became. Ali's voice too sounded sweeter and richer and more full of promise in the moonlight. She was the first true element of Africa that I really wanted to share with people at home. With everyone. She was like the oasis at Tamanrasset, unique, iridescent and staggeringly beautiful. I wanted the whole world to hear her. She asked us what we wanted to sing next. No one replied. We were under her spell.

"Let's sing something we all know," she said.

"We don't know your songs," Holly said sadly.

"But I know yours," she said. "All of yours are mine too. It is the only good thing slavery ever brought – our music went all over the world. Jazz, blues, rock and roll, hip-hop – it's all our music."

She launched straight into

> *"Well, since my baby left me,*
> *I found a new place to dwell.*
> *It's down at the end of . . ."*

We all joined in. Luke had by now given his water tank to Stella and was fashioning a rough *djembe* out of a piece of rubber and a spare tyre.

Lucy and Natasha were keeping time with brass bells they had bought in Morocco.

The singing went on all evening. It was a beautiful night; even the fact that Stevi insisted on singing "Who ate all the pies", at full volume, seemed more funny than pathetic. I decided to sleep outside that night under the stars, and I moved away a distance from the others into the trees to set up my mosquito net. I wanted to keep that sense of connection with my surroundings that I had felt all day.

As I was tucking in the sides of the net, Ami came over.

"It's not so good to sleep away from the fire," she said. "The animals might attack. It is safer when you are in the group."

"There are no animals here, are there?" I said.

"Sure," she said, shrugging. "It is Africa."

"Are there lion-men?" I said joking.

Her smile shrank and I regretted saying it. I had no idea what a lion-man was, but it was clear that to her it was no laughing matter. Later when I looked it up in books, all I could find was an indistinct photograph of a hunchbacked figure crawling on the ground in rags. The photo had been taken by a priest in Tanganyika at the turn of the century. There was very little known about what they actually were, but it was thought that mentally deficient or disabled children were reared in cages and made to believe they were wild animals. They were never allowed learn to walk or talk, and instead were trained to chase people on their hands and knees, attacking them using their long nails which were sharpened into claws. Sorcerers would dress them up in lion skins and hire them out as assassins to kill or scare people. As far as I know, the practice had died out long ago.

"There are always animals," Ami said to me with a forgiving look. "And if not, there are spirits."

I nodded ruefully.

"If you want, I'll sleep near by," she said. "We will be safer."

She rolled out her blanket and lay herself gently down a few feet away from me. She was humming softly to herself all the time.

"You have no mosquito net?" I asked.

"It's OK," she said.

We both lay there a while, looking at each other through the gauze of my net. I could hear Luke's drums playing in the background, accompanied now by a third one he had made out of a wheel rim that sounded jangly and Caribbean.

"You realise you brought us all together with your music tonight," I told her.

She smiled placidly. "It's what I love to do," she said. "More than anything, it's my passion. My gift from God. I want to give happiness always, to celebrate life. Here in Cameroon, it is difficult. They don't like for women to be singing. They want us in the home. They don't like for us to speak out. In Kenya it is different. Here, it is much harder. I really have to fight. But I pretend to them all that I will be a good quiet little teacher – and then they are happy!"

Ami was remarkably beautiful. Her lips were sullen and heavy, her brown eyes seemed enchanted and entirely too big for her long thin face. I found myself stretching out a hand to touch her cheek. There was a raised scar around the puncture wound which was just below her jawbone. It felt alive under my fingers, as though a current rippled through it. Perhaps a vein had knotted under the skin.

"Does it hurt?" I asked.

She shook her head, still smiling.

"Is it tribal?"

She laughed.

"No," she said, trying not to giggle. "It is not tribal, but you could say it is *African.* I got it when I was a baby. Hyenas attacked our hut at night and tried to take me into the bushes. They came right into the hut and dragged me out; luckily the dogs woke and frightened them. My father heard and came for me. I was very bloody, I think, but luckily I can't remember. The matron promised my mother that the wound would close, but it never did. I think maybe it helps my singing."

"It certainly doesn't seem to do it any harm," I said.

"Thank you," she bowed her eyes. "The head teacher thinks I should sing only for Allah, but . . ."

She fell silent and we both gazed at each other.

"You've had some life," I said, musing as much to myself as her.

"Just the usual," she laughed. "In Africa it is just the usual."

"What next?" I said.

"To sing," she said sadly, "that's all I want. I don't know for how long I will be able."

"And teaching?"

"Yes, teaching too," she said. "I want to finish training and have my own class."

I found my hand going to her cheek again. This time my mouth followed and I kissed her, my tongue brushing against her lower lip. It felt gently corrugated and tasted both sweet and salty at once. We pulled apart and she smiled.

"It's funny," she said with a hint of weariness.

"What?" I asked, but she wouldn't say.

I kissed her again, stroking her tight kiwi-textured hair. She wrapped her arms around my body and pulled herself in closer, then just as I was about to kiss her again, she turned her face away and lay it on my chest.

I ran my hand down her back and she looked up, her eyes glinting still, but with a new air of melancholy.

"What?" I said.

"We cannot," she said, still trying to smile, but with strain.

I said nothing, just let my hand rest on her waist. We both stayed quiet for a while. She began to hum.

"Why?" I said at last.

"I am sick," she said. "La Sida."

"Sida?" I said.

"It's a virus," she said.

"If you want medicine, we have paracetamol and penicillin onboard."

I had no idea what Sida was, but I knew our medicines could cure almost anything.

"It's OK," she said laughing. "The fetish priest sucked most of it out. He has given me potion."

We stayed quiet for a while. I was thinking how utterly different our lives were and wondering whether this Sida she talked of was real or just an illness she had made up as a handy excuse.

Suddenly a thought came to me and I asked her, "Did he have a little wooden box?"

"Who?" she asked.

"The spirit doctor."

"Yes," she said, surprised. "Why do you ask?"

"Just interested," I said. "What was it for?"

"I don't know," she said. "He just has it. Maybe it's for spirits. He felt inside it quickly before sucking the worm out of my womb, and then he burnt the worm in the fire to make sure it was completely dead. It was what was hurting me – a horrible, wriggling poisonous thing like a centipede. Already I am feeling better."

I stroked her head again and we lay down to sleep wrapped in each other's arms.

Early next morning we packed up and left. Ami said she'd stay on for a while and make her way back later. We went for a short walk together while everyone was packing up. I really didn't want to let her go. The connection I had formed with her over a few hours was deeper than any I had formed with the others over months. Dudley's decision to leave suddenly made more sense to me.

Chapter 16

O UR FOUR-WHEEL-DRIVE parade-float continued its stately progress through Cameroon and into the Central African Republic (CAR), engaging with local people about as much as a beauty queen might with her bunting-waving audience. Although to be fair, the guys had got on better with the football obsessed Cameroonians than anyone before and had played a few matches using balls of bundled-up bags tied with string. After each game, no matter win or lose, they had scoured the town to find a real Fifa-endorsed ball and presented it to the locals.

The Central African Republic had the same lush, mountainous land-scape as Cameroon – an enormous plateau looming over the Congo basin – but there was an oppressive sense to it. One could practically feel the tragedy of its history and of the corruption that was still endemic in every aspect of life. It had rich reserves of uranium, copper, tin, iron, chromium and diamonds, which could have made it fabulously wealthy, but the rot had set too deep for any enterprise to survive long. In ancient times, the CAR had a culture that outshone Egypt's. In the Middle Ages, its artwork was famous throughout Europe, but from then on things had been going downhill. It was as if the slave trade was a process of blood letting that had continued for centuries, eventually leaving the body so enervated that soci-ety could no longer function. By the early twentieth century when slavery was at last wiped out, the CAR was a mere ghost of its former self, and

France and Belgium divided it up between a few private companies, allowing them to exploit it ruthlessly, torturing and even executing the workers. In theory, the country gained its independence in the Sixties, but in practice no leader can survive without the support of France. In 1966, the French helped Jean-Bedel Bokassa become dictator, and his rule was one of the darkest regimes in African history. The French continued to back him, even after he had taken part in a massacre of school children who were protesting against a law forcing them to buy their uniforms from his own personal factory.

Bangui, the capital city, was the perfect model of a corrupt kleptocracy, with few proper roads or public services; instead there were blocks of gleaming glass offices built purely as a means of laundering money. The Avenue des Martyrs was a memorial to the hundred children the president had gunned down. It wasn't just that he had given orders to kill them; he himself had been out on the street shooting them. It was claimed he even ate some of them. He was tried for murder and cannibalism, and sentenced to death three years before we arrived, but the sentence was commuted to life imprisonment and he was still living in the city, in a palace that had been converted into a prison especially for him. His presence gave the place a pervasive sense of menace that was tangible in every breath. Suzi warned us that we were more likely to be robbed or attacked in Bangui than anywhere else in Africa.

We set up a three-person rota to guard the truck and drew up new rules of engagement, forbidding locals from coming anywhere near us. I was allotted a guarding period with Henry and Lucy, but first I had just enough time for a quick wander through the city.

One of the treats of a new capital was the chance to read papers again and enjoy croissants and *café au lait*. For others, it was the chance to get letters from home. I had long since given up on visiting *postes restantes* as it was too demoralising seeing the others collect thick bundles and coming away with nothing myself. They thought that there must be something wrong with me that there was no one at home who would bother writing. Secretly I thought the same myself. When I was feeling more positive, I tried to believe that the reason was simply because people at home couldn't comprehend the concept of my life here. Ireland had always had missionaries and emigrants, but the idea of wandering aimlessly around a continent was too farfetched to countenance. It seemed to them like a sick joke, which was possibly what it was. An exercise in fatuousness. Also, of course, my mother, brothers and sister were all coming to terms with my dad's death in their own way, and I think they felt I had abandoned them. In the first few weeks I tried keeping in touch regularly, writing long letters home whenever I could, telling them everything that was happening, but when I heard nothing back, I began to lose heart.

And so, when Stella came running up to me in Bangui saying there was a letter for me in the post office, I didn't believe her at first. I thought it was another cruel joke, but the chance that it might possibly be true made me take the risk. I grabbed my passport and hurried away. Sure enough, there was a letter there, from my brother, the Tiger, a full three pages of news, saying he was sorry no one had been in touch and how brave he thought I was for what I was doing. There was a short note from my mum too, saying she missed me and that she hoped to write soon. I could see the others were relieved for me. I had tried convincing them before that I had forgotten to give my family the list of *postes restantes* that we'd be stopping in, but it was clear they didn't believe me. They wondered how anyone could be so unpopular. Even Dudley got mail, and he wasn't even on the trip any more.

When I got back to the truck, everyone was fussing around Henry and Mildred, who had been accosted and had their bags slashed open. They were badly shaken. The robbers had honed in on the two oldest and weakest members of the group – just like their president before them had singled out the children. Fortunately, they weren't harmed and hadn't lost too much, just some local currency, old letters and Mildred's reading glasses.

I had been planning on giving Henry something to make up for the Baileys I had robbed, and I thought now would be a good time. I went to the locker under my seat and pulled out a bagful of miniature bottles of Baileys. I had got them from the mini-bar in the hotel, taking two from my room and trading with the rest of the group for the others. They knew I was desperate for them, and so most had held out for a high price. It had ended up costing me a lot in batteries, chocolate and money, but I figured it would be worth it to end the tension between us.

I handed the bag to Henry and he looked dolefully into it, nodding glumly as he saw what was there.

"Appreciate that, old fella," he said, at last. "It was the right thing."

"Yeah," I muttered. "I'm sorry."

"Bygones and all that, eh?" he said sonorously.

"Thanks," I said, and we shook hands.

Lucy came along, preening with pleasure. She had just made a reverse-charges call to her parents, who were in Barbados at the time. It was late at night with them, but they had been delighted to hear from her, and the line had held for a phenomenal nine minutes before breaking. She was brimming with news about her sister and Squibbles, the Siamese cat, and was now itching to go off and tell Natasha everything. We offered to let her go before she began her guard duty, but she was adamant that she wouldn't leave Henry and me guarding on our own. She was always so thoughtful and eager. Wayne had nobly offered to take Henry's place if he wanted to rest after his ordeal, but he too was determined to fulfil his commitment, to go on fighting until the last.

"Dunkirk, and all that," he said to Wayne, stoically. "On the beaches, in the air . . ."

Lucy raised a hand and hurrahed him cheerfully, although I don't think she got the reference.

Once the others had wandered off and left the three of us alone, a group of local boys drifted towards us from various directions. This was what always happened in any town; locals would come along to chat and stare, but this time we were so paranoid that we daren't let them near.

Henry told them to bugger off if they knew what was good for them. He was clenching and unclenching his fists compulsively and had the sleeves of his drip-dry polyester shirt rolled up in a style that I think was meant to convey an image of a pugnacious young buck. The boys giggled a bit, but they retreated after a while, and Henry looked around at us cockily before sitting down triumphantly. He was very wound-up, his arms fidgeting and his legs splayed like a warrior. I noticed the raised blood vessel on his forehead begin to throb a little. It looked like an earthworm burrowing through soil. I hoped that he was still taking his sedatives.

A noise rang out from beneath the buttresses of a nearby bridge. Henry shot to his feet and did a quick surveillance lap of the truck, jogging as he went and turning to look over his right shoulder every third step. He decided Lucy and I should be repositioned at more effective look-out posts and moved us to the apex of the opposing bumpers. By pointing to his eyeball then twirling his index finger in an outward spiral, he conveyed the information that he wanted us to remain eagle-eyed. We nodded solemnly at him and flashed a look between ourselves, trying not to laugh.

The whole situation was a bit ridiculous, and it made me very sad. Normally it was the presence of local children laughing and joking around us that made guarding bearable at all. They were like a chorus that followed us around the continent; playing and teasing us, and helping to teach us local ways and customs. Mostly they wanted nothing in return. They would call out for a *cadeau* or a *Bic* occasionally, but only because they thought it was expected of them. They never seemed to really want the pen once they got it. Sometimes they would even refuse little gifts, and they were for ever giving us things in return: a mandarin, a toy boat, a painting. One boy in Nigeria insisted I take his sister's hair clip.

"Because you give us fun all the time," he said when I asked why. "You are like the circus."

The Nigerian word for white man is *baturai*, meaning "man with no skin", and so I could see why we might have seemed like a freak show to him.

"Watch out, four o'clock," Henry called to Lucy, who checked her watch dutifully and said it was still only midday.

"Don't be stupid," Henry growled. "I mean all eyes right, over there behind the tree. Look sharp!"

A sweet-faced boy in a bright yellow Arsenal T-shirt was waving at us with a bow and arrow over his head.

"Get away from here!" Henry called.

The boy blinked and pulled up his cast-off soccer shirt to show a bundle of papers pressed against his belly.

"What's he got there?" Henry called to Lucy, who was nearest.

"I can't make it out," she said.

"Well, don't let him approach any closer. I'll get out the binoculars."

Henry got up onboard the truck and began rifling through his locker.

The boy was singing quietly to himself under his breath. I smiled at him and he shouted over.

"*J'ai un cadeau pour toi,*" he said. "*Quelque'chose que tu veux.*"

He waved the papers over his head.

Henry came rattling down the stairs, demanding, "What in God's name is up now?"

"He says he has a present for us," I said.

"It's a trick, the dirty whelp. Send him packing. I should have got one of those catapults they were selling in Togo."

I worried about the repercussions to Henry's health if the boy approached any closer, and so I decided to go over to him instead.

"*Bonjour, mon ami,*" he said. "*Je m'appelle Bonaparte. Et toi?*"

I told him my name and asked what he wanted.

"These," he said (in French), indicating the papers. "I think they are yours. I found them in the street after the grandma and grandpa were attacked."

I turned to Henry.

"He says he has your papers," I said.

"Damn it, the brat!" Henry screamed. "Bring the little urchin over here. I'll deal with him."

I led Bonaparte over to the truck, making sure to stand between him and Henry.

"You little cur," Henry bellowed. "How much, huh?"

"What's he saying?" Bonaparte asked me with concern.

"He wants to know how much you want."

"How much what?" he said.

"Money," I said. "How much do you want?"

"Lots and lots," he said, "but not from this poor grandpa. He has had a hard day."

I laughed and he did too, raising his hand and giving me a complicated handshake involving thumbs.

Henry, who hadn't understood what we were saying, was almost apoplectic by this stage. The earthworm was threatening to burrow its way right out of his head.

"What the bloody hell is going on?" he bellowed.

"He says he doesn't want your money and he's sorry about what happened to you and Mildred," I said.

"Yes, well," Henry muttered, snatching the papers back and carrying them into the truck with him.

Bonaparte pointed at Lucy and whistled admiringly.

"I give you a leg of mutton for her for one night," he said brightly.

"Don't be disgusting," I said. "What age are you?"

"Soon fourteen," he said, his chest held high.

"Don't you think she's a bit old?" I asked.

"She is beautiful," he said in her defence, as though it was I who had impugned her.

"You better leave," I said. "No one is allowed near the truck."

"OK, you win," he said magnanimously; "not for the whole night – just a few hours. I will bring her back to you in the evening. She will have a big smile on her face."

"You're disgusting," I said.

"I just want to give her pleasure," he cried, aggrieved.

"You're a child," I said.

"Maybe in your country," he said.

He pulled up his Arsenal shirt again to reveal a gold nugget hanging on a piece of twine around his neck.

"This I give you for her," he said, smiling again, his dimples spreading across his face.

"Just stop it," I said. "It's revolting."

"Sorry," he said, "I'm just joking. I have slept with all the girls in my village, and now I so badly want to know what a white girl is like. I am buying skin bleaching soap for my girlfriend for many months, but it is not good stuff. I want her to be like Michael Jackson. Maybe you lend me the money for good stuff?"

"No," I said.

"*No!*" he mimicked. "All the time no. Instead, maybe you let me swap my hair for yours."

He wound a finger through a kink in his wiry locks, smiling sadly.

"Is he still here?" Henry shouted down from the back of the truck. "Get rid of him for God's sake. Throw a stone or something."

"You better go," I said to Bonaparte.

"I know, *mon ami*," he said warmly.

As he was walking away, he stopped and turned.

"Perhaps you have some condoms for me?" he said.

"Don't you have any yourself," I said, "with all these girls you say you're sleeping with?"

He winked archly at the absurdity of the question. A condom cost a dollar back then. How could he possibly afford it?

"I haven't eaten anything since yesterday, you know, *mon brave*," he said brightly, turning to walk away.

I felt such an idiot. I called him back although I could hear Henry snarling behind me. I gave him a few francs and the pack of *pain au chocolat* I had bought earlier in an elegant patisserie. He insisted on giving me his bow and arrow in return and then formerly shook my hand and headed off in the direction of the Oubangui River. I watched him go with a choked feeling in my throat.

An ominous snuffling sound arose from the river. It was interspersed with louder barking, and when I looked I saw a hippopotamus rising from the water and stretching its front legs on the far bank.

Henry got down from the back of the truck and did another surveillance tour around the perimeter line.

"All quiet on the Western Front?" he asked.

I said nothing.

"Well?" he said.

"Yeah," I managed, trying to hold back the tears.

"I see you confiscated that little brat's bow and arrow. Good thinking."

I breathed in, forcing myself to remain silent. I didn't think I could deal with him just then. He stayed looming over me, rocking back and forth, waiting for an answer, and when I thought I could stand it no longer, I said, "Look, how about I just go and keep watch from inside?"

"Why?" he said suspiciously.

"It'll give me a higher vantage."

"Righto, good thinking," he said.

He took my seat at the bumper, and as I walked past the opposite corner, Lucy gave me a beaming smile, lightening my heart just a little.

Inside the truck, I wiped my eyes and tried not to think about it. All of it. Bokassa eating his own people. Henry and Mildred being mugged. Ami Ata's sweet, salty lips. Bonaparte screwing everything around him on an empty stomach. All this in a country that could be one of the richest in Africa, that once had one of the richest cultures in civilisation.

More as a distraction than anything, I glanced over the papers

Bonaparte had brought back. A few lines of poetry written on one caught my attention.

The Sun, the hearth of affection and life,
Pours burning love on the delighted earth,
And when you lie down in the valley, you can smell
How the earth is nubile and very full-blooded;
How its huge breast, heaved up by a soul,
Is, like God, made of love, and . . .

It was startling. Beautiful. I looked up and stared around me as though . . . as though, I don't know, I had been sucked through a filter and suddenly everything was different. I breathed in, trying to get my bearings, trying to fathom what the hell these beautiful words were doing on this stupid, dumb truck. Who brought them here? Who had written them out in clear handwritten script on a piece of vellum paper?

"Henry!" I cried urgently.

He sprang to his feet and began scanning the horizon in all directions.

"What's the matter?" he said, preparing himself for the worst. "What's wrong?"

"Nothing," I said. "Nothing like that. I'm sorry. I just got a surprise, that's all. I was reading these . . ."

Before I could say another word, Henry had come hurtling up the steps two at a time.

"What the hell . . . !" he was roaring in a panicked voice. "What are you doing?"

I was too startled to reply.

"Get out!" he screamed, batting my hand away from the pages that were covered, I noticed now, in more poetry. "Get out of here!"

I cowered back into the seat, with my hand up to my face in case he hit me.

"You've got some nerve," he fumed.

He was doing his best to gather the papers up, but his hands were shaking too much.

"I didn't mean . . ." I began.

He scoffed, as though clearing his throat to spit at me. Meanwhile he was yanking open the door of his locker and trying to stuff the papers inside, his eyes displaying genuine upset.

"It was all just lying here," I said apologetically. "I didn't mean . . ."

"Look, Paddy," he said. "I've had enough of your empty apologies already. Just can it, OK?"

He managed to get the papers safely stowed away, but it was another ordeal to get the lock to remain shut with his fumbling fingers. I wanted to help him but thought the better of it.

"It behoves you to . . ." he said, but he wasn't really focused on what he was saying.

It was clear that he felt embarrassed and upset. I felt a wretch, as though I were Dudley spying on the girls.

"I genuinely didn't mean to pry," I said.

The hippo cleared its sinuses again, snuffling with the combined power of a hundred geriatrics in a nursing home.

Lucy came up the steps excitedly.

"Did you guys see the hippo?" she gushed, then froze, noticing the tension between us. "What's up?!"

Henry and I were both staring at each other, saying nothing. Finally I broke eye contact and said, "Nothing, Luce, you're fine. Everything is grand."

"You better get back to your post," Henry said quietly.

She shrugged, then smiled and leapt back down off the step with a fine *entrechat*.

Henry and I were left looking at each other awkwardly, as though I had just caught him with his trousers down again. Neither of us knew where to look.

"Did you write all those?" I said to him in a hushed voice when she was out of range.

"No!" he snapped.

He stared at the ground for a moment, before looking up.

"Some of them, maybe," he conceded. "Most are by Paulin Joachim and Rimbaud – the French . . ."

"I know who Rimbaud is," I said.

"Yes, well" he said tersely. "Joachim is African, about fifty years later than Rimbaud, from Benin."

"I see," I said, staring at him in amazement.

I had never imagined such beauty could possibly be whirling through his head. I felt ashamed. I was hoping that he would explain more, but he kept his eyes focused on his fingernails like a naughty boy waiting for his punishment.

"Don't tell," he said at last.

"No, of course not," I said. "I'm really sorry. I just didn't . . ."

"It's my son, really," he said suddenly, as though the words were bubbling out of him involuntarily. "He's a poet."

He wiped his mouth like he had just burped.

"You have a *son?*" I said. "I never knew that."

"Not with Mildred, you understand," he said. "My ex-wife, Elizabeth. His name is Colin. We don't get on, but . . . he's, em . . well, he's away."

"And he's a poet?" I said.

"Yes," he said uncomfortably. "I don't imagine he makes much money or anything, but that's his decision, his lookout. He's a poetry nut, part of a collective in San Francisco; they write . . ."

"But you write too?" I said.

"Well, *now* I do," he said awkwardly. "Occasionally."

"Right," I said reassuringly, and continued cautiously. "And some of those works were yours that I was reading?"

He looked at me hard for a moment, then sighed and pulled open the locker again, yanking out a page and handing it to me brusquely. He got up and walked to the far side of the truck. I looked down at the paper.

Dust-motes, then straw-strewn earth,
Neon sun on plastic kettles in a hop-store shack.
Merc-truck flares, plantain fumes and more dust
the privileged rock binding its cropped head.

"It's not finished or anything," he said painfully.

"It's good," I said.

"Hardly," he said, with a nervous rasp. "It was the counsellor's idea, really. She said it would help bring us closer. When Colin got sick first, we all made an extra effort. He even took up ornithology for a while for my sake. Have to admit though, I still hate most of the stuff he churns out – dreadful rubbish about gym-toned abs golden in the evening light, that sort of thing."

"My father and I used to read poetry," I said.

"Huh?"

"We used to read together," I said. "Larkin, Yeats, Auden."

"Auden isn't bad," he said with a shrug. "Colin insisted I read all the greats before I came: Senghor, Jaochim, Tchicaya U Tam'si. Especially U Tam'si. I can see why – he's some man!"

"I've never heard of any of those people," I said.

"No," he said. "You wouldn't have, but believe me, they're the really big guys of poetry here . . . Just listen to this . . ."

He dug out another sheet and began to read from it.

"The flat horizon of this country splits my heart
If I recoil everything bristles suddenly!
I will stay at the gate with the wind in my side
but with tornadoes in my belly."

"Jesus!" I said.

"Indeed," he said. "I sent Colin some lines I'd written about the Sahara a few weeks back, and just today I got his letter back – but now I won't ever get to read it, will I?"

"Why not?" I said.

"It was in the bag, of course," he said. "The bag your street urchin friend stole."

"But he brought them back," I said.

"Not everything," he said sadly.

"The thing is," he said, "with the illness you never quite know what's next for him."

"He's sick?" I said.

"Well, not now," he said testily, "but his friends are dropping like flies."

I was busily trying to compute all this. It was no surprise to learn Henry had been married, but it was amazing he had never mentioned children. He was the only one of us to have any as far as I knew, unless Mildred was keeping hers quiet too.

"It brought it all back to me again the other day," he said, "when I was listening to that girl – seeing the marks on her face. It made me think of Colin's friends."

"What are you talking about?" I said.

"You know, that sweet little girl who did the singing?"

"Ami?" I said.

"Yeah, the baldie girl," he said. "Surely you noticed the marks on her neck. It was like a dried out jellyfish or something."

I had no idea what he was talking about. I had noticed a slight rash, but it was nothing out of the ordinary. Most of us had some form of skin irritation, a bit of ringworm or sunburn or heat rash or the jiggers that burrowed in under the skin.

"Ami Ata?" I said again.

"Yes!" he said, impatiently. "She definitely has lesions on her neck, and I doubt she's getting any treatment for them. Those singers lead risqué lives, you know."

"Bullshit," I said. "She had a slight virus, that's all."

"That's what I'm saying," he said. "Aids."

"No!" I said. "What are you on about? She told me she had *Sida*, but it was getting better."

Henry looked at me, shaking his head.

"Sida?" he said. "You didn't poke her one, did you? Tell me you didn't!"

"No!" I said.

Looking back, it seems amazing that I didn't know more about Aids or at least that it was known as *Sida* in French. There had been ads on the television in Britain and articles in Sunday newspapers about it, but it wasn't yet a big concern.

"The only real answer is condoms, of course," Henry said.

"That bloke," I said, "the one who brought back your poems, he wanted condoms."

"I hope you gave him some," he said.

"I don't have any."

"You don't have any!" Henry screamed. "You mean to tell me you came to Africa without condoms? Are you out of your bloody mind?"

"I'll get some," I said, mainly to calm him down.

"You better, son."

He grabbed his poem back from me and stuffed it into his locker.

Chapter 17

ONCE OUR GUARD duty was over, we had the rest of the day to ourselves. I went straight to the best hotel in town to escape for a while, lounging by the pool, trying to forget myself among the sun-creamed wives of mineral contractors, missionaries and government ministers. It was no use. The busboys all had Bonaparte's prowling stride, and I saw Ami's smile in the face of every maid. I had never felt so out of my league in Africa before. It was hard to imagine that Ami might have Aids, but the more I thought about it, the more likely it was. I often wonder what happened to her; I presume she must have ended up as another statistic on a World Health report somewhere, another member of that lost generation harvested by Aids. It seemed so random. Generally, I was able to assuage my despair at the hardship I saw around me with an adolescent belief in reincarnation. If every soul lived a series of lives, I reasoned, surely we must all choose challenging ones at some point. My duty in this life was to engage as fully as possible with whatever path I chose and not to obsess too much about others. That was what I had always told myself, but suddenly, amidst the reality I faced here it seemed so hollow and self-absorbed.

Lucy and Natasha joined me at the pool later in the day, and I was glad of their distraction. Lucy's lean, milky torso stretched out on a sun lounger was a visual treat to help me forget. She had a wonderfully straight back, and even lying down she had the poise of a dancer, languorous and aware. Her toned stomach reminded me of a well-upholstered armchair.

"I was thinking that now would be a good time to try our plan," she said to me, lifting up her shades.

"Sorry?" I said, caught unawares.

"Smoking, remember?" she said.

"Oh, right," I said. "But we don't have any grass."

"Sure we do," she said triumphantly, pulling out a little polythene bag from under her towel.

"Put that away!" I said, glancing around me in panic.

She was either clueless or fearless, although I think it was largely the confidence instilled in her by an elite education. She *knew* no one could harm her. She explained that the drugs were a *cadeau* she had been given by someone on the street. I just shook my head in disbelief. Had she any idea how dangerous that was?

"Well, can we try it?" she said.

"No, not here!" I said.

"OK, we'll go back to the campsite," she said.

In the hope that it might take my mind off things, I agreed. She and Natasha got up and started pulling me off my lounger towards the lobby. As we were leaving, Natasha spotted Duncan walking through the main doors. She stopped in her tracks and watched him pulling off his vest and flicking it casually on to a sun lounger before diving into the pool. Natasha was spellbound. She still adored him as only an eighteen-year-old can. She was blind to everything except her own infatuation and never seemed to notice him carrying on with other women. She took it as shyness when he refused to show her any affection in public. From what I could make out from the tent noises at night, they had spent a few evenings together, but Duncan was careful not to be seen too much with her during the day.

Natasha now made some excuse about needing to stay on to discuss something with Duncan. Lucy and I ended up going back to the campsite alone. Predictably enough, Lucy turned out to be an excellent student, and it took her little time to master the correct way of clamping the roach in her lips and inhaling slowly until she sensed the point at which to lock off the back of her throat and allow the vaporised THC crystals permeate the lung cavity and enter her blood stream. She never once burnt her windpipe by sucking too deeply or provoked a coughing fit by pulling too hard. She remained patient throughout the first few classes when the drug had no effect on her other than making her a bit dizzy. She accepted that it took time for the brain to learn how to be stoned and diligently kept up her practice until she got it right.

We held a class each afternoon for three days, and she insisted on repaying me by washing my towels and togs. During the third class, she began to notice trails lingering in the air when she moved her hand, and soon a whole range of other subtle sensations followed. She started obsessing about the texture of the tent lining and talking about how much she loved the lyrics of The Police's "Every Step You Take". In the end it was I who misjudged the dosage on one occasion and ended up getting far too stoned too quickly. I conked out and only awoke an hour later to find Lucy nuzzling up against me, singing to herself and drumming her fingers on my chest. The feel of her skin against mine and the scent of her breath was enough to send my arms reaching instinctively around her, and I clutched her to me, nuzzling my lips into her hair. We burrowed our bodies into each other, the curves and canyons finding their opposites, but with all our clothes still on.

She turned to me, seeking out my eyes and said, "From now on let's always feel this way."

I reared back. I didn't know quite what she meant, but I knew I didn't want to get involved. Not now, not here. I couldn't deal with the consequences. Looking back, now, I suppose I was afraid, but more than that I knew I didn't want to hurt Lucy, and I knew that it was likely I would end up doing so in the end. Her rose-eyed sweetness irritated me as often as it endeared her to me. It depended on my mood. I knew if we became any closer I would find myself lashing out at her when I was feeling down, sneering at her triteness, her juvenile waffle. Somehow she had managed not to be seared by cynicism yet, and I didn't want to be the one to ruin her, to blunt her blithe spirit.

I pushed her gently off me and turned away, muttering something about feeling dizzy. We both stayed quiet for a long time.

"Natasha and I are planning a reunion next Christmas," she said finally. "For all of us."

"You're joking?" I said.

"I've already written to Mummy. She says it'll be a bit of a squeeze, but we should all fit. We can cook African food and play music . . ."

I got up on my elbows and looked at her. Could she really be serious? Was I the only one who never wanted to see these people in my life again? I opened the tent zip and sat with my legs out looking around at the rainforest. The lushness of it was what struck me most, the sheer untrammelled fecundity. It was so at odds with my own pent-up sterility. The trees were like massive displays of vaunting sexuality – trunks soaring into the sky so that they could spread their seed as far as possible, and flowers swelling to the size of umbrellas to ensure they were pollinated. Duncan was just another big mahogany tree, I realised, whereas I was the dormant hybrid, grafted on to a weak rootstock; safely tucked up in my sleeping bag each night. Cocooned. Wayne was no better. We were both genderless, genital-less caterpillars sheltering beneath our polyester leaf of tent.

". . . and I'm going to make my almond spice cookies. Maybe Daddy will even hire a DJ . . ." Lucy was saying from behind me.

A shadow fell over my face, and I looked up to see Stevi looming down at me. He stuck his head further into the tent to see what was going on. I braced myself for the teasing, the snide remarks.

"Oh, it's you Steve, hi!" Lucy said brightly. "We were just talking about a reunion next Christmas. Wouldn't it be great?"

"Look at the two love birds," he cooed, ignoring her. "Ah!"

"Leave us alone," I said.

"OK, OK," he said. "Give her a lash for me, won't you, Mocha?"

"Get out!" I shouted.

"Hey chill, man," he said, imitating the drug dealer from *Withnail and I*. "It's all cool. We're all consenting adults here . . . I only came looking for a bit of bog roll. I've run out."

"I don't have any," I said.

"Really?" he said, dubiously. "What are you going to wipe yourself down with afterwards? You haven't gone *local* as well, have you? Duncan has, you know? He swears that just a quick wipe with the left hand and a dunk in a jug of water is all you need – Job's Oxo. He comes over all poetic about the squishy feel of the shit between his fingers and the odd nutty bits mixed in. Better than a rim job, he claims."

"Would you please just leave us alone," I said.

"Keep your hair on," he said, offended. "I wasn't asking for your left kidney or anything, just a stupid few squares of . . ."

A face leaned in over Stevi's shoulder. It was Suzi. She had her amenable, chatting-with-the-troops expression on. She didn't seem to want anything in particular. She was just doing the rounds, looking for distraction.

"How are you kids doing?" she said brightly.

"Fine," I said, perhaps too agreeably, as she bent down and stuck her head in through the flap.

"It smells odd in here," she asked, sniffing the air hard.

"Lucy may have farted," I said.

Lucy puckered her little face into a frown.

"No," Suzi said, sniffing harder. "It's not that. Has someone been smoking grass?"

"No!" Lucy and I cried in unison.

"Someone has been smoking," she said with more certainty.

"Definitely not!" I said, in a maligned tone. "Look, I'm glad you came by actually; there was something I wanted to talk to you about."

I knew I had to think fast, to come up with something to distract her. The vital thing was to stop her talking, and the only thing that came to mind was something that I had been mulling over a lot lately, but had promised never to address.

"It's about the mud holes," I blurted out nervously.

"Yes?" she said stiffly, sensing defiance.

There was no going back now. I charged recklessly on.

"I'm not prepared to stand by any longer while we cheat our way through them," I said.

It's hard to convey quite how dangerous this subject was. I knew Suzi would not like to be confronted on it. It had to do with a trick she had been using to get around the queues that formed on either side of the enormous potholes that regularly appeared in the road. These holes were more like mini canyons, as deep as a house and hundreds of feet long. They posed no problem to our powerful little war truck. We could plough right down into them and out the other side, our bulbous four-wheel drive tyres finding some strand of traction in the slushy mire at the bottom, the bigger trucks invariably got stuck and had to wait hours while they dug or winched themselves out. Long queues would form on either side as others waited to go through. Suzi had come up with the idea of driving to the front of the queue and promising to pull whoever was in the lead through if they got stuck. The drivers always looked at us in wonder and gleefully accepted the offer as though we were angels of mercy come to rescue them. They would allow us go ahead, and we would charge forward through the hole and continue on our way, never once stopping for them. Suzi would roar off, tooting her horn in thanks. The first time she did it, we all yelled at her to turn back, but she only laughed. We grumbled about it later amongst ourselves, but no one dared confront her openly. Not until now.

She looked down at me witheringly.

"What do you think this is?" she said in a tone full of sarcasm. "Are we charity workers or something? Are we missionaries?"

I was leaning back on my roll mat with the sleeping bag bunched up behind me as a bolster. I hunched myself forward and forced myself to maintain eye contact.

"Pulling them out would strain our engine," she said. "Do you really want to end up stuck in the middle of nowhere with a blown gasket? Do you want to take that risk? I remember you crying like a baby when you had a little tummy bug; how would you cope with the killer diseases you'd get if you were stuck here for any length of time, huh?"

I started into a long self-righteous speech about the legacy of white duplicity in the continent and how our duty was not to compound it any further, stepping out of the tent as I talked, leading her away from the smell of grass. I rattled on about the cycle of oppression that had gone on for so long and how vital it was for us to make a fresh start, to show integrity at all times. Suzi remained silent for the whole thing, letting me prattle on as if she were really listening. When I finished, she stayed quiet for another moment, seeming to digest it all. She ran her hand along the back of her neck a few times ruminatively. I was congratulating myself on how eloquent I had managed to be despite my drug-addled state when suddenly I felt a jab of pain across my chin and was thrown towards the ground and backwards against the tent.

I grasped at one of the tent poles and managed to pull myself up to look around, and saw Suzi standing over me with a big smile. There was the sharp salty taste of blood inside my mouth. I wondered what had happened, until suddenly it dawned on me that Suzi had punched me in the face. I felt a mix of humiliation and rage – the same rage that had gripped me on Christmas Eve. Fortunately, this time I had the sense not to attack. I could clearly see she wasn't in the least bit frightened of me. Henry had been frightened. Suzi's face only showed weariness. She turned her back on me and walked away, chuckling a bit to herself. I was about to scream abuse, but she turned around.

"And I swear, if I catch anyone taking drugs on this truck," she said, "I will castrate them."

Once we had our visas and supplies organised, we left Bangui and drove across the flat, forested plateau of the Central African Republic, seeing the Congo Basin stretching out below us towards the equator. We were now approaching the true core of Africa. This basin had once been Lac Zaire, an inland sea, until it burrowed its way through the Crystal Mountains and across the continent to the Atlantic. The river it created was the route through which white explorers had first entered the region, setting in motion the whole tragic train of events. From here on, we would be following in their footsteps, step by step. Zaire, the country we were going to next, was the nerve centre of nineteenth-century slavery; the land of Stanley and Livingston, and Conrad's *Heart of Darkness*. This was the most inaccessible and lawless part of Africa, and Suzi had warned us that if things were to go wrong at any point, we had to hope that it wasn't here.

From reading the few history books we had on board, I had some idea of the evils the West had committed here. The region had escaped slavery for centuries because its climate and geography were so forbidding, but eventually, when all the young blood had been sucked from the coast, the slave traders had made their way upriver, following the routes opened by Livingston and Stanley. I had a dark feeling about the place. If Africa was going to seek revenge anywhere, it was natural it should be here. Holly had brought along the diaries of one of the officers on Stanley's famous relief expedition of 1887, and I was spooked by how similar our experiences were. The officer's name was James Sligo Jameson, of the Irish whiskey family. He was a sensitive, good-humoured man who was described as "sweet tempered as a woman". He comes across in the diary as naïve but likeable. He had signed on for Stanley's expedition (the first to penetrate the heart of Africa along the Congo River) out of a sense of adventure and enlightenment. But his earnestness was soon dampened as he came to realise that he had paid £1,000 pounds (the same amount as me) to be little more than a slave driver and bully boy for Stanley, a ruthless schemer who had first gained prominence by scooping news of the British victory in Abyssinia for the *New York Herald*. (He did this by simply bribing the telegraph operator to send out only his report.)

Jameson's diaries had the same air of sanctimony as my own. We regarded our leaders as tyrants, although the more I learnt about Stanley, the more I realised that the traits I regarded as flaws in Suzi were in fact her greatest strengths. She was the real thing, well-informed, professional, ruthless – an expedition leader in the mould of the nineteenth-century greats. In another age, she would have made a brilliant conquistador.

Jameson's disillusionment with the trip made me feel slightly better about my own experiences:

"The last six months have been the most miserable and useless I have ever spent anywhere," he wrote, "and goodness knows when it is going to end . . . I have never been on a trip where there is so little enjoyment of any kind; it is all so serious, and a kind of gloom hangs over all."

His reasoning for going on the trip made me start questioning my own again.

"Ever since my childhood I have dreamt of doing some good in this world, and making a name which was more than an idle one. My life has been a more or less selfish one, and now springs up the opportunity of wiping off a little of the long score standing against me. Do not blame me too much . . ."

Certainly, he had more to feel guilty about than just cheating lorry drivers at mud holes. His days began with a public flogging of all the locals who had stepped out of line the previous day, and more serious crimes were punished on the spot with a bullet through the ear. The journey Jameson had so innocently signed up for proved to be Stanley's most calamitous ever, and its legacy played a major part in setting in train the next hundred years of exploitation and corruption. I think it was this diary more than anything that increased my own sense of foreboding. I thought back to what Mossallu had said about the spirits of every action living on in Africa and feared that we would inevitably become affected by the ghosts of his route.

Chapter 18

WE REACHED MOBAYI-MBONGO, the border town between the Central African Republic and Zaire (now called the Democratic Republic of the Congo) in the first week of February. After lunch of manioc soup and corn bread in a bamboo hut by the Oubangui River, we sought out the border guard who was to stamp our *carnet de passage*. We were told that he was having lunch and would be out to us when he was ready, so we lit a fire and boiled water for twenty cups of tea.

A few hours later, when there was still no sign of him, Suzi became impatient and went to find him. A woman selling banana lollipops told her he was in the bar – a wooden shack with two orange crates and a tea caddy as tables – but warned her that if we followed him in there, he might refuse to ever give us the necessary stamp to allow us cross over. We had the choice of either waiting it out, confronting him, or just ignoring him and going across the river without a stamp. We would probably be asked for bribes at future borders either way, whether we had the right stamps in our *carnet* or not.

Suzi considered for a moment and decided to give him another hour, but after twenty minutes she lost patience and went barging into the shack demanding that he come out and do his job. The guard had been drinking the profits of a bribe swindled from a French group earlier in the day and was in no mood to negotiate. He came out wielding his well-worn, ink-stained seal and waved it tantalisingly over his head. Suzi pointed to the printed circle in the *carnet* where it needed to go. He raised his arm obligingly to stamp it, but at the last minute his arm swung around and he imprinted a piece of leaf instead. He apologised half-heartedly and tried again, this time he got the side of the truck. He explained that his job only required him to issues stamps; he was under no obligation where to direct them. If we wanted his seal to land in a particular place, we would have to pay for the privilege. As usual, Suzi refused to pay bribes, so he shrugged and stamped the side of the shack a few times, then went back inside the bar. She stormed straight in after him, but he wouldn't listen to her and eventually had her kicked out. We had no choice but to pitch camp and wait out the impasse.

Holly rekindled the fire to begin boiling the sixty potatoes needed for dinner in two hours' time, while I took the opportunity to bathe in the wide, languorous waters of the Oubangui River, which looked incredibly inviting but turned out to be more like a sludge pit for the sewage of the towns and villages upstream. When I stepped into the water, my feet sank straight into the sediment, and a stagnant smell rose up, stinging my nostrils. I washed my clothes and body as quickly as I could and got out, retreating to my tent rather than suffer the ordeal of a dinner made up from the tins under the floorboards. Tonight it was fried Spam and HP sauce. Some of the group longed for the nights where we couldn't find a market and had to rely on our English supplies, but after months of fresh okra, peppers, chillies, plantain, peanuts and tomatoes, I found it hard to stomach the cheap catering tins of marrowfat peas, Spaghetti Hoops, etc. I preferred to go hungry. Holly saw I wasn't at dinner and came by my tent later with some potatoes. She noticed me reading her copy of Jameson's diary.

"Did you get to the mutiny bit yet?" she asked.

"No," I said.

"I was just thinking of it tonight watching them wolfing through the Spam," she said with a laugh. "When Stanley thought his officers were going to mutiny, he ordered a jam roly-poly pudding they had brought from England to be opened. It solved the problem straight away. We English would do anything for a bit of our own food."

The following morning I awoke to the sound of a stampede outside my tent. A herd of buffalo was being corralled into a concrete slaughter yard by the river. Their angular flanks made their bones seem like girders. From my tent flap, I saw a gold-toothed man select one animal from the drove and tether it to an iron hoop bolted to the wall, while the rest were led away. The border guard was slumped unconscious against the wall, and the gold-toothed man went over to him and shook him awake. The guard pulled himself upright and looked around him drowsily, hiding his eyes from the sharp eastern sun. The man was explaining something to him, and he nodded occasionally, seemingly trying to wrestle back control of his limbs from his stiffened muscles. They were both gesturing towards the buffalo and after a moment went over to examine it; the gold-toothed man taking out a bunch of *zaires* (the currency of the far side of the river) and counting them carefully into the guard's hand. The guard then swiftly unsheathed a Bowie knife from his belt. It sparkled in the low sun. With only the gentlest brush of its blade across the buffalo's throat, the flesh beneath was exposed, and from there, the guard dug it inwards until it had cut through the jugular vein. The animal immediately fell limp, slumping down near to where the guard had been sleeping with a plaintive sigh, and a high-pressure spray of blood shot forward. The guard then handed the blade to the gold-toothed man, who slipped it under the skin beneath the throat and along the length of its belly, opening a wound wide enough to stick his hand in. It was an act of flawless precision, beautiful in its own way. The bevel tracked between the fat and skin, separating them perfectly. The animal still looked fresh and clean, its hide shimmering black against the pale concrete. All that betrayed its condition was a steady purple trickle pouring down into the river. The herder gave the guard his knife back and, using a coarser, cast-iron one, hacked off the hooves.

Lucy called out to us that our morning porridge was ready just as the butcher was ripping away the hide to reveal the waxy, white fat below. I pulled on a T-shirt and went over to the truck. It was always great when Lucy made breakfast; she could make two gallons of Quaker Oatmeal stewed in powdered milk over a sooty fire taste better than anyone. She added so much palm sugar and pineapple jam that it seemed closer to pudding than cereal. As I was helping to put up the breakfast table, the butcher was busy eviscerating the entrails, and when Lucy had ladled out portions into our bowls, he sliced the animal's kidneys open, and a foul smell came wafting across on the breeze.

A ferry was due to cross the river in an hour, and Suzi was determined to be on it. She approached the guard and asked him again to stamp the *carnet*, insisting that all she would give him by way of an inducement was a dozen pawpaws to bring home to his wife. He held out for thirty French francs, and another long argument ensued. Finally, when the ferry was just about to leave, Suzi offered the guard a cassette tape as well as the pawpaws, and when he refused that, she straightened herself and brought her squeezed fist into the joint of her raised arm in the French gesture of contempt and called him "*un cochon*". She jumped into the cab, screaming at us to follow her, and then gunned the truck straight towards the ferry ramp and on to the deck with us still throwing the last of our things in while jumping on to the sides. The ferry captain, delighted with her daring, blew the whistle as soon as she had cleared the ramp. We pulled away from the bank with the guard screaming furiously behind us. We had left his jurisdiction for good, and he knew there was nothing he could do about it. We just hoped he wouldn't exact vengeance on the captain later. On the way across, Suzi got out a pill container with an embossed lid and some shoe polish and stamped the exportation docket herself. According to the records, we had just left the kingdom of Roche Pharmaceuticals Inc.

Fishermen had been watching us from their *pirogues* (dugout canoes) on the water, and they cheered us as we passed. We had outwitted the terrible river bank troll who tyrannised them all. Their fishing technique was entrancing – the men cast their nets into the air and allowed them open out and gently fall into the water before scooping them in again. The nets reminded me of wet butterflies trying to become airborne. It was beautiful and seemed relatively successful. With each throw they brought up a few sprats, but also the odd catfish with bushy whiskers and bulbous lips, fighting furiously at the indignity of being scooped from the depths.

As the ferry drew up at the shores of Zaire, Suzi's voice came over the intercom.

"Congratulations, children," she said in a menacing tone. "You've finally arrived in real Africa!"

She put a cassette into the tape player that she had been keeping for just this moment. It was a raucous pop song written for Muhammed Ali's "Rumble in the Jungle" fight in Zaire.

> *Once there was a battle there*
> *in Zaire, in Zaire*
> *Seven rounds of torture there*
> *in Zaire, in Zaire*

As the music blared across the river, the fishermen looked up from their nets. In our shades and bandanas, we must have looked like something out of *Apocalypse Now*. We were so alien to everything around us, as crass, if not as violent, as Jameson and Stanley. My anxiety about Zaire was growing. Every traveller we met had told us that this was the toughest, most humid, most corrupt, most jungle-tangled country in Africa. Inflation was running at 1,000 per cent, soldiers hadn't been paid for six months, food prices were rising daily – revolt was imminent.

To take our minds off it, Suzi had arranged for us to leave the truck for four days and take a riverboat down the Zaire River (formerly, and now once again, the Congo River) to the old capital, Kisangani (formerly Stanleyville), while she and Joe drove the 200 kilometres by truck. It was said to be one of the great river journeys in the world, on a collection of barges lashed together with vines and propelled by an old Rhine tug. Suzi said that it was always the highlight of the trip, and we were really excited. She was excited too, as it meant she would have four days without us. In fact, she had been counting down the days to this time when she could at last get a break.

The drive south from the Oubangui River to the Zaire River was an eye-opener. Having heard so much about the country's poverty, it was a surprise, on leaving the riverbank, to find the mud track had suddenly segued into a beautifully tarred dual carriageway, complete with neon signs and street lighting. It was as if we had tapped our heels and been transported to Europe. If the infrastructure was this good in such a remote part of the country, we could only imagine how great it must be further on. We reached the first town in record time. It was a small, remote backwater called Gbadolite which was gleaming with swanky buildings, tall glass office blocks, modern supermarkets and even an international airport. Outside the town there was a pristinely clean, backlit sign for a Swiss dairy farm.

"Don't believe anything you're seeing," Suzi warned us, when we pulled up for lunch. "This isn't Zaire – it's a sick joke. President Mobutu was born here, and he's spent billions building all this."

"But, it's beautiful," Dorothy said.

"It's a lie," Suzi said. "There's nobody in the offices or the restaurants. There's no food in the supermarket. It's all a charade. This is one of the poorest parts of the country. The locals can hardly feed themselves. They get nothing, while he's built two huge palaces for himself – both of them empty – and he's planning a Disneyland next."

We decided that we didn't want to eat there. We just couldn't stomach it, and instead drove on out of town where the road soon turned into a dust-track winding through the bush. Mobutu Sese Seko was another dictator, like President Bokassa, who had killed people with his own hands, but the difference between them was that Mobutu was still in power, aided by the Americans and the Belgians. He had siphoned off four billion dollars into his own accounts from the country's vast potential wealth of industrial diamonds, gold, copper and cobalt, and had bankrupted the country in the process. Again, as in Bangui, it was hard to overlook his sinister presence wherever you were. His portrait loomed down from every wall, in leopard-skin cap and cloak, and thick glasses fashioned out of the horn of some endangered species. Often the image was so sun bleached that all you could make out was the dark leopard spots and glasses frames, like some abstract Miro painting.

The words of the song kept running through my mind and I hoped that they weren't prophetic.

> *Once there was a battle there*
> *in Zaire, in Zaire*
> *Seven rounds of torture there*
> *in Zaire, in Zaire*

We had arranged to join the Congo riverboat at Lisala, but when we got there we were told the two-way radio was broken and they had no idea when the boat would be leaving Kinshasa, the new capital. They advised us to travel on to the next town and take it from there; so we drove on to Bumba, which on first sight seemed a pleasant little town of a few blocks of modest bungalows in the French colonial style arranged along the riverbank. It was a sleepy, jungle-nestled place that revealed no trace of the turbulent events that had happened there a century before. Perhaps, if we had been more aware of them, we would have been more careful. It had been a centre for illegal trade for centuries: first for ivory (the white gold that was hacked off elephants and shipped downriver in vast amounts for Belgium's King Leopold), then later for real gold. Now it was a docking point for oil tankers of black gold heading upriver to Kisangani. Cannibalism had always been a problem here. As late as 1912, a steamer suffering mechanical problems was attacked and four of the crew eaten; two others managed to escape and were discovered living in the forest, driven mad from fear and exposure. Baptists had founded a mission in the area to curb the man-eating tendencies and, at first, were reasonably successful; although the locals still insisted on being allowed sell the bodies they captured to other neighbouring cannibal tribes. Joseph Conrad had written about the place in ominous terms, and Stanley had written in his diary of attacking fifty-four war-canoes here and massacring 2,000 locals dressed in ivory and parrot feathers. He had set alight whole villages on each bank and had stolen everything of worth from them, including the pillars of a temple made of thirty-three enormous tusks. This place had been treated worse by white men than anywhere else we had been to on the trip so far, and if Mossallu was right that everything in Africa really was connected through the spirits, what happened next should have been no surprise.

As soon as we pulled into Bumba, Suzi went straight to the quayside to check that the boat was on its way upriver and that we could get tickets for it. She came back assuring us that it was due the following day and explaining that she and Joe would have to leave right away as their journey might take longer than ours if the road was in bad repair. So we gathered our sleeping bags and toothbrushes and stuff and waved goodbye to the truck. I had rarely seen Suzi look as happy as she did when pulling out of town. She was like a child again, eager to begin her big adventure.

We were left alone and leaderless for the first time in the trip. It felt exciting, but daunting too. From now on we would be completely in charge of our fate – not that there were all that many decisions to be taken: Suzi had assured us that getting tickets for the boat would be easy, and once we were aboard, it would be an idyllic three days of living like

Humphrey Bogart and Katherine Hepburn on the *African Queen*, slowly making our way upriver and enjoying the great food on board. She said there would be whole markets laid out on deck with everything from monkeys, crocodiles, parrots, maggots and tortoises for sale. All we would have to do was pick what we wanted and bring it to a woman who would kill it and gut it over the gunwale for us, then cook it on a charcoal brazier.

Henry said he would arrange accommodation for all of us for this single night in Bumba, and we let him do it because he got such pleasure from being able to use his, by now, semi-atrophied managerial skills again. After looking at the few options available, he chose a boarding house and booked three rooms in it, telling us we were to divide up six to a room to save money. The rooms only cost a few cents each, but we were all so used to sleeping together by now that the idea of wanting one to ourselves never occurred to us; some had even complained of feeling lonely in the hotel in Nigeria. I teamed up in a room with Luke and Holly (who were still managing to be more-or-less a couple, at least when they needed to be), Lucy and Natasha (the two London girls) and Wayne (my cranky, though long-suffering tent partner). Stella, my cooking partner, joined us later as she grew exasperated with the two other nurses whom she was sharing a room with. I noticed that the three rooms reflected the three different subgroups that had first emerged in the Sahara over the tobogganing incident. There was the sensible and moderate room of Henry and Mildred (the oldest couple), Felicity and Dorothy (the nurses), and Stevi, who were all a bit scared of Africa but knew that if they kept their wits about them and didn't do anything rash, they were liable to get through it in one piece. The second room had Rita and Vinnie (the couple who fought in the first week), Rodney and Marsha (the willowy soldier and his wife), and Norman and Duncan (the Cornish brothers) who were torn between the desire to open themselves up to the continent and to protect themselves from it. They sensed the need to step beyond the narrow ruts of their upbringing, but were nevertheless terrified of what they might find. Lastly, there was my group of messers and oddballs, who just wanted to enjoy ourselves.

Each group retired to their room and marked out spaces on the floor with our roll mats and mosquito nets, then went out for dinner all together in a rice-and-bean shack that had a bamboo gazebo out the back with benches and a reed-mat fence. Afterwards, the three groups separated to their various rooms. It was at this point that I made the single most stupid and most fateful decision of the entire trip – a decision which would have repercussions on all of us, and which would change my outlook on life for ever.

My group were all back in the room, lying on the double bed, which none of us were actually going to sleep on as it looked even dirtier than our sleeping bags. We were bored and restless, and I suggested we go out and get some grass. They all jumped at the idea, and I slipped out on to the street, careful not to let the people in the other rooms know what I was up to. They would have been furious.

It only took a few minutes to locate someone willing to sell me a bag stuffed full of buds of the crude local variety – the sort that grew wild on the roadside. I brought it back to the room, and Lucy, whose delicate, origami-skilled fingers had quickly mastered the art of joint rolling, began rolling one using the flimsy Zairian bank notes as cigarette papers.

I couldn't possibly have known that the drug would be spiked; laced with some form of hallucinogenic plant extract that soon had us all hurtling off on wild mental slalom rides. Mobutu's face on the rolled bank notes came alive and began taunting me, laughing at my foolishness. He was followed by demons that came rushing in through the air vents and then fled out through the window before I could catch them. A dead cockroach in the corner swelled to elephantine proportions. It was being eaten by flying ants – and the ants took on the shape of pterodactyl hyenas devouring a dinosaur. It was terrifying, but thrilling too. All of us experienced different things, but occasionally our mind-tracks crossed, and we laughed so hard and with such relief that everyone in Bumba must have heard us. It was a memorable night, gripping and delirious. I don't remember going to sleep, but fortunately I had the presence of mind to tuck the mosquito net around me and put my money belt and passport under my head beforehand.

Next morning we were all feeling pretty low. The room looked a shambles, and we avoided making eye contact with each other, uncertain of what exactly we might have done the previous evening, what Dionysian excesses we may have been lured into attempting.

I noticed Lucy looking around her anxiously. She was pulling things out of her bag and shaking her clothes.

"Are you OK?" I asked.

"I can't find my shades," she said.

"Oh," I mumbled, without interest. My head was throbbing a bit from the after-effects.

Stella was rummaging too, furtively pulling up her roll mat and mosquito net.

"I think my passport is missing!" she said. Her voice was dry and her eyes still bleary from the drugs.

"Natasha might have it," Lucy suggested. "Luke and I gave ours to her for safety. She locked them all in her bag."

"Where's Natasha?" Stella asked.

I pointed to the bathroom and Stella called in to her. "Where's your bag?"

"I locked it to the bed frame," Natasha said.

We all looked over at the bed frame, but there was no sign of any bag there. It was then that we began to worry.

"It might be just Duncan playing tricks," Luke said. "He could have come in and taken it."

"My camera is gone too," Holly said, looking around her, "And my bag with my contact lenses. I had put Luke's watch and all his cash in it too."

We got up and went outside. The others were all up and dressed; they looked at our dishevelled appearance and made no effort to hide their disapproval. I think they suspected we had been up to no good and were looking for proof. They couldn't have not heard all our laughter. We asked Duncan had he by any chance come into our room and taken things.

He shook his head, and Mildred said, "Don't look at us! I wouldn't go in there if you paid me. It stinks. I'd be afraid I'd catch something."

Gradually, it dawned on us that something bad had happened. Someone had got into our room during the night and taken things, almost everything, except my money and passport which I had fortunately tucked under my head. They must have stepped right over us as we slept, as though they knew for certain that we would be out cold.

"Make a list," Henry said, "of everything you're missing."

"I'm missing my mum," said Natasha with a smirk.

"For God's sake," Henry snapped, "can't you guys ever be serious. Do you know how bad this is?"

We got out a pen and paper and made a list: five passports, two cameras, a few hundred French francs, all our malaria tablets, medical supplies and the girls' sanitary towels. Of these, the passports were definitely the most important. Without them, we couldn't leave the village. We would be arrested at the next roadblock if we didn't all have some form of valid identification papers with us. Yet, to have the passports replaced, we would have to get to a city. A classic bind.

It was clear the rest of the group secretly thought that we had got what we deserved for disobeying group orders. We had been warned from the very beginning not to take drugs, and now it was up to us to suffer the consequences. The local people were slightly more sympathetic. The owner of the hotel let on that he was shocked by the news, but I suspected he knew exactly who had robbed us and how. The front door of the hotel hadn't been broken in. Either he had let the robbers in himself, or turned a blind eye while one of his staff did, but I didn't dare accuse him of this straight out.

He advised us to go straight to the army barracks and report it, and on the way there, we stopped and told everyone we met what had happened. They all feigned disbelief and outrage, wringing their hands and shaking their heads dramatically, but in their eyes you could see they weren't all that surprised. Bumba was a small place, and they probably all had a fair idea who had done it, but it took me many days to realise this. At the time I was too addled and bleary to make sense of anything.

The barracks was a parched field on the outskirts of town with a few patchy, bleached-grey tents and a lookout tower made of split bamboo. The munitions store was laid out in the shelter beneath the tower. It consisted of twelve tarnished machine-guns pointing barrel-upwards and a single box of bullets. Paint was flaking from the guns' chipped chambers. A commanding officer was leading his men through morning manoeuvres when we arrived, and on seeing us he had the men halted in their tracks and a bugle sounded. The men lined up diligently along the side of the field, and the officer walked us down along them as though we were important dignitaries performing an official inspection.

They were a dishevelled-looking group, as scruffy and dead-eyed as us. I had no idea why we warranted such a ceremonious welcome, but then I remembered that they hadn't been paid in six months, and I realised they were probably desperate for any outsider who might be encouraged to part with some money. The whole display instilled in me a certain degree of confidence in them, a feeling that these men, despite being a little shabby, would have no problem tracking down a few petty thieves. Again, it was only later that I reflected on how quickly they had lined up for us, how choreographed the whole thing had been. They had clearly been expecting us.

The officer came forward and introduced himself as Hercules, bowing and shaking hands with each of us in a bewilderingly excessive manner, as though his future lay in our hands. We lapped it all up, of course – it's precisely how anyone wants to be treated after he's just been robbed. His face was withered and bucolic, suggesting a character from a Velasquez portrait. As he spoke no English, I explained the situation in French. He reacted like everyone else, with insincere surprise, turning to his troops and translating my words into Lingala.

They too cried in horror. *"Quelle horreur! Mauvais chance!"* (In French for our benefit.)

Although their concern was reassuring, unconsciously I began to see that something wasn't right. The timing was off, their responses seemed programmed. I looked into Hercules's face and noticed his eyes bulging from their sockets, pushing forward his pupils which were narrowed into pinpricks. I realised he was off his head on something very potent.

Hercules led us to a bench on the side of the pitch and, kneading my hand maternally, assured me he would get to the bottom of our distress. He called forth two soldiers, who he said were the most skilled in his regiment, and sent them off towards a settlement of shanty huts beyond the camp. The soldiers looked at him quizzically as they accepted their orders in pidgin French. They had the look of dogs being scolded, and when they ambled off in the direction he had pointed, they veered from side to side as though they weren't entirely sober either. They were dressed in a hotchpotch of the world's combat clothing, but from the way Hercules gestured towards them, like a master of ceremonies in a burlesque club, you would swear they were an elite commando force dressed in the latest neoprene kit. We stared wanly after them until they shuffled out of sight, each of us hoping that they were more capable than they seemed. Hercules continued waving manically at the spot where they had been long after they had gone. It was as if he couldn't help himself – his arm was like a serpent out of his control.

There followed a long pause. Hercules finally managed to pull his waving arm down and began rubbing his belly in a convulsive fashion. After a while he excused himself, bowing graciously and backing away from us until he too was out of sight. We were left there for the next hour on our own – all the soldiers had disappeared. Had an enemy attacked the camp at just that point, they would have presumed that it was us who were guarding it.

Shortly after lunchtime, Hercules returned, breathless and bristling with pep. He waved his arms in another flourish of courtesan pageantry and said he had great news for us, gesturing over towards the horizon from where we saw the two soldiers returning. They were pulling behind them two young boys with rope fettered around their ankles, forcing them to take small steps. They were being jolted forward by another rope tied around their necks. Hercules was delighted, his moustache bristling with the drama of it.

"Ha, ha!" he said triumphantly. "They are here!"

The boys were about my age. One of them wore nothing but a pair of shorts, the other had a ripped T-shirt on.

"The robbers!" Hercules said. "My men have caught them for you; you can give them *un grand cadeau*. Something for all of us. We are all working hard for you. *Un grand cadeau*."

When the soldiers drew up to us, they threw the boys at our feet.

"*Bravo!*" Hercules said. "*Bravo, mes braves.*"

Hercules lifted his boot, and after stretching his ankle back and forth a few times in preparation, he swung it languorously into the belly of the bare-chested boy. The boy winced.

"Bravo!" Hercules cheered again. "You are very lucky Englanders, we are always efficient and successful in Zaire. You have been fortunate, yes? In your country the army is not so efficient, am I right?"

I didn't know what to say. Hercules kicked the boy a few more times for emphasis.

"Am I right?" he said again, breathlessly.

"Do they have the passports?" I said.

"The passports?" he said, quizzically. "We have the robbers!"

"The passports are what we really want," I said.

He looked at me as if I were a child who had just smashed a birthday gift on the ground.

"We have found the boys for you," he said. "This is not good? Would you like to kick them? You must – they are a menace to Zaire."

"I don't care about the robbers," I said testily.

"Oh-la-la," he said, laughing at the innocence of it. "First we need to catch the robbers, then we do the investigation. It is always this way. Only later does the investigation begin. Much later, maybe. It takes planning and diesel for our truck, and also money to help write the report. This is our system."

"Tell him to stop beating the boy," Lucy cried in English, and he stopped immediately as though he understood exactly what she said.

"If you excuse us, now," he said in French, "we must get to work."

"What are you going to do?" I asked.

"Interrogation," he said. "You come back later, maybe tomorrow or the next day, then these robbers will give us all the information. At first they won't want to, but soon . . ."

He took one of the machine-guns from the shelter and started hitting the boy with no T-shirt. I tried to stop him, but it was as if I wasn't there. Finally, there was a whistle from behind us, I looked around and saw a head jutting out from a trapdoor in the ground. The soldiers all stood stiffly to attention, including Hercules, who was stiffest of all. This figure was the camp commandant.

Without asking who we were or what we were doing there, he threw back the trapdoor fully and told us to follow him down. I looked to Lucy. She shrugged and began bravely making her way toward the bunker and climbing down steep, steel steps into a musty concrete room, empty but for a line of tall metal lockers and a heavy wooden desk with an old type-writer on it and an unspooled ribbon. The commandant sat down carefully behind the desk, spat on a length of the ribbon and threaded it delicately into the typewriter. Then, craning his neck out towards us, he squinted one eye and over-dilated the other in a gesture that was meant to convey that he was ready for us.

I began to tell him what we were doing there, but he hushed me, saying he just wanted a list of everything that was stolen. His typing was neat and methodical, but the keys kept getting caught around each other and then jamming on the roller, so it took over an hour to compile the list, after which he demanded a fee per person from each of us for typing expenses. We had no money on us, and he pointed out that this was regrettable as no more work could be done on the paperwork of the case until the payment had been made. And only once the paperwork was done could the case begin. I promised we would get the money and bring it to him straight away, but he said the office was closing now and we would have to wait until the morning. I told him I could have the money there in ten minutes, but he said that even if I had it there in ten seconds, it would be too late. There was nothing more we could do. We made our way back up the steps again just as the two boys were being led down.

Hercules pushed them in and shut the trapdoor behind them, then turned to us, reiterating his determination to help, letting rip a histrionic bout of fervour that showed no sign of abating until we were all shocked into silence by the sound of the boys' cries rising up from an air vent somewhere in the ground near by. He looked to the ground then and said he had better get back to work, ushering us dismissively towards the exit.

We went back to the hotel feeling completely demoralised. I think that day was the first time I truly became aware of the intensity of African heat. Up until then we had always been sheltered from the midday sun, either by the truck canopy or by trees when we were in a campsite. It was cripplingly hot, hard even to summon the energy to move. We filled the bath with water and took turns soaking ourselves in it.

Chapter 19

O F COURSE, WHEN I went back to the army camp next day, no progress had been made. We paid the fee, but nothing much happened the following day either, or the day after that. I spent five days in total going back and forth, conducting futile and gradually more outlandish negotiations. Each day Hercules would haul in a few boys, claiming that these were the robbers and beating them vigorously in front of us. It never brought us any closer to anything. Meanwhile, the days just got hotter and the countless trips back and forth along the dust track to the camp more enervating.

We tried making contact with the embassies to get them to issue new papers, but making a phone call was not an easy matter. The missing passports were British, New Zealand and Australian, but only Britain had diplomatic representation in the country – some 1,000 kilometres downstream in Kinshasa. After days of effort, we managed to get through to someone in the embassy, but they told us there was little they could do at such distance. They stressed that under no circumstances should we risk leaving town without some form of official identification and advised us to get down on our knees and beg the local Secretary of Justice for temporary papers. Unfortunately, we had already tried that. The Secretary's secretary had refused to allow us see him, and she only relented later when the British ambassador himself telephoned personally on our behalf. Grudgingly, she promised him she would try to fit us in in four days' time, insisting that it was the first free slot the Secretary had.

The biggest problem was that we had no idea what was really going on. If we had we might have known what to do. Everyone seemed to be playing us, but I couldn't tell for what or why. Some of the locals in the market told me the passports were most likely still in Bumba. They were of no value to anyone else, except perhaps to criminals in the big cities hundreds of kilometres away, and since there was no proper transport or even postal system working in the country at the time, there was no way to get them out. I longed for Suzi. She would have known exactly what to do – what tack to take, whose back to scratch. Everyone, from the rice woman to the blind knife-sharpener, assured us that things would work out if we played the game right, but none of them could tell us what the rules were. It revolved around money, that much was clear – almost every-one advised us to bribe someone, but they never agreed on whom.

The problem was that we didn't have that much money. That was the single biggest misconception in the town: everyone was certain we were rich, and we couldn't make them believe that we had left most of our funds on the truck. A third of what we had brought had been stolen, and the rest was being whittled away by trunk calls to embassies and extra nights in the boarding house. Henry had done some calculations and worked out that if we kept enough aside for eighteen passages on the boat, we should have just enough left for a bunch of bananas and two bowls of rice and beans each for another week.

It soon became clear that money and passports weren't our only problems. Although Suzi had assured us that she had checked with the transport office at the port and that the boat was due the following day, when we went down to the office ourselves, we were told there had been no ferry service on the river for a month as the motors of the old Rhine tug were being overhauled. It wouldn't be back in service for another few weeks, but even then it wasn't certain it would operate, as the water levels were too low. The shipping agent assured us that there was no way anyone in his office could have told Suzi that a boat was due. She had lied to us.

This was a lot to come to terms with – Suzi had driven off and aban-doned us, knowing that there would be no boat. We knew she had been keen to get some time to herself, but still it seemed a bit drastic to leave us stranded here just so she could have a break. I hadn't realised quite how much she must have disliked us until that moment. In her defence, I suppose she may have thought that we would be picked up by some other boat going upriver. She wasn't to know that the dry season had come early and that the water was unseasonably low. The smaller, shallower boats that could make the journey during the dry season were all out of action because of the economic chaos in the country. The Gulf War and the country's bankruptcy meant that there was almost no diesel left in Zaire. The country had run out of foreign currency to pay for it, and the borders to the oil producing countries had been closed.

Even when the rains came and the Rhine tug was fixed, it was unlikely the ferry company would be able to pay for diesel to make the journey. The whole country was gradually grinding to a halt. It was only when we started looking for alternative routes out of Bumba that we became aware of this. We learnt that no train had passed through the train station in a decade, and no plane had landed on the airstrip in months. There hadn't been a boat along the Zaire River in weeks.

The only way in and out of Bumba was by road. By using the foreign currency we had kept aside for the boat passage, we could possibly buy enough diesel to get us away. All we needed was a vehicle and someone willing to drive. But this proved near impossible to find. The route was so potholed with craters that only a four-wheel-drive vehicle could possibly cross it, and the only four-wheel-drive jeep in town belonged to the army. It was shared between them and the barracks in Lisala, 120 kilometres away, and we had already had to pay for the tank of diesel it took to drive it over from Lisala, so that Hercules could parade up and down the main street searching for the robbers. There were two old Mercedes trucks in town which had somehow survived World War Two and ended up here, but they weren't in any condition to make the journey. In most parts of Africa, there would have been cargo trucks driving by regularly, but the roads were so bad in Zaire that most trade was done by river. People just stopped trading when the water levels were low. There would also normally have been other European missionaries or overlanders passing through, but because of the Gulf War, Algeria and Nigeria had closed their borders (one on religious grounds, the other on commercial), thereby cutting off the route from Europe to Central Africa. We were some of the last foreigners to get through.

On the first day of our second week in Bumba, a messenger boy was sent by the secretary of the Secretary of Justice to tell us our meeting, which had been arranged by the British ambassador, was being put back by another four days. It was then that I became convinced that not only were we being toyed with, but actually strung along in a carefully planned game of cat and mouse. Zaire was a military dictatorship after all – by definition the army controlled everything. In a small town like Bumba, of less than 2,000 people, nothing happened without their direct involvement, or at least without their knowing all about it. In such a place, the Secretary of Justice was little more than a puppet. I became convinced that Hercules and the commandant were leading us around in circles and that we would never get to see the Secretary of Justice until they permitted us to. But, what I couldn't see was why they were doing all this. What else could they want from us? They already had our money and passports. Why wouldn't they just issue us identification papers and send us packing? Hercules seemed actually to enjoy my daily visits. His exuberance would rise a notch every time I arrived, and he would eagerly bring new young suspects to beat up in front of me.

I asked the woman who cooked our rice and beans what she thought we should do.

"Just wait," she said. "*Monsieur le Commandant* will sell your things back to you. It is always the same. It is easier for them than bringing them to Kisangani or Kinshasa."

"But, he hasn't asked for money," I said. "No one has."

"He cannot ask," she said, with a laugh. "They are the army. They are above reproach."

I thought about this. It made some kind of sense, but I had no idea how to go about telling the commandant that we wanted to buy back our passports. I was so weary at this stage that I could no longer think straight. We weren't eating right or drinking enough water. Water was available only a few hours each morning, and no matter how much of it we stored, we still ended up running out in the evening and having to drink the murky bath water we had been soaking in all day. The unvarying diet of rice and beans was leaving us weak and disorientated; none of us had any of our daily malaria tablets left, and some people began to get hysterical over every mosquito bite. There was supposedly a particularly deadly strain active in the area which had killed two Swiss girls a few months before. We all had our own private hardship. Natasha had had her contraceptive tablets stolen, and was having to deal with her period coming unexpectedly and without her having any tampons.

After talking to the rice and bean woman, I decided that my only option was to try and confront the Secretary of Justice. I went straight to his bungalow, knocked on the door and kept knocking until eventually his secretary let me in. The building appeared to be completely empty except for her desk in the hall. There was no activity anywhere other than a gardener out front spraying a bed of geraniums. Suddenly I noticed movement through Venetian blinds on the far side of the veranda and went over to see what it was. Straining through a set of tall double doors, I saw the Secretary leaning back in a leather armchair in front of an ornate hardwood desk. His eyelids were closed and he was swinging back and forth, trying to stay within the draft of a fan that was swaying elliptically overhead. I coughed and he looked up at me distractedly, then, guessing who I was, he stood up and called out for his secretary. She came running in and grabbed my arm, saying in a scolding voice that the Secretary was preparing for an important meeting.

"But I need to see him!" I said.

"You're lucky the guard wasn't on duty today. He would shoot you," she said pulling me firmly away. "The Secretary is a very busy man. He has planned his timetable to see you at the soonest time."

"In four days?" I said.

"Hopefully, yes," she said hesitantly.

It became clear at that point that the meeting would never happen, and I went straight back to the boarding house and called the whole group together for a strategy meeting. The money Henry had budgeted for the seven days was all gone by now, and we only had the French francs for the trip to Kisangani left. We were no nearer to finding the passports or a way of getting out of Bumba. From now on, anything we spent would lessen our chances of ever leaving, and we would have no option but to wait until Suzi finally decided to come back looking for us. That might take weeks. It could have taken up to a week for her to reach Kisangani if the roads were really as bad as people said, and provided she turned around immediately, it would take the same to drive back.

It became clear over the course of the meeting that our only hope was to put ourselves entirely in *Monsieur le Commandant's* hands, to do whatever he wanted of us. It was he who held all the strings. The problem was we had no idea what he wanted. It was most likely he was after money, since he had everything else of ours. Somehow he must have known we still had a bit more. We would have to hand it over – the problem was finding a way of doing so without causing offence. If we misread the situation and acted inappropriately, we were liable to end up in jail for attempted bribery.

I felt that our best bet was to work through Hercules, and with the agreement of the others, I went straight to the army camp after the meeting and announced that we were all so appreciative of the work he and the others had been doing that we wanted to give them a token of our esteem. I handed him some foreign currency wrapped in a little watercolour sketch of the quayside that Mildred had done.

Hercules made no attempt to hide his pleasure. "*Argent, argent!*" he roared approvingly. "*C'est merveilleux!*"

He turned to his soldiers, explaining to them about this noble gesture that the Englanders had made, and how they all must now prove themselves worthy of it.

"*Nous devons trouvez les passports,*" he said in French, again largely for our benefit, then switched back to Lingala.

As soon as he had finished talking, the soldiers scattered in all directions, snatching guns, jumping on bicycles, lacing up their boots and racing off. It was yet another impressive display. Hercules sat back on a bench and assured us he would not let us down.

True to his word, the following morning two of the passports were handed in to our boarding house. They just appeared out of nowhere with no explanation. I went straight to the army camp to thank Hercules, but he looked bashfully at his toes, insisting adamantly that he deserved no thanks until he had recovered all of the passports for us. I handed over another watercolour full of francs, and by the time I made it back to my room a man was on his way to the boarding house with some of our malaria tablets. All day a steady stream of foreign knickknacks were delivered:

a watch, envelopes, a diary, lip balm, sunglasses . . . Most weren't even ours, but had evidently been taken from other travellers or missionaries long before. A third passport arrived the following morning after I handed over another painting. By this stage we had very little money left. Henry said we couldn't afford to give Hercules any more the following morning, and so no more passports were returned. We had finally cracked the code. Money equalled passports. No doubt, we could have got them all back straight away if we paid enough, but Henry was determined to keep a few hundred francs aside in case we ever found a way of escaping from Bumba. Hercules and *Monsieur le Commandant* must have known we had a bit more, or else they were just biding their time, waiting to see whether we would offer more or if they had really exhausted our supply. By this stage we were spending no money on ourselves and were surviving on a large stalk of bananas that the boarding-house owner had hacked off one of his plants for us. It was a game of high-stakes poker between us and the Commandant, and it continued for two more days until finally we won. On St Valentine's Day 1991, after two weeks in Bumba, a man claiming to be an officer of the *Service Secret d'Information Militaire de Zaire* turned up in our room with the remaining three passport in his hand. We were finally free to leave. That is, if we could find a way out.

Chapter 20

ABOUT SIX HOURS after the last passport was returned, a miracle occurred on the banks of the river. A cargo boat appeared on the horizon. It had been sailing upriver for three weeks from Kinshasa and was on its way to Kisangani – travelling as slowly as it could, to avoid hitting sandbanks along the way. Somehow it had scraped together enough diesel for the journey and was now making a fortune charging exorbitant rates to those who urgently needed to be brought upriver or to have their goods brought up. It was the first boat to pass by in a month. Within a few hours, it would be pulling up at the dock, and already there were hordes of people making their way down to the river to await it. We said goodbye to the boarding-house owner and raced down to join them.

The quayside was like an evacuation scene, with crowds of people hauling bundles and crates, desperate for the chance to finally get themselves or their belongings out of Bumba. We all stood jostling for position as near to the edge of the water as we could without being pushed in. We stood there for two hours as the boat made its way agonisingly slowly through the sandbanks towards the quay. As it manoeuvred through the shallow water in towards the bank, the propeller rose out of the water now and then when it hit sand; and the smell of burning oil and spray of grey water would send us heaving backwards.

It was only when the boat docked that we got to see how crowded it was. The deck was a seething mass of tight-cropped heads and shiny black limbs. There must have been a few hundred people on board, all of them eager for this one chance to travel upriver. The ballast was sunk worryingly deep. When the gangway was dropped, all of us on the quayside lunged forward, and the captain had to wave an oar above our heads to keep us back. He reversed the engines and pulled away from the bank, shouting at us that we were to line up with our money in hand. He promised he would take as many of us as he could. Of the group in my room, I was the only one who had not been robbed, but I waited back with them while the others joined the queue, promising to buy tickets for us. The gangway was lowered again, and with a little less tumult the crowd boarded one by one. Soon the gunwale was almost touching the water, and the whole boat was listing dramatically to starboard. The captain, fearing for the stability of the vessel, sounded a horn and pulled away from the quay again. He called across the water to us that the boat was overloaded and he couldn't take any more passengers or cargo. The others in our group had been some of the last to get on.

"Did you get us tickets?" we called over to them, but they were too busy commandeering space for themselves to hear. Finally Mildred turned around to us.

"What?" she yelled.

"Did you get us tickets?"

She shook her head. "We tried," she screamed, "but . . ."

The rest of her sentence was drowned out in the disorder. We now found ourselves on the quayside looking out wanly at the others. I wondered should I have stayed with them and bought myself a ticket? Although theoretically we had pooled all our money, Henry allowed us all keep our own portion, as we didn't trust one person to handle the whole lot. With the amount of money I had left, I could have bought myself a ticket and guaranteed a place on the boat, but it wouldn't have been right to leave my friends. It was partly my fault we were in this mess anyway.

"What do we do now?" Lucy said to a local man beside us.

"Beg," he said, pointing to the locked gangway, where the captain was allowing certain people through to petition him for one of the last few spaces onboard. If it really was a matter of life and death, or you had enough money, he would find space for you. Looking around us at the harrowing state of some of the others, we knew we didn't stand a chance. I realised that it was best for at least some of the group to get to Kisangani – they could let Suzi know what had happened and tell her to come for us. But the thought of being left behind had me close to despair. We would have to fend for ourselves somehow – it might be two weeks or more before help arrived.

Gathering our belongings, we waved goodbye to our friends and slumped back to the boarding house, hoping to throw ourselves at the owner's mercy for another few nights. A vivid red sunset was setting fast over the village like some speeded-up reel in a movie, and into the newly cooled air the sweet warm smell of evening was released. By the time we had laid out our roll mats and mosquito nets, it was already dark and we were able to seek solace in sleep.

Next morning we made our way back down to the river and to our surprise saw the boat still there. It appeared that there were goods to be loaded and unloaded, payments to be collected and the usual stamps to be issued by errant guards. The boat remained docked there for two whole days while our friends sat beneath the blistering sun the whole time. We brought them water and bananas a few times a day, and tried to chat with them from the quayside to buoy their spirits. Each had a segment of deck no bigger than a newspaper to themselves; it was far too narrow to lie out in.

On the third day, as the boat was about to leave and its passengers about to wilt, Etienne, a local man with a handsome, slender face and squirrelly eyes, came to see us. He told us he had an outboard engine and knew where to find some diesel and offered to ferry all eighteen of us to Kisangani in a motorised *pirogue* for a huge sum – about ten times what it would have cost on the ferry. We told him there was no way we could afford it.

"No problem," he said. "You pay a little now and the rest in Kisangani."

We wondered why no one had mentioned Etienne to us before.

"I am living in Lisala," he said. "And the engine was in another part of the country. It is not mine; it is my uncle's. It is the only one."

We were amazed that suddenly this man could appear out of nowhere offering us a way out, but we didn't question it too deeply. We were just thinking how we could find the down payment that he claimed was need-ed to pay for diesel. We calculated that if the group on board sold their tickets, we could just about cover the cost, and we raced down to the quay to tell them.

"We can leave in a few hours," Natasha shouted across excitedly. "Once he gets the diesel, we'll be off. He says you'll be able to sell your tickets for double what they are worth. We will all be in Kisangani togeth-er in a couple of days!"

Our friends said nothing. They remained silent while we stared out at them, waiting for their assent. It was odd that they didn't react. We couldn't understand it, and so we explained the situation again, thinking that perhaps the sun had blurred their minds. We told them how this man was willing to bring all of us upriver in a giant dugout canoe propelled by an engine. Granted, he was charging a lot, but wasn't it worth it? We would all be free. Still they said nothing. They looked in dishevelled con-dition; the days of naked sun had taken their toll. They were red with sun-burn and pale with hunger.

Finally Mildred spoke up.

"It's just that," she began, "how can you be sure he's for real?"

It was a fair point.

"He is!" Lucy cried.

"Yeah, but how do you know?" Rita said.

They needed proof, and so I hurried off and got Etienne to bring down the outboard engine for them to see. There were *pirogues* scattered all along the bank. It was easy enough to imagine the engine being bolted to the back of one of them – a few even had a flat stern carved out espe-cially. But they still weren't convinced.

"An engine needs diesel," Henry said, "and there is none."

"It doesn't need much," I said, "and Etienne promises he can get it."

They looked at me dubiously, and so I asked Etienne if he could bring the diesel tank to show them. He doubted he could get it without the money first, but I begged him, and finally he did manage to get three men to wheel the barrel down on a cart for the others to see.

"Do you want to taste it?" Luke said sarcastically.

It was hard to tell what the group were thinking, but the sight of the diesel barrel hadn't made as much of an impression on me as I'd hoped.

It seemed that they had already made up their minds. The ferry boat's engines had been switched on an hour before, and it was likely it would set off soon.

"We've been waiting here for so long," Rita shouted across to us, as though this were a reasonable explanation for not helping us, "and the boat is finally leaving – it really is!"

They shot furtive glances between each other which were difficult to read from our position on the bank. It was hard even to hear what they were calling to us above the din of the engines and other hordes of restless passengers.

"We know you want to get away," Felicity shouted over to us at last, "but we just don't think canoes are the answer."

I shouted back that there was no other answer. We had finally found a way for us all to escape together. We could be in Kisangani within a few days; all it took was for them to get off that horrid rusty boat and join us. If they didn't we might end up being stranded here for weeks. There was no way we could afford the diesel without them.

"I know it seems harsh," Dorothy shouted to us, "but . . ."

"We can all be free!" Lucy cried. "Etienne says he will be ready in an hour. He just needs to prepare the *pirogue* and pay for the diesel . . ."

They weren't listening any more. They had already made their decision. Their boat was leaving, and it was certain to reach Kisangani in the next few days. And although it would be slow, it was more comfortable than a canoe and, most importantly, had its own lavatory onboard. Also the captain had promised some food once they got underway.

I noticed that Rodney and Marsha, the soldier and his wife, were looking the most shifty of those on board. They were having doubts about what to do, and finally Rodney called out to us.

"Will your guy really leave in an hour, do you think?"

"We believe him," I shouted back.

He looked me in the eye as I was talking, and I knew at that moment that he wouldn't abandon us. He turned to his wife and they discussed the issue in a whisper. I noticed the others trying to interrupt them, and tempers seemed to flare for a moment until eventually Rodney and Marsha got up and dug their bags out from the pile stacked against the galley wall and came forward.

"They want to get off!" I shouted to the guard. "Lower the gangway. They want to get off!"

I grabbed their bags and Lucy hugged them both as they stumbled down on to the quayside.

"Don't worry," Rodney muttered into my ear. "We wouldn't have left you."

"Thanks," Lucy said. "What about the others?"

"Don't hold out hope," Rodney said sadly.

"Please!" Lucy shouted out to them, "please!"

After a while Norman and Duncan got up shakily to their feet and made their way towards the gangway, handing their ticket over to the guard and clambering down. Natasha ran up to Duncan and hugged him tightly.

"I knew you wouldn't," she cried. "I just knew it."

"Yeah, sure," Duncan said distractedly.

"We'll pay for the rest of you," I shouted out to the remaining seven onboard. "Once we get to Kisangani, we'll pay you every penny back, I promise."

"Canoes are simply not a viable option, Mocha," Rita said. "You know it as well as I do. You're putting everyone at risk."

"At risk?" I screamed. "You're prepared to abandon us here to die!"

"Don't be childish," she said.

"Mocha's right," Rodney shouted back. "What chance have we unless we stick together?"

"For God's sake," Henry shouted at him. "You're a military man; be realistic. Sometimes you have to make the pragmatic decision. This way we can send the warning out and get help for you guys."

"But we have an engine and a *pirogue*," I said, "and you've seen the diesel."

"It might seem harsh to you guys now," Vinnie said, "but you'll see it's for the best. And anyway, Rita's sick. She needs a doctor."

Rita did look worryingly flushed. She had a fever and bad stomach cramps. The nurses, Felicity and Dorothy, claimed they were obliged to stay on the boat and help her. Stella, the third nurse who was with us, scoffed at this. Mildred claimed her leg suffered spasms and needed to be kept straight; she couldn't cope with days cramped in a canoe. Stevi was taking no part in the discussion. He had secured himself a comfortable patch on deck and was sprawled out contently playing cards with some locals.

The siren sounded three times and the boat's engines suddenly grew louder. The gangway was pulled up a final time.

"Please!" roared Natasha. "What happens if one of us falls ill? What then?"

They could no longer hear us. The boat was shunting out towards midstream, and our former friends all kept their eyes averted, staring down at the water or at the deck; all of them that is except for Mildred. She never once took her gaze off us. It was as if she wanted us to see what she was thinking, that we had only ourselves to blame. We had been warned often enough and had failed to listen.

I couldn't face the walk back to the boarding house in public sight. Everyone in town knew us by now, and they would be watching us. They had heard the boat leaving and knew that our friends had abandoned us. I couldn't face the shame of it. Instead I went the long way around, along the jungle path that skirted the town, an ochre dust path that was favoured by snakes. I felt so sad, so miserable; not so much for myself as for all of us, for our group, for our flawed humanity. We were a microcosm of humanity, and we had behaved entirely predictably. After all these millennia of evolution, we were still as ruthlessly self-serving as ever. If existence really was a grand test of mankind, of good versus evil, then we had just failed.

Tears began to fill my eyes, and as I wiped them away I looked up ahead around the bend and saw something that stopped me dead in my tracks. It's hard to explain it, but the path looked so serene suddenly, so achingly magical with the morning light filtering through the broad dancing leaves and the mist rising through a cloud of golden white butterflies fluttering above a mud pool, that I was simply overcome. It was so beautiful, and I felt all at once grateful to be allowed witness it, to be in the presence of such perfection. I was only twenty years old after all and from an entirely different world; by rights I should never have gotten to see any of this. Few Irish people ever had. Why was I so lucky? My heart glowed, and I felt a tingle through my body. It was impossible to feel any sense of animosity after that. I realised that no doubt those on the boat had felt they were doing the right thing. We were all just following our hearts, I suppose. Who could blame them for wanting to hold on to this sacred world?

Back at the boarding house, I collapsed on my roll mat and slept. There was little else to do, and the hunger and heat were less noticeable in one's sleep. I dreamt of Jameson, who ended up dying here on Stanley's cursed expedition, and also of the men who had escaped the cannibals and gone mad living in the trees. They blended with Johan hanging himself in the boathouse. I realised how alone they must all have felt – confused, harried, haunted. That was the common link. They all felt abandoned and hopeless, just as I did now. If my father were to ask me again why I thought Johan had committed suicide, I would say that it was because he had felt so alone. I wanted to know that this wasn't the case; that there was someone or something out there helping us; somewhere to turn to when you were at your lowest ebb. Whatever that force was that had cured my sprained ankle, and had turned the path incandescent yesterday and sent tremors of love through me. What was it? Spirit? I hoped it had come to those poor sailors as they fled from the cannibals. Had it made them feel like I did yesterday? Accepting, swooning. Like how they say a mouse feels no fear when it is being swallowed by a snake – just acceptance and possibly even a twinge of excitement. I wanted spirit. I needed it. Was that the common weakness of both Europe and Africa: that we believed too little in spirits and they believed too much?

When I woke I saw a local boy in shredded shorts staring in the window at me, a shrivelled testicle peaking out between the seams. I pulled the sheet over me and shouted, "Go away!"

"It's funny," he said in French, "you are so pink, like roasting pigs – all red and crispy from the fire."

I threw something at him, and he said with great joy in Swahili, "*Assanti Sana!*"

From behind him I heard music approaching. It was rock music, not the normal circular *soukous* music that lingered on the breeze throughout Zaire. It was the first rock music I had heard since we left the truck. It was coming from the outskirts of town, growing louder as it approached, bouncing back and forth off the bungalows on the main street. I could hear the unmistakable sound of synthesizers and a mandolin; the authentic, integral tones of American alt-rock. As it came closer, I realised it was REM, and I heard Michael Stipe singing:

> *Sometimes I feel like I can't even sing*
> *I'm very scared for this world*
> *I'm very scared for me . . .*

I leant up on my elbows, startled. It was just so unexpected and so out of place. I had the strangest conviction that he was singing the words directly to me, the way people at revivalist meetings claim a psalm suddenly comes to life and talks to them personally. Michael Stipe continued:

> *All you hear is time stand still in travel*
> *And feel such peace and absolute*
> *The stillness still that doesn't end . . .*

The boy turned to look at where the music was coming from. I jumped up and followed him out with just the sheet around me. There was a bright orange truck driving down the main street. It was an overland truck somewhat like ours, but newer and bigger, and far better in every way. It pulled up in the square and the music died.

"No shiiiit?!" I heard someone say from the back of the truck, in those instantly recognisable, elongated vowels of the Californian dialect.

The steps were let down and a bunch of clean, sprightly Americans came bouncing out, chatting and jeering with each other and looking around bemusedly at their new destination.

"Hey, there! How's it goin'?" one of them said to me, seeing me standing on the roadway, bleary-eyed in my sheet. "The route been treatin' you good?"

I made no reply. My brain couldn't accept the sight of these rich, white people in this, our own personal purgatory. Where the hell had they come from? No one else could possibly be here. The Gulf War had caused the border to close on every side – Central Africa was determined not to be a launch pad for either group.

"You OK?" he said to me. "Know when the boat's due?"

I suddenly felt very dizzy and put my hand out to grip the wall. It was all too much. One of the Americans reached out for me just as I was about to fall.

"English? Anglais?" he said to me anxiously. "You OK, man?"

"The boat . . ." I said finally. "There is no boat. I mean, there hasn't been . . . there won't be. . . ."

The man was looking around him concernedly, wondering what he should do with me. I tried to compose myself. I knew it was important that I kept these guys on side. We needed them. I wanted to bring them to meet the others, but had no idea where I would find the strength to put this resolution into action. I had just formed the words "Come with me", when suddenly a wave of nausea overcame me and I slumped to the ground.

"Hey, man, you OK?"

"Sometimes I feel like I can't even sing," I muttered unintelligibly. "I'm very scared for this world. I'm very scared . . ."

"Go get a saline drip," I heard someone say.

Lucy came along at just that moment and saw a white guy trying to put a needle into my arm.

"Get away from him," she screamed.

They told her who they were and what had happened, but she still didn't want them messing with me. She asked them to help her carry me into the bathroom, where they pulled my sheet off and dumped me in the bath.

About an hour later I came round, and Lucy told me that the group was part of a Peace Corp contingent on an end-of-duty break. They had been camped along a stretch of no man's land between the Republic of the Congo and Zaire when war broke out and all the borders shut. Neither country would take responsibility for them, and they were passed like a shuttlecock from one to the other until eventually Zaire took pity and allowed them enter. They were disappointed to learn that the riverboat was cancelled, but Etienne's offer of a *pirogue* trip sounded even more exciting. More like a true Tarzan jungle adventure. They offered to pay the entire cost and bring us along with them if we liked.

Lucy went straight to Etienne to check whether he could carry more people, and he assured her that if he tied a few *pirogues* together he should be able to fit everyone in. He said the most important thing was that we leave as soon as possible, before the army got to hear about the arrival of the Americans. As soon as they found out that they were in town, they would start planning to ensnare them. They did it to everyone who passed through, Etienne said. It was as much out of boredom as a way of getting money.

The Americans weren't at all keen to leave right away. They wanted to explore Bumba first, and they couldn't see why they needed to be scared of the army, who had always been helpful to them so far. They thought we were just being paranoid, but we begged them to listen to Etienne, who promised them they were bound to end up in the same position as us if they didn't leave.

It was evening by the time we had convinced them, but meanwhile Etienne had been preparing the vessel, lashing three huge dugout trunks together, and it was now waiting for us in the water. He had it hidden downstream a bit in a muddy patch with overhanging trees where it would be less noticeable to the army. He had asked the American driver to hide his truck under the cover of some weeping branches that soared out from plinths of visible roots that had been eroded by floods. Pelicans and egrets fished in the shallows, and I saw sprats jumping up to escape the grips of water rats.

The twenty Peace Corp workers looked like something out of a mail order catalogue, with flashy new outdoor gear that was in stark contrast to our dishevelled state. Etienne loaded us all into the boat as quickly as he could – fifteen into each of the outer *pirogues* and all our supplies in the centre one. It was surprisingly stable considering it was basically three trunks tied together. The huge mound of luggage in the central *pirogue* (consisting of two thirty-gallon barrels of diesel, innumerable rucksacks, sleeping gear, water vessels and cooking utensils, all belonging to the Americans who were used to travelling in style) acted like a weighted keel.

Just as we were about to leave, a boy came running up to Etienne warning him that he had seen Hercules with a group of men making their way towards the quay. Etienne said it was vital that we set off immediately, and the truck driver had better leave too or they would come after him. The driver made some last minute arrangements with his people to meet up in Kisangani in a few days' time, and then he gunned up his big orange monster (a glowing carbuncle, even more ridiculous looking than our own), and drove off towards the main street. Etienne, meanwhile, checked the lashings that were keeping the *pirogues* together one last time, and after tinkering with the outboard, he tugged the ignition chord and we glided out slowly into midstream. It should have been a moment of great elation and triumph, but we were all too anxious about Hercules to feel anything but fear. We thought he might find some way of coming after us if he found out that a new group of wealthy whites had just slipped from his grasp.

It took an hour, and constant reassuring by Etienne that Hercules could never get his hands on another outboard in time, before we truly began to relax. I reckoned we were far enough away by then that no rower could catch up. We settled ourselves down into the hollowed-out trunks, which felt like clogs two sizes too small. No matter how we tried curling and unfurling our limbs into various foetal positions, we couldn't get comfortable. There wasn't enough room to sit lengthways, so we had to crouch sideways like hatchlings in the hours before the egg cracks. We reassured ourselves with the knowledge that it wouldn't be for long. Etienne promised the journey would take only two days: two days until we were safely back in civilisation again, with access to money and medicine and some control over our lives. And to be honest, snuggling up had its consolations – pressing in close to Lucy and Holly made me think again of Lucy and Natasha in the first harsh weeks of the trip and how they had overcome it by cuddling. After a while, I began to close my eyes and savour the feeling of being on the move again, moving towards safety and abundance, with the keels slipping through the water with soporific ease. It must be the feeling a fly gets on finding an open window.

Around midnight I was jolted awake by a violent crash. Looking around me, I realised the *pirogues* had hit a sandbank. I noticed a gap appear between them, and it gradually widened until it was clear they were slowly edging apart. The vines binding them had snapped, and each canoe began to drift off in separate directions. Only the middle one with the engine on it could be steered or powered. The other two, with all of us onboard, drifted off into the darkness, heading back downriver from where we had come, propelled by the current. All of us panicked, but Stella, my cooking partner, was the worst. She stood up in the canoe and began to scream, rocking the log violently from side to side. I grasped her to me and pulled her down, but she was hysterical and didn't seem aware of what she was doing. I hugged her tightly, hoping to crush the panic out of her, but it didn't work. She didn't even seem to know I was there. She was staring blindly forward with locked eyes and screaming from the depths of her lungs. Wayne got at her from behind, clutching her belly so tightly that she could hardly breathe, and finally he managed to half choke her back to consciousness. Etienne, who was still in the central *pirogue* with the engine and all our bags, yelled at us all to jump overboard and try to pull the logs back to shore, but manoeuvring a nine-metre log through a strong current in a deep river at night wasn't easy. Even coordinating the fifteen of us to push and pull in the right direction at the same time was challenging. It took an hour before we had all three logs safely tied up at the bank. By that stage we were completely sodden and the logs were full of water. We had no option but to set up camp and stay the night where we were. It would just add more time to the journey, but at least we'd get a night's sleep. We had been hoping to do the whole journey in one go, to get as far away from Hercules as quickly as possible.

Etienne went off into the jungle to find the local chief of the area and to ask his permission to camp for the night; otherwise, he said, we risked being disturbed, or possibly attacked, in the night. The Americans began unpacking their supplies and lighting a fire to cook dinner. Obviously, our group had no food with us, but for some reason we didn't want the Americans to know. It's hard to explain why; but basically we were all feeling so low about ourselves that we felt it would only have added to our shame to admit to hunger and have to beg for food. We had seen them pack only enough for themselves and knew that if they shared with us they would be left hungry, and they would have felt that more intensely than we ever would. They had done enough for us already without that too. Although I know that none of these reasons can really explain our behaviour, they're the best I can come up with for why we kept our distance that night, setting out our roll mats and mosquito nets a distance away so that they wouldn't notice us. We told them we were exhausted and needed to go straight to sleep, and they seemed to accept this. We hoped that if we buried our noses deep enough into our sleeping bags we wouldn't smell the sweet mango and turmeric rising from their tins of gourmet chicken curry.

It was virtually impossible to get to sleep, but eventually I managed to doze off, ignoring the spasms of hunger that racked me every time a breeze wafted over. I slept fitfully and sometime before sunrise woke to find Holly's lucid, doe eyes staring down on me. She didn't say anything, but her eyes tracked across to where the Americans were sleeping and to the pans and dishes scattered around their fire. The minute I laid eyes on them, I knew what she was thinking and nodded imperceptibly to her.

Slipping out of bed, we both snuck over to their side of the camp, checking that they were all still asleep before approaching the cold fire and grabbing a pot and pan each and shoving our faces down into them to lick the last of the congealed curry out. At some point Rodney woke and, noticing what we were up to, came scurrying over to join us. When I saw him with his face stuck in a plate, I thought of Bobby Sands and felt like saying something, but in the end I kept quiet. The thought of the hunger striker who had endured sixty-five days without food without ever debasing himself to the animalistic level to which we had so easily succumbed was sobering. I grabbed another plate and tried pushing the thought from my mind, focusing all my attentions on my licking, lapping, slavering tongue. But my mind ricocheted back and forth through various states of shame and a type of hyper-awareness, like a fox stealing the last few moments of opportunity before the dawn. Thoughts of Bobby Sands made me think of my own grandmother, who had endured thirty days on hunger strike as a political prisoner fighting for Irish independence, and that made me think of my dad and how we used to smash crab claws with a hammer and suck out the meat. I avoided looking at Holly and Rodney; I didn't want to acknowledge the shame in their eyes, to be a witness to their debasement.

Eventually, one of the Americans, whose name was Rick, stirred in his sleeping bag, and before we had a chance to retreat, he opened his eyes and began looking around him.

"Hi," Holly said guiltily after a long pause. He was staring straight at her, and she knew she had to say something. She had looked behind her a few times first to see could she get away, but it was too late for that now.

"What the hell . . . ?" he muttered sleepily.

"Huh?" I said, wiping my lips.

"What are you guys up to?"

"Nothing," Rodney said, getting up casually and beginning to walk away. "Just checking the fire."

Rick looked around at the pots and plates, and suddenly it dawned on him what was going on. He looked as if he wanted to say something, but no words came. It seemed he was as embarrassed as we were. An hour later, when everyone was up and about the news of what we had been up to spread through the camp. The Americans were appalled.

"Why didn't you guys say something?" one of them said. She sounded really upset.

We shrugged awkwardly.

"Shit, I mean, I know we shoulda figured it out," she said. "Of course, you have no food – you have no money, for Christ-sake. Duh! But you cudda said something. We would have given you everything we have. You just needed to say."

We stared at the ground, feeling worse than ever. It was all our fault, and we felt terrible for having made them feel more uncomfortable.

"Listen, I swear to God," Rick said, "the minute we get to a village, we'll buy whatever the hell you want, OK? I mean it, *no problemo!*"

Etienne and his men rebound the boats, and we slipped back on to the river. They had brought no food either, of course, but for them it was normal.

Chapter 21

THE DAY SEEMED hotter than any we had experienced so far, the sun pounding unremittingly down, and with no shelter whatsoever on the open water. The rays came at us from every angle, even reflected back up from the surface, so that even if we covered our heads with towels we still ended up getting burnt. The sweat flowed from us, and by mid morning our water bottles had run dry. The Americans had brought along a five-gallon drum of purified well water, but once again we didn't feel we could ask them for some. Why should they have to go without for our benefit? It was even more important that they avoided dehydration than hunger.

And it wasn't as if there were no other water available; we had the third largest river in the world flowing inches from our fingers. When Etienne and his assistant were thirsty, they just dropped a cup over the side and drank as much cool, fresh water as they wished. But it was a little different for us. It had to do with "gut flora". Every white man who ever sets foot in Africa is told not to let even a drop of Congo (Zaire) or Zambezi River water pass their lips. The consequences could be instant, and eventually fatal.

We said nothing and did nothing for a while, but slowly as the day wore on we began to wilt. By noon, when the sun was bearing down right above our heads, our bellies had begun to stab with pain as the acidity of the enzymes in our stomachs became ever more concentrated. Our heads grew dizzy as the blood cells began to weaken. All of us succumbed at different rates, growing more lethargic, crumbling in on ourselves. Again, the Americans noticed nothing until it was too late. They just presumed we were tired and not as accustomed to the sun as them.

Natasha was the first one to get really sick. Heatstroke overcame her and she collapsed, foam spewing from her mouth. We were all too weak to help her much, and so we turned to the Americans. They stepped in, siphoning litre after litre of their precious water into her until she regained consciousness. She went on coughing convulsively and dry retching for the rest of the day, but she looked like she would make it through.

We knew after that that it was too dangerous to hold out any longer; we would have to drink something. It was Rodney who plucked up the courage to ask the Americans if they happened to have any spare purification tablets with them. Straight away they handed over a whole pack of Puritabs, looking at him in a strange manner as they did so. They knew as well as we did that purification tablets were of little use against the water in a river like this. They might clear up some of the sediment and possibly kill off the giardia and other micro-organisms, but they were powerless against the most evil parasites like bilharzia or the diseases that were latent. Nevertheless, Rodney took the tablets and began to fill our water bottles from the river, dropping a tablet into each. He then handed the bottles out to us one by one, without saying a word, just staring us straight in the eye until we drank.

"It's your only hope," he murmured.

The Americans looked on in guilty silence, but they had nothing to feel guilty about. There simply wasn't enough water for all of us, and they had already used enough on Natasha. It wasn't their fault. It was no one's fault, or if anyone's, it was mine. It was I who had bought the grass.

Now, faced with the situation that the creepy-crawlies would inevitably invade our bodies, we sat back and awaited our fate. I imagined the dreaded microscopic bilharzia worm entering me with the very first gulp of water. I could feel it burrowing its way deeper into my bladder. I knew exactly where it would go and what it would do. It would carve its way over a series of weeks through my gut until it reached my kidney and, from there, would set about establishing its dominion. I knew there would be no pain during this stage, just maybe some gentle flu-like symptoms. But once it had carved out its territory, it would begin reproducing, gradually coating the kidney and the surrounding organs in a layer of coral-like calcium. Eventually, my entire innards would be turned to stone, like some fossilised sea mammal or a victim of Medusa the Gorgon whose evil eye solidified everything it saw.

I knew all this would happen, and yet strangely I wasn't too bothered. The sublime relief of the cool, sensuous water flowing through me was too intense to care about anything else. It was the indescribable euphoria of resurrection, of death delayed.

We kept on going all through that day and night, and by the end of the following day, we were supposed to be drawing near to Kisangani. Our skin was raw red by this stage, and both we and the Americans were in a bad state, but we were excited by the idea of reaching the city and were already planning a big party where we would gorge ourselves on ice cream and chocolate and beer and Coca Cola. As the sun began to set, we were surprised that Kisangani hadn't appeared on the horizon yet. One of the Americans asked Etienne if there was a bend in the river which might hide the city. (She had read the V.S. Naipaul novel about the area and hoped that the eponymous "bend" might be here.)

"I don't know," Etienne said.

"What do you mean, you don't know?" she said.

"I don't know, I've never been."

"You've never been to Kisangani?"

"No," Etienne confirmed.

"What about you?" the American said to Etienne's assistant.

He shrugged and looked toward Etienne.

"So how do you know which way to go?" the American asked.

Etienne shrugged.

The river broke into numerous forks every few kilometres creating tributaries sometimes as wide as the river itself that then went off meandering in all directions. Etienne had never once paused at any of these branches, just continued confidently along as if he knew exactly where he was going. For all we knew, we could be kilometres off course by now; anywhere at all in the intricate filigree of rivers that roughly made up the Congo.

"One more day, I think," Etienne said now, standing at the tiller staring ahead with the rapt absorption of a helmsman.

"A day!" we cried. We couldn't believe it.

"Possibly," Etienne said with a shrug.

He had sworn to us in Bumba that the trip would take no more than two days. We had never thought to ask him whether he knew how to get there. It hadn't occurred to us that the river mightn't be straight and neatly banked.

Now the prospect of an extra day seemed almost unendurable, yet we knew we had no choice but to endure it, and somehow we did. We slumped down into the heel of the boat with our limbs draped over the sides, too hot and weary to even brush the flies off our faces. That evening, as the first mists began to fall on the river and we began counting down the hours until the end, Etienne announced that it now looked like it might take another day. We looked at him aghast, but there was nothing that any of us could say. Etienne wasn't being purposefully deceitful; it was just that the amount of time a journey took was of no relevance to him. The only important thing was to get there. It was the same for all Africans. In *Lingala*, the language he spoke, the words for yesterday and tomorrow were the same. He thought we were crazy to be focusing on the time it took to get somewhere, rather than on the fact that we would be getting there. Everything was based on the idea of *now*, not the past or the future. *Now* we were on the river; at some point in time we would be in Kisangani. It was futile and childish to think of anything else; a version of *Are we there yet, Mum?*

On the fourth day we felt we couldn't stand the discomfort any longer, and we ordered him to pull over for the night. We needed to stretch our limbs and get a proper night's sleep and possibly even to find some food if we were lucky. Nobody in the riverside huts or fishing *pirogues* we had passed so far was willing to sell us any. A few of them had rowed out to greet us, but when we asked for food, they said they didn't have enough for themselves. There was no way of knowing if this was true or if they just didn't want to encourage travellers in the area. The former was more likely the case, as most Zairians practised a form of subsistence agriculture which basically meant growing just enough for your family and neighbours, while leaving a bit to go to seed for the following year. There was never any surplus, other than the small amount that could be offered as a token to a neighbour in a time of need. This was one of the biggest problems that Stanley's expeditions had encountered a hundred years before. He came into the region with 600 people, certain that supplies would be plentiful in such a fertile place, and as a result many of his men ended up dying of hunger and malnutrition.

We docked at a sandy spot on the shore, and after pulling the boats up into some bushes, we cleared a patch for our roll mats and settled down to our first sprawled-out sleep of limb-extended luxury in three days. In the middle of the night I felt a body brushing up beside me. Opening my eyes, I saw Lucy.

"Are you OK?" I said.

She nodded.

"Sure?" I whispered.

She nodded again. I stretched my arms around her and she nestled into me, pulling herself in close, and we slept like that, hugging each other through the night.

Next morning some locals appeared out of nowhere, having somehow intuited our presence, and again we tried getting food off them, the Americans even waving dollars in front of them as an added impetus. But the locals just laughed and looked out on to the river sadly. Stanley had had to resort to kidnapping women and children and then ransoming them back in return for food, but even that sometimes didn't work; the tribe wouldn't pay the ransom, and he would be left with more mouths to feed.

Before we set off again, the Americans tried to extract an estimated-time-of-arrival from Etienne, but it was futile. He had about as much idea as we had. We asked him to ask the locals, but few of them had ever been as far as Kisangani, and certainly none had ever made the journey in a *pirogue*. They all pointed upriver and said 'a day or two, maybe three".

"I don't know about you guys," Rodney said to the Americans, "but we're certainly not going to last the pace much longer. We're at breaking point. Our skin is peeling off us – if we go on like this, some of us are going to start dropping like flies. We just don't have the reserves left."

"He's right," Stella said. "It's pure luck that only one person got heat-stroke so far. It'll get us all in the end."

"What are you saying?" an American said. "You want to give up? You want to head back?"

"I'm just pointing it out," Rodney said coolly. "There's no point getting to Kisangani if it kills us."

"Personally speaking," the American said, "I don't think that's a very helpful observation. Do you want to just sit here and die? Is that what you're saying? Or do you have a more constructive alternative?"

Rodney said nothing.

"I thought not!" the American harrumphed. "Do you want us to put down roots like Kurtz or something? Pair off and start a new settlement?"

"There's no need to be cynical," I said.

"I'm being realistic, man," he said. "Sorry if it rocks your boat, if it shakes your ship."

"That's a good idea," Lucy said. "A great idea. A ship! Why don't we make the boat into a ship?"

"What?!" someone said, a bit impatiently.

"A ship," Lucy said eagerly, "or a cruiser anyway."

"What the hell are you on about?" I said. I was worried for her sanity.

"Convert it," Lucy said, "into a really comfy place, where it becomes nice to travel in."

"Is she on drugs?" the American said.

"What do you mean exactly, Lucy?" Natasha said, ignoring the American.

"I mean, that we have plenty of drinking water now, although it's a bit yuck and might kill us, and we're so used to being hungry that we don't even feel it, so the only thing that's really bothering us is the sun. I think we should shut the sun out. It makes sense. We build a canopy with lovely fronds like in a beach hut in Barbados or something. It could be really nice."

"You mean like in that Tom Cruise movie?" Natasha gushed. "Where he's mixing drinks and dancing and they're all just chilling out."

"Didn't see it," Lucy said, "but my big sister put a roof on to our tree house, and it made it a thousand times better."

The rest of us stayed quiet, slowly coming to terms with what she was saying. It wasn't such a bad idea at all.

One of the Americans got out a piece of paper and began to draw up some plans. It would be a simple enough matter to construct a frame with poles and bind them to the *pirogues* using hemp. We could notch out holes for larger poles between the *pirogues* which would increase the stability of the whole structure.

We agreed to give it a go. Forming two teams, we headed out into the jungle looking for bamboo, or any other straight branches that might be of use. It took a while to haul them all back to the river. Etienne then hacked them down to size with his *panga*, and we set about swiftly erecting the scaffold and cladding it with large leaves. It took some hours to ensure it was solid and well-braced against the river winds and storms that could whip up occasionally. There were numerous arguments about whose technique was best, but overall we worked impressively well together. There was a feeling of excitement that had been absent for a long time.

By midday it was all built, braced and tightened, and we pushed out on to the river again, all of us slapping Lucy on her bony back in thanks. With the sun no longer bearing down on us, the journey took on a whole different feel. We began to actually enjoy ourselves. The landscape was breathtaking. We were moving along a strip of silver-blue ribbon through pristine equatorial rainforest – massive swathes of undulant greenness arising from olive cotton-swab banks. The forest was so all-encroaching and the river so bendy that it seemed as if we were only ever sailing through a tiny, though never-ending, pond. The forest would shut tightly around us as soon as we had passed through, and you would swear that it had never been there and that you had literally come from nowhere.

A few of us decided that since we were now drinking the water we might as well swim in it too, and Etienne agreed to steer the boat further into midstream for us, away from the crocodiles and hippos that tended to congregate along the banks. We dived in and immediately became aware of the great quiet power of the river tugging at us, eager to sweep us back downriver along with the ten million gallons it was pushing past us every second, with a force so powerful that even once it had reached the ocean 4,300 kilometres away, it still could gouge a 1,000 metre canyon in the ocean floor. So powerful as to shoot African soil and vegetation 200 kilometres out into the Atlantic. It gave me a whole new respect for the river which looked so placid and pool-like on the surface; this "immense snake uncoiled," as Conrad described it, "with its head in the sea and its tail lost in the depths of the land."

The sunset that evening was the equal of the dawn over the Sahara in Tamanrasset. It appeared slowly over the solid-green, soaring, cliff-like trees and danced a while above the canopy in a bulb of red fire, setting the entire mercuric reel of water that spooled out on either side of us aflame in chromatic splendour. We became just a dark burn in the endless reel of film, an insignificant frame bar passing by the lens of the mighty projector.

Etienne tried to tell us that the intensity of the sunset meant a storm was coming, but we ignored him. It was too calm, too beautiful to ever imagine such a thing. Nothing could disturb such tranquillity. Of course, we were wrong. By midnight, when the wind began to whip up and spit water back at us from the river, it was too late to seek shelter. The air exploded with a crash of thunder, and lightning began ripping down on us, lighting the river and sending raindrops so big that they tore the canopy to strips in minutes and filled the boat as quickly as we could bale it. We huddled down, shivering in the pools of water at our feet as the sky and water flashed through colours of blue and white. All we could hope for was that the poles wouldn't act as conductors and electrocute us all.

In the morning, the dysentery that had affected a few of us spread through everyone, as though it had been carried between us by the static electricity of the night before or, more likely, through the water sloshing at the base of the boat. We spent the day with our bottoms hanging over the side. Some of us were so weak that we couldn't hold on and had to ask a friend to grab our arms as we dangled our bottoms over the side. At mid-day, the river sent us a sign not to lose faith. Far ahead in the distance, we saw a grey dot on the water. It was too tiny to be a town, and as we motored towards it we realised it was a boat, a large metal cargo vessel.

There was only one cargo vessel it could possibly be, but we didn't dare raise our hopes too high until we knew for sure. It took the entire day before we drew near enough to be able to see for certain that it was the one our friends were on. We had caught up with them. It was what we had been hoping for all along, but never believed would actually happen. The boat was listing dangerously to starboard, and Etienne said it was impaled on a sandbank. We were still perhaps five kilometres away. It was unlikely they could have spotted us yet, sitting low on the water in our notched-out tree trunks. Suddenly we heard the sounds of drumming rippling out across the water, ebbing and flowing in the heavy evening air. We looked around us and realised it must be coming from the far bank, although all we could see was the usual thick drape of vegetation rising up out of the water.

"It is a village," Etienne said. "Somewhere in the trees. They are calling each other – maybe, telling about us."

"Would they have food?" Rick, the American, asked.

Etienne shrugged. "I don't know."

"Can you understand what they're saying?" Lucy said.

Etienne shrugged again.

"We ought to check if they've food," Rick said. "It seems like the first proper village we've come across."

"Maybe they're not friendly," Rodney said.

"On the river everyone is friendly," Etienne said, "as long as you are."

It took an hour to sail across the river, which was almost three kilometres wide at this point, and we were moving further away from the cargo vessel all the time. It was drawing dark by the time we pulled up at the far bank. The drumming continued sporadically until we landed and then fell eerily silent. We expected someone to greet us, a welcoming party perhaps, but no one came. Yet I felt them watching us, or at least I thought I did.

In the moonlight, the remains of a vast brick warehouse loomed over a rusty disused winch. Two of the walls had caved in and were festooned with drooping fronds of climbing palm, which were slowly eating away at the mortar. Behind it were the shells of smaller buildings, crumbling back into the red equatorial mud from which they'd been moulded. We walked into the forest and came upon a few huts made of leaves and branches. There was a fireplace with embers still smouldering but nobody around. We looked to Etienne for guidance, and he signalled to us to just sit and wait, which we did.

After about twenty minutes, a young albino girl came wandering along the path waving sticks gently around her head. Etienne went to greet her, but she ran away. We were left alone for a further period until she returned with a pygmy elder wearing a crocodile-skin hat and carrying a stout staff.

I couldn't take my eyes off the albino girl. I had seen albinos in Africa before, of course – they are more common here than anywhere else, particularly in isolated areas where the genetic diversity has been weakened. And, of course, they were far more visible here than they would be in Europe. This girl was not so much pale pink as cream coloured, and speckled with dark black spots like a cross between a panda and a tiger. The pygmy elder stood behind her at all times, as though she were a protective talisman, or perhaps just a common bond between us – an intermediary point between our two skin tones. A sign that we were not so different.

Etienne tried addressing him in various local languages until they found one they both spoke, and after a moment he turned to us excitedly.

"Good news! The grandpa says Kisangani is only a few hours away," he said. "He says it is dangerous to arrive at night, but if we leave in the morning we will be there by midday."

We cheered.

"Does he have food?" Rick asked.

Etienne asked the elder and then translated his reply. "Not much – just some rice and beans."

"Does he know anything about the other boat?" I asked.

"He says it has been there for some days. It is waiting for a tug boat from Kisangani, he thinks. It will take time."

"How much time?" I asked.

"Time," Etienne replied, with another of his shrugs.

The Americans, who had heard all about what the others had done to us in Bumba, insisted that we ought to think of a way of getting revenge. They said it was the only way we would get over it and move on; otherwise it would fester inside us for ever. We were too weary to care. All we could think about was the rice and beans. We asked the elder to give us as much as he could spare, and about twenty minutes later the albino girl came back with two pygmy boys carrying a blackened pot slung over a pole. She instructed them where to set it down and then began ladling out small portions on to large waxy leaves for each of us. We gulped it back immediately, even chewing the leaf-plates which had become soggy with the juices. The portions were small, but our stomachs had contracted so much that it filled us, and we were able to go to sleep that night feeling full for the first time in weeks.

The elder had refused to accept any money for the food, but he said that in the morning he would bring us a rare luxury that he was willing to sell us if we offered him the right price. It was a treasure, he said, the only one of its kind in the region.

As I was laying out my roll mat in the trees, I heard faint sounds of crying in the distance. When I went to explore, I found Lucy sitting on a stump with tears running down her cheeks. Standing behind her was the albino girl, crouched over and plaiting strips of cloth into her hair.

"What's the matter?" I said.

"Nothing," Lucy said, quickly pulling her teddy bear smile back in place.

"Is she hurting you?"

"No," Lucy said, managing a laugh. "I'm just a bit sad, that's all. I was thinking of my dad. He used to plait my hair before school every day."

"Oh," I said.

She began to sniffle a bit, and then said, "Mocha, I don't want to study law! And my dad really really wants me to. He wants me to continue the family tradition, but . . . I don't even know what I'm doing here any more. I think we're all running away. You know, you're lucky you don't get letters from home; they just make things harder, more confusing. I can't go back to the old me now. What am I going to do?"

"Didn't you tell me something before about the road teaching you everything your parents couldn't?" I said.

She nodded stoically, biting her bottom lip.

"Well?" I said and stroked her lower back.

True to his word, the elder sent the two boys back to us in the predawn of the following day, pulling a covered handcart from which we could hear bottles clinking. We all gathered around to see what it was, and once they were sure they had our attention, the boys triumphantly pulled away the covering to reveal a bright red plastic crate of twenty-four perfectly formed, curvilinear bottles of Coca-Cola. One of the boys stood protectively over it lest we might grab one and run for the river. The other boy called out for the elder, and when he didn't respond, he went over to a drum that was hanging from a gallows erected in the trees and beat it a few times until the elder appeared. He repositioned his crocodile-skin hat regally on his crown, looking proudly between the Coke and us, certain of the allure of his offering. He smiled with stirrup-like dimples gouging into his cheeks and gathered us around the bottles as if they were sacerdotal offerings, telling us to inspect them carefully: the quality of the glass, the integrity of the seals, the precise tint of the liquid. He wanted us to assess every detail, to see beyond their mud-spattered exterior to the core integrity. These were prime bottles of Coke, he wanted us to understand. He proudly pointed to the sell-by date, which was only seven months out of date, an impressive achievement in a place like this.

Once he was sure we had taken full cognisance of the exclusivity of his offering, he asked us to name our price. No one said anything at first. Clearly our group hadn't the means to acquire it, no matter how much we might want to. The Americans seemed dumbstruck by its sudden appearance in this godforsaken place. It was beyond their comprehension that their national drink could suddenly turn up out of the blue here in the infamous Heart of Darkness, the setting for the vilest scramble for money and power that ever polluted the history of geographical exploration. The perfect redness of the crate and glacial greeny glint of the bottles had cast a spell on them; it all pointed towards the promise of the black nectar inside. The elder said nothing more, biding his time, knowing precisely the power of what he had. All he had to do was give it the time to work on us.

Finally, Rick, the American who had caught Holly and me licking the plates earlier, cleared his throat and solemnly mentioned a figure. Etienne nodded a while over it, before conveying it to the elder. It was a large figure, about half as much as we were paying for the whole boat ride. The elder said nothing, just stared at Rick, his eyes and mouth rigid. He signalled to the boys to jangle the crate a bit more, a way of reminding us all of just exactly what was at stake here, what he had in his power to give or retract. Some of the Americans tried to feign indifference, looking casually away, but no one was convinced; you could feel the yearning radiating from them, the waves of covetousness arcing towards the great prize.

The elder grabbed a stick and began making calculations in the earth. After a moment he stood up again with legs slightly bent like a warrior preparing for battle and told Etienne he wanted double what was offered. This was translated for Rick, and without a second thought he agreed. He did so eagerly, as though it were the elder who was doing him a great favour. He opened his backpack and began pulling out wads of crumpled Zaire notes and handing them over breathlessly. It's hard to know exactly how much he was giving, as the value of the currency could have soared or plummeted many times over during the few days we had been on the river. The exchange rate had been rising and falling like a springtide while we were still in Bumba. Yet, no matter how much it was, it would be worthless within a few months, as the currency was once again devalued. I just hope the old man had spent it by then – maybe bought some sun cream for the young girl whose skin had no natural pigmentation to protect it against the sun and who was bound to end up with skin cancer at some point in her life.

Once Rick had taken receipt of the crate, the old man bowed and led his boys back into the forest. We all stood for a moment looking down distractedly at the crate as though we had just woken up from a bout of delirium and didn't quite know how we got here. Rick's eyes suddenly focused, adopting a resolute gaze, and he carried the crate over to us and laid it at Holly's feet.

She looked at him quizzically.

"It's for you guys," he said shyly.

We stared at him.

"All of you. It's for you. Share it however you want," he said. "I told you we'd help when we could."

"No . . ." Natasha managed, the first of us to process what was being offered and manage a response. "We're OK . . ."

She fell silent, too weak to say any more.

"Seriously . . ." Holly backed her up. "We're OK."

"I want you to have it," Rick said. "It's not just from me, it's from all of us. But there's one condition: you're not allowed drink it yet. You've gotta wait till we're on the water."

"What?" Rodney said.

"You have to wait until you're passing your friends," he said. "And then look them straight in the eyes and start drinking."

"What do you mean?" Lucy said.

"It's to make you strong again," he said, "so you're not losers all your lives."

"Screw you," Duncan snapped. "We're not losers."

"I don't mean it like that," Rick said. "I mean that one way or another, you're going to remember this for the rest of your lives, and you'll either see yourselves as having won or lost. My dad was in Korea, and he came back a loser. I had to grow up with the effects of that. I just don't want you guys, or your children, to have to face the same."

Stella started to cry.

"Thank you," she managed, tears and mucus dribbling down her face. "From the bottom of my heart."

She tried to hug him but he backed away.

"Seriously, it's nothing," he said, embarrassed.

The rest of us were too dazed to take it in. All we could focus on now was the imminent meeting on the river and what we would do. We got back onboard the *pirogues* and began making our way slowly upriver towards the vessel. Etienne loved the whole idea of the Coca-Cola plan, but he said it needed more; he wanted us singing and clapping while we were drinking. It should look like we were having the time of our lives, he said. The Americans liked that idea, and they started suggesting songs we could sing. We didn't really understand what was going on. We lacked the perspective to make sense of it all, but we went along with their ideas. Finding a song we all knew was hard, and we spent most of the next hour trying out various things mostly getting through the first verse and chorus and then realising that that was all we knew. Tempers got a bit frayed over some of the lyrics – we couldn't decide whether Otis Reading had been "sitting on the dock of the bay, watching time rolling away" or "watching the tide rolling away". I found I couldn't concentrate much on anything; my nerves grew tenser the nearer we approached the others. My stomach was tightening. I couldn't be sure how I would react on seeing them, how I would feel. I just wanted to get it over with.

In the end Etienne suggested, "By the Rivers of Babylon". He had been taught it by a nun at school in Lisala, and although his pronunciation was poor, he was able to prompt the rest of us with the lines we were unsure of. He had a beautiful singing voice, and he led us through the whole song a few times, quietly at first, with him singing lead vocals and us following. He wanted us to clap along with the words, but we weren't able to practise this beforehand as we wanted to attract as little attention to ourselves as possible. We were hoping to sneak up on them. We knew that it was likely that someone of the hundreds on board had spotted us by this stage, but we were far enough away that they wouldn't have been able to see our faces.

The nearer we got, the more transfixed I became by the crate of glinting bottles with their treacly bubbles all choked up inside, yearning for their moment of release, of fulfilment. They wanted to be in my mouth, I was sure of that. Etienne and the Americans were far more excited by the singing idea than the rest of us; we were too conflicted and sad to know how we felt. Again and again, my mind sought solace in the thought of the drink – the sublime syrup that would soon be bubbling over my lips, coating my tongue, slipping down my throat. It was hard not to just reach out and grab a bottle right away, but Rick made sure he kept it safe until the time was right. Once we were within shouting distance of the other vessel, he suddenly whipped out his Swiss Army knife and began cracking open the bottles one by one.

By that stage, we could see the whites of the people's eyes on deck. The boat looked even more crowded now than it had in Bumba, but I knew that it couldn't be. There had been nowhere else to stop along the way, unless people were being ferried out in *pirogues*. The passengers looked completely worn out, staring at us dispassionately as though the sight of thirty white people in dugout canoes was a normal one. I could see no sign of our friends at first. There were too many people crowded together to be able to see through them, but after a while some of the people recognised us from Bumba and they must have passed the word back to our friends. Suddenly I saw Henry pushing his way towards the edge. When he caught sight of us, he froze for a moment, and I could see the whole thing dawning on him. He stared blindly at us for a moment and then looked around him and called something back to the others.

To my surprise, a sense of pity rose within me. It didn't seem fair to watch him in his humiliation and I turned away. When none of the others came forward, I saw him turn around again and scream something at them. Felicity was the next to come forward. Her reaction was less visible, her stony, sun-beaten face hardly flinching, but nevertheless you could see her jaw hardening a fraction further. The crowd on deck parted to allow the others through. Dorothy and Vinnie appeared carrying Rita between them. They all looked in a bad way – withered and sick, and even more sunburnt than us. Rita's face was sweating feverishly, and her skin was coated in beads of pus-like oil. She looked almost green, despite the sunburn. I heard Stella mutter "malaria" to herself, echoing my own suspicions.

While we were silently taking it all in, the Americans were already putting their plan into operation. They got Etienne to hand control of the tiller over to his assistant, and he took up position at the bow of the middle *pirogue*, while Rick handed out the Cokes to each of us, dividing up the fourteen remaining bottles between the twenty people in his group. On a signal from Rick, Etienne raised his arms above his head and began clapping out a slow rhythm.

At the end of the first bar, he gave us all a signal with his eyes and began to sing, "By the rivers of Babylon . . ."

We all looked at him, wondering how the hell we had got to this point and what we were doing with these Cokes in our hands. Seeing our former friends had wiped our brains of everything else.

". . . where we sat down . . ." Etienne continued.

Natasha began to sing, and that jogged our memories and gradually we all joined in.

". . . And there we wept, when we remembered Zion."

We looked away from our friends and didn't look back. The curvaceous bottles of Coke focused our minds, and we gripped them tightly, savouring the gun-barrel feeling between our fingers. All our concentration was on the song now, belting out each line with all our hearts, and after each verse being rewarded with a quick swig of bubbly eruptions of lava. Our voices were buoyant and bold, rising ecstatically as we went along. When we got to the last verse, we just started straight in at the beginning again, louder and wilder this time, with more clapping and whooping. We were delirious. It felt too delicious to think of stopping. The caffeine and sugar had swamped our minds, and we were spinning sky high. The fact that Rita most likely had malaria and might possibly not make it back to Kisangani didn't worry us at all. We were drunk on the heady, savage moment of revenge. The guys on the cargo vessel never once tried shouting out to us or calling for our attention, not that we would have heard them if they had. On their faces was written the knowledge that within hours we'd be in Kisangani, savouring fresh white linen,

Perrier water, French patisseries – anything we might wish for. Whereas they would still be stuck on that cursed river for eternity.

Chapter 22

I'LL NEVER FORGET the first sight of Kisangani's decrepit skyline rising up out of the jungle, pushing out into the river as though it were some monstrous stone giant that had eaten its way through the jungle and stopped here to drink. This was the place we had fixated on for so long. It alone could answer every need and desire we had: food, medicine, telephones to the outside world, possibly even flights out of this cursed place. The city was one of the few places we had an image of before we got there, as it had been the model for Conrad's Inner Station in *Heart of Darkness*; the place where Mistah Kurtz "confronted the horrors of his limitless power and corruption" in Coppola's re-imagining of the tale in *Apocalypse Now*.

As our *pirogues* pulled up at the quay, all I could think of was the scene from *Apocalypse Now* when Martin Sheen's Captain Willard arrives at the riverbank lined with poles topped by human heads and Dennis Hopper is saying, "Come along. It's all right. I am glad." This wasn't just an image from Coppola's imagination: fourteen slaves had actually had their heads cut off here and boiled to remove the flesh before being placed on poles.

I jumped out of the *pirogue* as soon as it touched the quay wall and leapt up the steps on to the dock. It was early evening by now, and the sudden equatorial sunset had cloaked the world in murky grey. An old woman was watching us, and I reached out to her, asking in slurred, desperate

French where the campsite was. Her eyes were hazy with conjunctivitis and her head was thrown back as though she were trying to suck up every spare inch of breath, like a fish in an oxygen-starved tank. I knew she understood French, I was certain of it, but she didn't give me any indication that she had heard what I had said. Then finally she raised a slow hand and pointed towards a street stretching inland. I set off straight away, without looking back to see if the others were OK. I didn't even bother to tell them the directions. I figured they could just follow me, and to be honest I was beyond caring. All I could think of was my stomach, of getting some proper food into it.

I called to anyone I could find in the dirty, abandoned streets, asking them for more specific directions, but most just ignored me. Finally after running about four or five blocks inland, I heard pop music and saw two huge metal gates that I imagined must be the entrance to the campsite. They were bolted shut, and I hammered against them until someone heard and fetched the gatekeeper. As soon as he opened it, I charged straight past him, racing through the multicoloured dome tents and the rugged overland vehicles until I spotted our Bedford. It was empty, but I knew Suzi and Joe had to be somewhere near by.

A Swiss girl came up to me and touched me lightly on the cheek.

"Are you OK, my friend?" she said radiantly.

I looked up into her bright moon face and then around at the glittering wonderland of fairy lights strung from trees and at all the healthy, happy Westerners in shorts and singlets drinking Primus beer and dancing to the strains of Bob Marley blasting from massive wooden speakers. I was still trying to take it all in when I heard Suzi's voice behind me. I spun around and saw her standing at the bar. She was shrieking at me.

"Mocha!" she bellowed drunkenly, as though I might be an apparition and could vanish at any moment.

She came and dug her fingers into my belly. Joe soon followed, bounding over and hugging me exultantly. They were both very drunk.

"Where are the others?" Joe asked.

"You know, we've been trying to find you!" Suzi began without even waiting for my answer. "Yeah, we heard rumours a group of foreigners were stranded downriver, slowly succumbing to disease, and we thought it might be you guys. God, it's good to see we were wrong."

"Are the others OK?" Joe tried asking again, but Suzi just went straight on with her torrent of justification.

"Christ, it's been so hard," she said. "We were so worried. Just tonight we decided that we would have to ring home and tell your families what had happened, that you were missing and all. We were going to start first thing in the morning."

My mind wanted to shout out, "Why didn't you come for us, you bitch!" but my belly vetoed the urge – it demanded food first.

Suzi kept spouting on, saying the only reason they had got so drunk tonight was to strengthen their resolve for the task ahead. She told me in great detail about how they were planning to set off in search of us really soon and how they had already contacted the authorities for help, but I had difficulty taking any of it in. All I could think about was food, and as soon as she paused for breath, I grabbed whatever money Joe had on him and raced back on to the main street to find the nearest restaurant.

When I got there I laid all the money out on the table and begged the waiter to bring whatever he had. A crowd of Westerners came in just after me, and the waiter went over to them before relaying my order to the kitchen. I knew there was no guarantee that the restaurant would have enough food for all of us. At any moment they might run out and stop serving. It had happened before. I shouted over to him to please, please tell the kitchen I needed food. I needed it immediately. Anything! Just as long as it was food. Lucy and Luke came in a while after and joined me, and I tried to wave down the waiter again, but he had gone back into the kitchen. I got up and followed him in there.

"Please!" I said. "I'm begging you. We need food. We haven't eaten. Please!"

He pushed me out of the kitchen, and I shoved him back. I was ready to punch him, but Lucy came and took my hand, steering me sweetly back to my seat. I collapsed on the table, but as soon as Lucy was out of the way I was back on my feet again, calling to the waiter,

"It doesn't matter what food. Anything! Just . . . !"

He brought me a Fanta which quietened me for a while, then the plates started to arrive; plates of everything: rice, eggs, sausages, chips, tomato salad, fish stew, beans, cake. I stared at it all in wonder, not believing that so much food could ever exist in one place at one time. It was awesome. I reached for my fork, but as soon as I brought it to my mouth, my stomach clenched and wouldn't allow anything come near it. My arm wouldn't even allow me bring it to my mouth. My whole body seemed to have shut down, everything except my nose, which had become hypersensitive to the smell of food and was finding the whole array repulsive. I tried tricking my mind into thinking of something else and then sneaking a chip to my lips, but for once my mind and body were in synch, and I could sense bile making its way up my throat before I even lifted the fork. I knew I would gag if I stayed there any longer. In the end I had to leave it all behind and stagger back to the campsite, where I collapsed in my tent which Joe had kindly erected for me.

Next day I ate. I practically did nothing else, just ate from when I awoke mid morning until late that night. Most of the food went straight through me, but I didn't mind. All I wanted was the sensation of food in my mouth, of chewing and swallowing, of feeling my belly swell. In fact, it was better that I didn't keep it in because it meant I could just go on eating. I went to the Italian ice cream shop off the Avenue du 24 Novembre three times that first day, and I arranged for a street seller named Tucker to track me down every hour or two to deliver vegetable samosas whenever I asked. He took it as a personal mission to have hot, freshly fried food waiting on his tray for me. Whenever I would hear his catchphrase of "Bloody Good Tucker" echoing through the campsite, I would go and fill myself once again with oil-sodden parcels of pastry.

After dinner Suzi and Joe, who had hung nervously back from us for most of the day, tried taking us aside in little groups to explain what had happened, to lay out their defence. They had begun drinking sundowners in the late afternoon and were drunk again by this stage. I didn't want to hear anything they had to say: their leaky justifications, their mealy mouthed defence. I just wasn't ready to have to make a judgment call yet. Knowing Suzi, I was sure she had come up with some clever way of extricating herself from all blame, but I didn't want to hear it. Instead, I snuck off with Etienne to a nightclub.

It was more of a bar in someone's back garden than a nightclub, but it had sheets of plywood laid out under a banyan tree for dancing on and lights shining down from the branches that flickered in time to the generator. In place of a bar counter was a tall fridge with a working motor and five openers dangling on chains. You helped yourself to the large brown bottles of Primus whenever you wanted and left the money in a jar that rattled happily on top of a huge quaking speaker made of hessian and hardwood planks. Although it was still early evening, people were up grinding their hips to the music – women mostly, in outrageously decorated fabrics with patterns of flowers, tractors, cardiogram squiggles and what looked like an array of acid tabs. Their bodies moved so freely, as though their pelvises were connected to their torsos with rubber bands, but they kept their hips taut so that they could grind them in a circular motion like the well-oiled cogs of an industrial mill. It was as if gyrating were as natural an involuntary response as tongue wagging or blinking.

The whole scene shared something with the speakeasies in America where the rich had partied hard to forget the ravages of the Great Depression. Zaire was plummeting towards bankruptcy day by day, and the currency was still roller-coasting – yet people nevertheless needed to have fun, to spend their money as quickly as they could before it lost all value.

I could have watched the Kisangani girls dancing all night. Even the largest women managed to swing gracefully, standing steady and letting their waists loll about like clappers on bells, shimmying, looping, chicaning and arcing, while their hands waved gently to a far slower beat. A girl in a bright mauve headdress saw me watching and offered to teach me how. She took hold of my hips and started swirling them while I tried to keep the rest of my body still. It was hard. She was directing my attention to muscles and tendons that I had never even noticed before. After a while, she told me to forget about my body and to focus instead on the music. She held me close to her, and I felt the rhythm of it coming through her. This was *soukous,* or Congo rhythm, an infectious spiralling, unstoppable sound that was said to be originally the preserve of witch doctors. There was a sense of ecstasy to it, a hypnotic beat that circled around me, luring me in. She claimed that it wasn't so much music as medicine, powerful medicine. And gradually, during the course of the night, it managed to take hold of me, unlocking blocked pathways and inhibited circuits and whirling me along with it. I couldn't help smiling at the simple joy of it, and I noticed the same smile on everyone else's face. *Soukous* had us all under its spell, regulating our pulses, bringing us into harmony. I didn't want the feeling to ever end and went on dancing until well after dawn.

When I woke the following afternoon, *soukous* melodies were still rippling through me and all I could think about was getting back to the club again, losing myself once more in *soukous,* in its geometric maze of pulses and patterns. It was like a door had been opened, and I had gone spiralling through. I spent the next few days dancing all night and sleeping most of the day. It stopped my mind thinking about what I had been through. If the clubs didn't eventually close each morning, I probably would have just gone on dancing. No matter how tired I was, new waves of energy would come and carry me forward.

Late one night in one of the dance bars, I noticed Etienne stiffen at the sight of two soldiers drinking in the corner. He was about to pull me away, but they spotted us and came over, embracing Etienne fondly.

"My friend, life is good?" one of them said. "It's sad we see you here so rarely now."

They spoke in French, possibly for my benefit or because they didn't think they shared a common local language. Etienne answered in an African language, Lingala I think, and after a short exchange, he insisted that we were just about to leave, that we had only called in briefly looking for a friend.

He practically pushed me out the door.

"I thought you said you had never been to Kisangani before," I said to him as soon as we were back on the street.

"I didn't," he said.

"You did," I insisted.

He gave one of his signature shrugs. "Never by *pirogue.* Normally I come by ferry."

"So you have been here before," I said. "How often?"

He didn't reply. In all the time we had spent in the city, he never once mentioned that he knew the place.

"Those soldiers seemed very friendly," I said.

Etienne laughed and said, "So?"

I was suspicious immediately. Something wasn't right. I was trying to think back to Bumba, wondering if he could in some way be linked to Hercules. It all seemed too fortuitous now: how he had suddenly appeared out of nowhere when we most needed him. We walked on in silence, but later that night when we were dancing in some other bar and the sullenness that had overtaken us had been forgotten, he put his mouth up close to my ear and said, "This is Zaire, my friend, the army is everywhere."

"What do you mean?" I said, but he wouldn't say any more. He was standing beside the sound system, its valves, copper wire and transmitters so hot that smoke was rising from them. I wanted to focus on what, if anything, he was trying to tell me, but my mind was spinning again with the music, my eyes darting about following the glinting lights ricocheting off beer bottles.

"Please," I said. "I need to know."

"It is Zaire," he said at last. "The army rules everything, everyone. I know them, they know me. So what? They know Hercules, I know Hercules . . . Of course we do."

The huge throbbing bluebottle-eye of a loudspeaker was belting out music behind us, and it was hard to make out what he was saying. I signalled to him to follow me outside, and reluctantly he did.

We walked awhile through the market saying nothing. The place was lit up with fairy-tale flames dancing in the glass chimneys of kerosene lamps that were hanging from straw-roofed stalls. Hawkers were selling cigarettes and fried food to nighttime revellers. As usual, Etienne picked out some morsels that he thought I might like: salty fried palm grubs and a mush of okra-paste balls. The grubs were crunchy, like prawns, and the balls tasted like stale croquettes.

He sat me down on an old crate and said, "You are worried, Mocha. You think I am working with Hercules."

"I don't know what to think," I said. "It is strange that you turned up just when you did, just when the ferry came."

"It's not important, Mocha," was all he said in reply. "You *mindele* are so caught up with finding out the facts. Life is not like that. It's like *soukous;* you roll with it, don't strain against it. Your friends on the cargo boat, they got scared in Bumba and they fled, but you didn't; you rolled with the blows. If you punch me, I will double in pain, but punch a white man and he steels himself. That is why we will always survive longer than you, because we bend. We keep on breathing. We are strong like grass; we never snap."

Chapter 23

ETIENNE'S WORDS HAD a big impact on deciding what I should do next. I knew I should escape home. I could do it quite easily now. The insurance would pay for a first-class flight if I had contracted a serious disease from the river, and it was almost certain that I had. But I could see from what Etienne had said that leaving now would be a form of buckling under, instead of bending, and I refused to do that. One way or another, I would see this thing through. The few days' recuperation in Kisangani had given me a renewed sense of myself, of my direction and potential. I was reminded how lucky I was to be here, especially at this time. It was a unique period in Africa's history, the point at which the continent was still teetering between its gracious, old life of small-scale herding and farming, and the inevitable repercussions of the modern age which was bringing industrialisation, medical intervention and subsequent population explosion. Within a generation, the landscape and culture would have changed irreparably, and I owed it to myself to see and learn as much as I could while I had the chance.

Jameson's diary actually played a part in my decision too, if only in that it put our own ordeal into perspective. He too had been abandoned by Stanley on the banks of the river, a little bit upstream from Bumba, near to where our pirogues had split apart on the first night. Stanley had left him with four officers and 200 sick porters there, promising to return for them in four months. He had been abandoned exactly 103 years to the day before Suzi had left us. They too had run out of food and water, and many of the men had died, most of the rest succumbing to fever. Jameson managed to hold out for fourteen months, but three days before Stanley finally returned, he collapsed and died, riddled with fever and dysentery. He had spent his last nine days curled up inside a pirogue being lashed by tornadoes and downpours in a final desperate trip to seek help.

Reading about his death had a profound effect on me as it reminded me so vividly of my dad's dying hours. An officer who had cared for him wrote about bringing hot bricks to keep him warm and rubbing his thighs with mustard leaves.

7.20 p.m. His pulse grows weaker and weaker . . . 7.32 p.m. As I supported him to administer brandy with a spoon, he drew a long breath, and his pulse stopped.

I cried over that bit, thinking back to the ward in the Dublin hospital with my dad bound with canvas straps to a metal bed, his mind delirious, under siege by a mysterious infection that was eating through his brain tissue. I could smell again the hint of chloroform, the rich steam of coffee brought by a neighbour and the Gucci No. 3 sprinkled like holy water to mask his incontinence. Poor old dad.

Poor old Jameson too. I felt I knew him at this stage; we had been through so much together. It made it all the more startling when I read later about the scandal that had followed his death. Even before his wife and children had learnt that he was dead, it was being claimed in London newspapers that he had paid to have a young girl killed and eaten so that he could sketch the scene. He stated in a letter home that it had all been a big misunderstanding, and that although he had paid six white handkerchiefs to see someone being killed, he thought it was a joke. When they really did begin to chop up the girl and eat her, he decided he ought to make the best of a bad situation and drew her anyway.

After almost a week in Kisangani, the guys from the cargo boat began to turn up at the camp in dribs and drabs. We kept as far away from them as possible. None of us were ready to deal with the consequences yet. It was all still far too raw. I couldn't foresee a way of ever mending the schism. As a group, we had barely managed to remain amicable up until now, and I reckoned it was inevitable we would descend into rival factions from here on in, spending the remaining weeks simmering with animosity and occasionally erupting into outbreaks of violence. Suzi's leadership skills came into their own at this point. She deftly managed the whole situation by erecting tents for the newcomers on the far side of the campsite and making sure we never needed to come into contact with each other. She spent most of the day going back and forth to the hospital, where Rita, Dorothy and Mildred had all been brought as soon as they reached the town. I never bothered asking them how they got off the boat or what was wrong with them, though Stella, who with heroic magnanimity had gone to see them, told me that only Rita was really sick. She had malaria, but the doctors thought she'd make a full recovery. We acted as though the other lot didn't exist, and they seemed equally willing to stay out of our way. It was up to Suzi and Joe to convey information between us.

Finally, once Rita was discharged from hospital, Suzi ordered us all on to the truck. We filed obediently in and sat down opposite each other, avoiding making eye contact as we set off towards Nairobi and the Indian Ocean. We drove for two days hardly saying a word, but surprisingly there were no unseemly incidents in that time, or at least my diary doesn't record any. It records very little of those two days – I think I wanted to blot it out. Somehow, we managed to keep our cool. It was possibly the act of being driven that lulled us into a stupor again, like children in pushchairs. Eventually Suzi judged the time was right to confront the issue, and she pulled into a wildlife reservation for okapis (shy forest animals, thought to be a cross between a giraffe and a zebra) in the south of the country and told us we were going to have a party whether we liked it or not. She said she would do all the cooking and make all the preparations.

There was a British couple camped there who offered to share their crate of Primus with us as Joe had helped them fix their gearbox. I noticed a tension between the couple that was almost as intense as our own, and I realised they were using us as a distraction from the widening crevasse that was slowly destroying their relationship. Suzi invited them to the party, and she set about actually preparing and cooking a full meal for the first time in the trip. She made sure we all sat together around the fire as she peeled and chopped the vegetables and encouraged the British couple to open a fresh bottle of Primus as soon as we had finished the last. It didn't take us long to empty the crate. Afterwards a few of us got up to wander off again, but Suzi called us back, insisting we stay around the fire until dinner was cooked and eaten. It was a mark of her unshakable authority that we still did as she said. She pulled up the floorboards and started handing out the last of the spirits, unscrewing the bottles and literally pushing them into our hands in a manner that made it clear that we dare not refuse. We looked at each other, shrugged and began taking slugs straight from the bottle, gulping back mouthfuls of whatever was offered, whisky, Cointreau, gin, before passing it on. It was like a college initiation ceremony, but the stakes were far higher. This was about avoiding civil war.

We kept drinking until our words slurred and the world began to blur.

"Let's talk,' Suzi said, handing out plates of spaghetti Bolognese. "I want to know what happened. Everything."

Nobody said a word, and so she reached for another bottle, opened it and passed it along.

"I mean it," she said. "We're not leaving here until we've done this. You've got to have this out."

It took another whole bottle before Vinnie finally got to his feet, teetering a bit and sucking in his stomach, then jutting out his chin to steady himself.

"I wanna say, I just wanna . . ." he said, looking around him searching for inspiration. "Personally speaking, yeah? I'm fuckin', well, sorry about the whole sorry, em, mess, yeah? That's just how I see it."

"You guys screwed up," Henry said to no one in particular. "But you know what? I think you're OK and if I could choose a group of tossers to go through all this with, it would be you lot!"

Both Vinnie and Henry had been on the cargo vessel, and some of the others from that group echoed their words with similar vague sentiments. Our group didn't feel we had anything to apologise for. We weren't the ones who had abandoned them to die on the shores of Bumba. Not that they saw it in those terms, of course. Yet, the alcohol softened us all, and after some more emotive and incoherent declarations on both sides we made mollifying noises about there being fault on all sides, and agreed to try and put the incident behind us, or at least to pretend that we did. (Secretly we would probably continue to resent each other for decades.) We agreed to carry on with the charade – our ticker-tape parade – like a loveless couple going through the motions for the sake of the children, infected by too many past hurts to ever heal. We would put our faith in alcohol from now on to get us through. Suzi said that the kitty money we had saved during our time on the river would be spent on crates of spirits. I suddenly saw the wisdom of her insistence back at the Moroccan border that we buy as much drink as we could afford. Years of trans-African travel must have taught her that it was the only way to get a group of disparate individuals across the continent.

Next morning a forest warden named Patrick turned up with an AK-47 slung over his shoulder, offering to bring us into the jungle to look for okapis. We all agreed and set off on a new adventure. Unfortunately we didn't manage to find any, but at least it proved that we could still do something together. At lunchtime Patrick surprised me by speaking a few words of Irish.

"*Pádraig is anim dom,*" he said. "*Conas tá tú?*"

He had been raised in an orphanage by Irish nuns. I could see Lucy found him attractive right from the first moment. He was fairly tall and thin with barely visible tribal markings on his jowls. She had kept pace with him the whole morning during the forest walk, eagerly asking him questions – even more eagerly than usual – and finding reasons to brush up against him whenever she could. It was she who had insisted that he join us for lunch; the rest wanted to pay him off after the forest trip and be rid of him.

"You have the best job in the whole world," Lucy said to him after he told us about his role looking after wounded okapis and gathering plant specimens to send to laboratories abroad to test for new medicines. "You're like Indiana Jones."

He told us he was going into the forest in the afternoon to check on a pygmy tribe that had recently set up an encampment in the area, and Lucy asked could she come with him.

"It is very far," he said hesitantly, "and they are sometimes afraid of strangers."

"Please!" she cried.

He said he'd ask his supervisor.

In the end, Suzi arranged it that Lucy and the rest of our group from Bumba would go and spend the night there. She thought it would be wise to give both groups some time apart. We set off back into the dark forest, following the few shafts of light where the sun managed to penetrate the canopy and send beams of white heat down that raised wispy steam off the ebonies and mahoganies. Lucy kept asking Patrick questions about every butterfly and orchid we passed – playing the dumb blonde flawlessly.

The camp consisted of a few huts made of saplings and large leaves in a small clearing in the forest. The tribe gathered around when they saw us coming, and in their eyes I saw the same questioning gaze as in those of the children of the Sahara, wondering what the hell we were doing there. They were about to go out hunting – the young men with great manes of twine netting draped around their shoulders like Elizabethan courtesans or Jedda warriors. Patrick asked us if we wanted to join them, and when we agreed, an elder insisted that we smoke a pipe first, as it would help our endurance and dull the pain of the branches in the undergrowth. He lit some dried leaves in a tiny bowl, which he placed at the end of a very long bamboo pipe, and passed it around. Everyone took a few mouthfuls from it, even the children, the mothers helping to hold the pipe for them. The whole camp was infused with the smell of cannabis. I wondered what Suzi and the others would have said. The adolescent males had a second small-er pipe which they used to supplement their draws on the long one.

Once the pipe was finished, the hunters ran off into the forest and we followed as best we could. The trails were low as the pygmies tended to crouch when running, so we were left to smash our way through the thick tangle of bush. We just kept running until we reached a tiny deer trapped in a net. It was called a dik-dik and looked like a lanky hare but with huge Bambi eyes. The hunters looked at us with ebullient eyes and slit its tiny quaking neck, before heading off after another. Once they had three dik-diks suspended from a pole, we all headed back to camp, where an old woman came and dabbed palm oil and crushed leaves on our wounds. The pygmies set to work, chopping wood, cooking manioc, fixing the nets and skinning the dik-diks, while we sat around the fire until nightfall dis-cussing whether or not it was right to eat the tiny animal. In the end, we weren't offered any of the meat and had to make do with tinned tuna that Stella had fortunately thought to bring. Afterwards we went straight to sleep, exhausted from the hunting. Lucy and I had been paired up togeth-er to sleep in the chief's house, a small circular building of arrowroot leaves with an earthen floor. I set up both our mosquito nets, but Lucy told me she didn't want it. She had been offered a different hut by one of the women. I just shrugged and pulled down her net again, handing it sullenly to her. I didn't really care. The hut was tiny and I was glad of the extra room. As it was, my head was touching one side and my feet the other.

I went straight to sleep and if I dreamt I don't remember it. I had given up on the dream diary after Bumba, realising there were better things to focus my attention on. At some point in the night, I awoke and sprang up with the feeling that I had just heard something worrying. I looked around and found there were six bodies all around me: pygmies curled up in every spare inch of ground of the tiny hut. It suddenly dawned on me that I had taken it for granted that Lucy and I were being given the chief's house to ourselves, whereas in fact it seemed we were meant to share it. My roll mat and mosquito net took up so much space that two of the sons were sleeping with only their heads inside the door. I must have been so tired that I didn't notice them coming in.

I heard the sound again, a whimper, that I recognised immediately as Lucy's. I got up on my knees and made a lunge for the door, crawling over the bodies as fast as I could. It was like playing Twister (a game I was never very good at), and I ended up kicking the chief's wife in her stomach and then stepping on her fingers.

"Sorry," I whispered at her bleary, sleep-sewn eyes. I wished I knew the word in their language.

By the time I had got myself out, Lucy was already emerging from another hut in a distraught state.

"What's wrong?" I cried, but she batted me away and ran right past me.

"What . . . ?" I began, then fell silent as I saw a figure rising from the back of her hut. I peered hard into the darkness before I realised it was Patrick. He came lumbering out now, looking lost and confused.

"What happened?" I screamed.

He looked at me distractedly, then stumbled off towards the edge of the forest.

"What did you do?" I yelled.

He wouldn't meet my eye.

"What the hell did you do to her?" I said, chasing after him.

I caught up with him and pulled him around towards me. His eyes were red with anguish. He was gasping, deep rough breaths from the back of his throat.

"What the hell did you do?" I cried.

"I don't know . . ." he said. "I didn't mean . . ."

He paused and wouldn't say any more.

"Oh Christ!" I whispered and went off to find Lucy.

I couldn't see her anywhere in the camp, and I was just about to raise the alarm when I thought of Natasha and hoped she might know. I went around each hut until I found the one she was in, and sure enough Lucy was with her. They were curled up in each other's arms with a crowd of sleeping pygmies around them.

"Lucy?" I called quietly, hoping not to wake the others. "Lucy?"

Natasha looked up and shot me a stare.

"Lucy?" I tried again, but Natasha waved me away.

I went back to Patrick, getting angrier with every step.

"What did you do?" I spluttered.

He was still very upset. He said nothing.

"Tell me!" I screamed.

"It is my father," he whimpered. "My father always says it is important to have blood, so there is no disease . . ."

His words were like a steel bar against my forehead. I looked around me dazed and felt my fist tightening. I looked back at him and noticed that he had stopped talking, then realised my knuckles were sore. I had hit him. He didn't react, just dropped his head and fell quiet. We sat there in silence, and I must have dozed off at some point as suddenly I was startled awake by loud crying. Many people wailing. It spread from person to person right throughout the camp. I looked around me and saw people crawling out of their huts to join in. For a split second, I thought I was still dreaming, but this was real. Someone in the camp must have died. I thought back to Mossallu's aunt and worried at the frequency with which death seemed to follow me.

"What's wrong?" I asked Patrick.

He looked around him.

"Why are they crying?" I said.

"Every morning they cry," he said. "It's tradition."

"Why?"

He shrugged.

Lucy was emerging from Natasha's hut, and I went over to her, approaching hesitantly. She stopped when she saw me, and I tried to put an arm around her shoulder. She frowned and made to step back, but then softened and allowed me take her by the hand, and we walked off into the trees a short distance.

"Are you OK?" I said.

She tried to smile.

"What was with all that wailing?" she asked.

"They're sad too," I said.

She smiled, and then a tear came to her eye and she turned away. I could see she was as much angry as sad. She pushed me gently, then pushed again harder and started slapping my shoulders.

"What's wrong?" I said.

"You!" she said, biting her lip.

I just looked at her.

"Why weren't you . . . ?" she said harshly. "Oh God!"

"What?"

"I thought you were going to . . . you know, look after me."

I couldn't think of anything to say. She looked at me again, sadder this time.

"I'm sorry," I said at last and tried to say more, but the words wouldn't come.

We stayed like that in silence for a while until Natasha came along, glowered at me and led Lucy away.

Chapter 24

THE ROAD WORE on. It seemed as if we would never leave Zaire. At some points, the track disintegrated into a mire of pure mud that even our truck couldn't pass, and we would have to turn into the jungle, knocking down trees to make a path. At other times, we would be coaxed along by a slim, smooth ribbon of black tarmac that tore through the jungle like a Scalectrix track, built by foreign logging companies to whisk the oldest and rarest timber out. The relief one would feel at the few hours break from the choking cloud of orange dust and gluey mud was tainted by the sight of the juggernauts hauling perhaps two thousand years of mahogany towards the coast.

One time we were laying waste to a section of ancient forest to make a track, rather than have to wait for the other trucks to plough through the mud, when we got caught on the stump of an enormous tree that we had just felled and we broke our driving shaft. It took us a day to fix it. There was no real reason for us to ever have to knock down trees. We could have looked around for an alternate route, but Suzi was still eager to maintain the pace. She still considered the trip as some kind of race, or else she knew she was only being paid for six months and wanted to make sure we didn't take any more time than was necessary. After we had broken the driving shaft, I went to her and asked could we possibly avoid felling more trees unless it was absolutely necessary and, to my astonishment, she agreed. She had become more docile since Bumba. Perhaps she felt guilty.

She certainly should have. She was largely responsible for the whole thing. She had left us in Bumba knowing there was no boat. Of course, she never admitted this; in fact she denied having ever told us the boat was due at all. I'll never know the truth for sure, but the question will always remain: why didn't she come to help us when she heard rumours about our troubles on the river?

Gradually we emerged from the forest into a landscape of rolling emerald hills and lush meadows grazed by Friesian cows. The weather changed dramatically from hot and humid to wet and misty. We had entered the Virunga Mountains: a volcanic land where Uganda, Rwanda and Zaire meet – a distinct region, neither jungle nor grassland, which marks the border between the equatorial rainforest of Central Africa and the savannahs stretching east. It looked and felt remarkably like northern Europe of a century ago, even down to the rustic Flemish cottages and patchwork allotments of cauliflowers, leeks, spinach and other temperate vegetables. It reminded me of a pastoral scene from a Dutch painting.

In the town of Rutshuru, we accidentally knocked down a Frenchman who was speeding down a hill on a child's scooter. It was hard not to hit a scooter somewhere in the town as they came at you at speed from every direction, usually laden with vast bundles of vegetables precariously balanced on the footboard. Once they picked up speed on an incline, they became practically uncontrollable.

Fortunately, the Frenchman was unhurt, and he accepted full responsibility for the accident as he was still learning to drive the scooter.

"I was good as a child," he said, "but . . ."

He had been sent by an aid organisation to examine the local transport system. They had heard rumours that there was a revolutionary new form being used here. They thought it might be ideal for other regions – a solution to Africa's transport problems. He was surprised when he came to find only scooters, children's scooters, with reinforced wheels and a lengthened footboard to carry a bigger load. He had been expecting something more, and was about to turn back dejectedly again, annoyed at the wasted journey, when he realised to his surprise that the system actually worked quite well. It was crude, but efficient. The farmers lived in the mountains and only came to town once a week to sell their produce. They couldn't afford trucks, and it was a waste of resources to have a mule or pack pony for a once weekly trip. The scooters proved the ideal solution for transporting produce to market. Once a few planks were placed cross-ways on the footboard, they could carry a surprising amount of goods. The Frenchman calculated that they handled five times more than a bicycle and twice as much as a handcart, and were far easier to push back uphill than either.

He was now eager to get his report back to the office in the capital so that they could start spreading the idea across the region, and he asked if we would be able to give him a lift eastwards to Nairobi with us. To my surprise, Suzi said she would ask the rest of the group. It turned out that everyone was more or less in favour. We were all sick of the sight of each other by then and desperate for new blood.

Relations between Lucy and me improved considerably in the following days, largely thanks to the mountain gorillas which we came upon up near the Rwandan border in the Virunga Mountains. We climbed up into the hills with a warden in search of them, and after about an hour hiking through a mossy, gnarly, deciduous forest on the edge of oxen-ploughed fields, we came across a monstrous, rust-brown gorilla staring out at us from a leafy grotto in the undergrowth. She was cradling a tiny baby in her arms, and they looked for all the world like a Renaissance Madonna and Child. We peeked in at her through a veil of vine-bound bromeliads, feeling somehow sanctified by her gaze, her soft inquisitive eyes and placid, gaunt expression. I felt that curious blend of exaltation and serenity devotees feel in the presence of a master. Everyone felt their hearts soften a little. The group photo we took that morning is the only one in which we all are smiling. Our eyes are eager and open, and we are standing close together as a team, a single nurturing family, united on the adventure of a lifetime.

A sudden crashing in the trees spun us around, and we scattered at the sight of a gorilla, almost twice the size of the first, moving swiftly through the undergrowth on his knuckles and knees. He stopped and stared between us and the mother and child for a heart-stoppingly long time, his black plastic face indecipherable. He tore at some branches in a half-threatening way, and I became aware of the smell of our fear mixed with his sweet, dungy aroma. This gorilla was a silverback, the head of the family, one of only fifty left in the wild. He must have decided we were not a threat, as he squatted down and began swiping a length of cane through his great yellow teeth, dismissively spitting out the stem and chewing on the leaves. Lucy leant over to me and put her hand in mine, just like she had that day in the market in Fez. This time I didn't pull away; rather I drew her to me and she pressed her bony thigh into mine. The silverback lay out on his belly with his chin cradled in his hand and called out in a coughing, absent way to some young gorillas that appeared out of the trees and began to play on the deep, silver carpet of his back. I brought Lucy's hand to my mouth and kissed the tips of her fingers, and she cradled deeper into me. One of the young gorillas looked up from picking at his fur and, noticing us, he pointed a stubby grey fingernail straight at us. Lucy looked up at me and beamed. It was an imprimatur. That night I asked her to be my girlfriend and she agreed. We decided not to share a tent as she was still getting over the incident with Patrick, but we promised that we would look out for each other in the days and weeks that remained. We wouldn't hide our feelings any more.

We finally crossed into Uganda on St Patrick's Day, leaving Zaire behind after more than a month. Lunch was in a lean-to against the back wall of the immigration office, with sacks of kidney beans and planks of wood as chairs and tables. Pale maize in sheaves lay drying on the roofs. The immigration office next door was indistinguishable except for a hand-painted sign above the door. We spent our remaining Zairian currency on bananas, buns and a casserole which could either be goat, chimpanzee or river rat, depending on what we most wanted it to be, according to the owner. I opted optimistically for the first choice, though I knew it was most likely the last. I hoped it wasn't chimpanzee; nothing was worse than eating something with humanoid fingers. I was taken aback by the cook's slenderness. We hadn't seen a tall thin figure during the entire time in the Congo Basin, but from here on in until Kenya, it seemed the people just grew taller and thinner.

In fact, everything looked different the moment we crossed the border. We entered the comparative affluence of East Africa and benefited immediately from the billions of pounds Britain had splurged on the area in its vainglorious attempt at empire building. There was a paved road most of the way from here to the coast, built by the British, with a little help in the early days from rhinoceros-hide whips. The markets had a range of food that was unimaginable to us after a month of bananas, eggs, manioc and peanuts. Suddenly there were aubergines, pasta, peppers, chocolate and coffee available. These seemed wonderfully extravagant compared to what we were used to, but Suzi told us that they were nothing in comparison to the riches this part of the world had known during the Twenties and Thirties, when the region experienced a bout of intense hedonism. The British elite were given ranches on 999-year leases and came out en masse to create a high-living, trophy-hunting culture, revolving around perilous, cocaine-fuelled safaris and cocktail parties at which pet lions mingled with the guests.

We drove straight to one of the last remaining vestiges of these old glory days, the Queen Elizabeth National Park, a vast wildlife reserve that had been one of the great hunting grounds of the region. We camped beside a white colonial hunting lodge and had breakfast of buttered toast and marmalade with Earl Grey tea on the geranium-clad veranda. The waiter, who was dressed immaculately in a black and white uniform, told us that we were the only visitors – the first to pass through in two weeks.

Idi Amin had frightened off the last of the colonial hangers-on a decade before, and tourists had long since stopped coming. Amin had allowed his soldiers to shoot the wildlife for target practice, and the unpaid Tanzanian soldiers who deposed him had carried on the practice. When they left, the locals killed whatever remained. It was only recently that some animals had finally begun to return.

The waiter offered to arrange a game warden for us to show us around the park, and we sat back in wicker chairs under a grand plaster colonnade to await him, sipping tea from peacock-decorated cups.

The warden was about sixteen, but he knew the park well. Within minutes of leaving the lodge, he pointed out a quiver in a thorn tree beside us and told Suzi to stop the truck. We looked around us, but could see nothing until he gestured upwards. An elephant trunk suddenly appeared through the trees, grabbing leaves off a branch above us. I had seen elephants peek from behind tufts in cartoons before, but never realised it could actually happen. It was a cow elephant. She was watchful and silent, observing what we might do, her heavy grey flanks quaking gently, scattering the dried earth of a distant pool. The warden steered us into the bush: she retreated a few steps, then tracked alongside us on her lumbering columnar legs as we followed a trail of spoors and lacerated leaves down to a murky pool. At the far side were five more cows – two with calves – sloshing in the mud. None of them seemed particularly concerned by our appearance. They raised their trunks inquisitively, looking over to the elephant who had accompanied us, and she quickened her pace to reach them before we did. We stared on humbly, sensing their dignity again, as we had with the gorillas, and the mystery that lay behind their heavy-lidded eyes. It felt good to know the matriarch had judged us acceptable, had deemed us worthy.

Lucy and I sat up on the spare tyre which we had tied to the roof bars to be as far away from the others as possible. I hugged her to me. This was what I had hoped Africa would be about: antelopes grazing in golden grass, waterbucks playing beneath baobab trees – not a six month psychological experiment in a moving cage. About a kilometre further along the track, we saw a pair of lionesses, their lithe bodies stretched out to soak up the sun. They lifted their heads only very slowly towards us and then, in no apparent hurry, picked up an errant cub and bounded off into the trees in one perfectly choreographed movement. We took our first photographs of frightened animals running away from us; and in the following two weeks we gathered many more. (They reminded me of us at the beginning of the trip, fleeing south, looking back to make sure we had really escaped from whatever it was that had made us run. I knew a lot more now about what each of us was hiding from; but I was still no closer to solving the mystery of Henry and Mildred. They were fleeing something, but I had never got to find out what.)

We drove on through Uganda and into the parks of Tanzania and Kenya, inching our way in awe across the landscape through herds of herbivores and their predators, breathless in expectation of the next encounter with wild nature – as random and repeatedly thrilling as a shooting star. Its rawness never waned, whether watching a flock of flamingos rising up in a fluffy pink cloud from a waterhole or a vulture craning its neck into a carcass. There was something about the unpredictability of life here that grabbed me, finally cracking irretrievably the illusion of the conventional veneer that I had been taught to believe in. The sight of a lion leaping on to a zebra, sinking its teeth deep into the spine, staining the earth with blood, is something you don't forget. At its heart lay a truth greater than any I had been taught by teachers or priests, prompting questions in my head about who and what I really was.

Dominic, the Frenchman, kept to himself most of the time, but his presence was a stabilising influence. It kept the worst of the animosity and bitterness between us in check, although even he couldn't stop all of it. On one occasion, Wayne accused me of breaking the zip of our tent, on purpose.

"Don't pretend otherwise, you cretin," he said. "You've been trying to screw things up for me right since the start. I wish to God I had never had you as a partner."

Someone else left an envelope of human excrement in Rita's locker with a note saying, "You know who . . ."

Felicity, the meek nurse who had remained prim and proper throughout the journey, threw herself on Duncan one night, demanding that he sleep with her. Whatever cohesion there had been between us had crumbled, and were it not for Dominic's presence, I'm sure things would have been even worse.

"If I had come across you all a year ago, you would have disgusted me," Dominic admitted to me when we were out on the savannah watching warthogs one morning. "Your ignorance and the pointlessness of your journey would have sickened me."

"Oh," I gulped.

"Now it's different," he said. "Now, I can see your heroism."

"Heroism!" I exclaimed.

"You are heroic," he said. "All of you."

"Thanks," I said, "but I don't see it."

"You've come the whole way here," he cried, "seen things, experienced things few people ever do. And this is only the beginning. The world awaits you. You must decide what you want to do, and choose carefully. My advice is, don't think you have all the answers. That was the mistake I made."

Dominic had been a missionary until two years before when a crisis of faith had caused him to flee Africa.

"I was arrogant," he said. "Interfering. You guys, you're not doing that. You're just doing nothing. That's good. Look at me, I'm back here sticking my nose in again after saying I never would. I just can't help it. They don't need me! Who the hell really needs scooters? Scooters aren't the answer to Africa's problem. Why are we so obsessed with giving advice? They never ask for it. Africans don't see the problems we see; they just see life."

"Why did you come back here if you didn't want to?" I said.

"Where else could I go? I tried living in Marseilles, but I had never cooked or shopped or cleaned before. I am no good in the real world. Here I get a small salary. It's tax-free and paid into a bank in Strasbourg. I will need it when I retire. I wish I did what you did – nothing! Just watching, maybe learning a little."

It was strange to think he saw our trip as worthwhile, or at least not as damaging as his. Perhaps I was too close to it all. Salade told me the Tuaregs had an expression that the further your tents are separated the closer your hearts are to each other. Maybe the problem with us was that we had simply spent too much time together. I was too close to the group and to Africa to see things clearly.

"Look out there," Dominic said, pointing out on to the sun-beaten plain where a Maasai herder was standing on one leg, stork-fashion, carrying a tall spear. His body was covered in an ochre pigment making it glow golden red in the sunlight. Behind him Mount Kilimanjaro rose like a classical image from Oriental art.

"What do you see?" he said.

"A herder," I said.

"Yes, but what else?" Dominic said. "What does he look like?"

"I dunno, he's wearing something like a toga, I think, and beads around his neck."

"Is he rich or poor?" he said.

"I really don't know," I said. "He's got a nasty wound on his face, and even from here I can see the flies. Why doesn't he swat them away?"

"That's not a wound," Dominic said. "It's dried blood."

"Same thing," I said irritably.

"No! It's not his blood. It's his cattle's. He's just sucked his breakfast out of the throat of one of his cattle. And he's ignoring the flies because they're his ancestors, and he doesn't want to be disrespectful to them. And comparatively speaking, he is rich. Those cattle provide milk, cheese, blood and everything else: dung for fuel and plastering, hides for leather, urine for cheese-making, bones for jewellery, horns for fishing spears – I could go on."

"What's your point?" I said.

"Just don't make presumptions about Africa, about what you're seeing, about what's wrong and right. Don't feel pity. That's all I'm saying."

Whenever we camped for the night, I would head to the nearest waterhole to watch the continual struggle for survival. All the different species focused on the water source, cooperating and compromising. They all had to take a risk, and the stakes were high. Languishing in the waterhole often was the grey-green corralled form of a crocodile which could rise up and strike at any moment. The animals seemed to dare each other to advance and slurp a few agitated mouthfuls before darting back to safety again.

One evening Dominic and I were watching a herd of zebras undergoing this heroic game of Russian roulette when suddenly the place erupted into a brown cloud as a hyena came thundering through from the opposite direction, scattering the herd wildly in all directions and raising heavy swathes of dust. All I could make out was a quiver, a shadow of black mane and the feeling of panic rippling through the herd – the nostrils distended in terror, those horse hearts palpitating. It was mostly just an impression left on the mind, of something seen but not focused on. Bright, protruding eyes turned cold. Savage energy. The glass beads of glinting saliva suddenly turning blood-red. And the hyena retreating, dragging its heavy load.

Those few scenes, so elemental, so profound, changed me for ever. I just felt so lucky to be here, experiencing all this when I was still so young. There was something sacred about the whole landscape: the endless vista of lion-coloured grasses, elephant-grey boulders and black silhouetted oleanders and acacias webbing the sky in zebra patterns. The place was like an altar to the integrity of beingness, and I hoped I could incorporate some of it into my own life.

After the zebras had fled and the dust settled, I noticed the rib cage of a gazelle – a Gothic cathedral of bones picked bare of meat – rising starkly up from its wilted carpet of skin. It seemed to have been placed there solely for me: a sign to say that sometimes you had to risk death to be fully alive. I thought back to the moment when the ferry had pulled into Bumba and I had made the decision to stay back with my friends and not push my way to the front of the queue to get myself a ticket, and I felt suddenly immensely proud. I knew the risks of not getting out of Bumba, but I preferred to take my chances than leave the others behind. Like the zebras, sometimes you have to walk towards danger to be fully alive. Death couldn't dictate one's life. I think I was already realising that in relation to my father. It was time to leave him behind.

"If you want to know whether the trip was worth it, you have to ask yourself some hard questions," Dominic said to me at one point.

"Yeah?" I said.

"First, ask yourself whether you've enjoyed it," he said.

I thought about it and decided that on balance I had.

"Then ask yourself if you learnt anything about yourself."

I certainly had.

"And most importantly," he said, "are you more likely now to look someone in the eye and smile when you pass them in the street? That's the ultimate question. The only one."

I considered the question.

"Just answer that," he said, "and you'll know if the whole thing was worth it."

As soon as we got to Nairobi, the group split up into separate hotels. Three different going-home parties were held by three different sub-groups. I didn't bother going to any. Lucy and I had broken up by that stage; we had barely stayed together a week. No one in the group was keen to spend much time together. Occasionally, over the following days as we arranged our flights home, I met one of them in the bank, or the bakery, or the Thorn Tree Café, and we greeted each other courteously, but there was nothing much left to say. Natasha and Lucy were still pushing their idea of a reunion the following year and tried to get us all to swap addresses, but no one was keen.

Suzi informed us that she would be bringing the truck down to the port in Mombassa, and any of us who wanted to come were welcome. I decided to take the train there instead and got to spend a glorious few days swimming in the Indian Ocean and sleeping in a hammock on the strand.

During those last days, I paced the shoreline thinking about the future. I was as excited as I was scared. I prayed to God that the depression and lack of direction that had set me off on this journey would not return as soon as I got home. On my last night, I got stung by a wasp, and a feeling of both pain and peace overcame me. I lay down against the trunk of a swollen baobab tree and rested, finally falling asleep there and only waking at dawn. Above me the limbs of the baobab were gently swaying, and I realised that this tree was possibly aware of me. All leaves are equipped with light sensors that can detect sun, shadow and shapes. This tree could feel me in this place and at this time. I knew that baobabs could live for a thousand years, and a shiver ran through me as I thought of how long it had been here and of how much it had witnessed over the centuries, and of how it could now vouch for the fact that I had been present here and had accomplished this journey. Centuries hence, when Africa had changed completely, had reached its full potential, this tree might still be standing, and in its cellular memory would be a snapshot of me.

The sun rose above the horizon, racing across the sea and inland towards the plain, tangling itself in the black lace of a clump of acacia bushes. I stood on the shoreline and let it beam at me, charging me with light. I imagined it honouring me, vouching for my potential. A chorus of crickets were chiming melodiously, and I thought back over the trials I had endured and the people I had shared them with: Norman and his UFOs, Holly and her hard chewing gum, Stevi and his strangled chicken, Henry and his butterfly-wing shirts. I owed them all so much. They had helped transform me into the person I was now. I recalled the paint-box colours of the dye pits in Fez and remembered something the guide had said about the tanners who spent their days immersed in the baths and how they were more fertile and able than others; they were infused with its potency. That's what Africa, and indeed the group, had done for me. They had infused me; pickled me with experience. From now on everything would be different.

ACKNOWLEDGEMENTS

The James S. Jameson diary extracts are taken from James S. Jameson. *Story of the rear column of the Emin Pasha relief expedition*, edited by Mrs J. S. Jameson (London 1890).

"The Sun, the hearth of affection and life,
Pours burning love on the delighted earth"
Arthur Rimbaud. *Collected Poems*, edited and translated by Oliver Bernard, London: Penguin Classics, 1962

"The flat horizon of this country splits my heart
If I recoil everything bristles suddenly!"
Tchicaya U Tam'si. *Le Ventre* (1964) *The Belly*

"In Zaire" by Johnny Wakelin, from the album *Reggae, Soul and Rock'n' Roll* (PRT Records 1975)

SOME OTHER READING

from

BRANDON

Brandon is a leading Irish publisher of new fiction and
non-fiction for an international readership. For a
catalogue of new and forthcoming books, please write to
Brandon/Mount Eagle, Cooleen, Dingle, Co. Kerry,
Ireland. For a full listing of all our books in print, please
go to

www.brandonbooks.com

MANCHÁN MAGAN

Angels and Rabies: A Journey Through the Americas

"[Magan's] writing is unashamedly sensual and he has an engagingly confessional narrative voice; his adventures are as poignant as they are hair-raising. And while exposing the chaotic workings of his own soul, Magan reveals the underbelly of the colourful cultural and sociological jigsaw of these two great continents."
Sunday Telegraph

"Frightening, funny and lovable." *The Sunday Times*

"A cross between Joseph Conrad and Frank Zappa." Gerry Ryan

"Somewhere between *Lost* and *Heart of Darkness*." Ryan Tubridy

"The charm of the book is that, no matter how wacky, the story is all about people. Faraway lands can be hard to visualise, even with detailed descriptions, but love and loneliness are things we can all relate to. Mocha's vulnerability and naivety make him likeable. Very strange, but very enjoyable." *Ireland on Sunday*

"Each chapter is gripping because truly insane things happen around the author: war breaks out in Ecuador; a famous Hollywood actress falls into his arms. Then there are the near death experiences... It is a warm, well written and entertaining book which will keep readers happy." *Village*

"His writing is intimate and immediate, perceptive and humorous."
Books Ireland

"This travelogue exudes an attitude that is unmistakably rock 'n' roll. Fuelled by the same wild abandon as Jack Kerouac, Magan journeys through the Americas with nothing but adventure on his mind." *Hot Press*

"This is never dull, and always genuine." *Irish Homes*

ISBN 9780863223495; paperback original

MANCHÁN MAGAN
Manchán's Travels

"The book's scope embraces the sublime and the ridiculous…Often humorous, at times hilarious, Magan never opts for a cheap joke at the expense of the situation he is describing…He has an evocative and elegant turn of phrase…Most intriguing are the sporadic discourses on Irish history and the Gaelic language. While these may seem jarring in a book about India, the two cultures are in fact skilfully interwoven. The ability to bring together such disparate elements with such lucid conviction is key to Magan's skill as a writer." *New Statesman*

"His fans will not be disappointed…While the local colour is entertaining, it is the writer's personal journey that makes this book so compelling. It's a funny and occasionally sad, but ultimately satisfying read." *Sunday Telegraph*

"Magan has a keen eye for the hypocrisies of elite urban India and artfully evokes the 'fevered serenity' of the Himalayas." *Times Literary Supplement*

"As off-beat as it is entertaining, taking a look at the often surreal nature of life in modern India." *Traveller Magazine*

"Mad, brilliant and often hilarious." *The Irish Times*

"An irresistible read. From beginning to end, I chortled, chuckled, gasped and held my breath." *Gerry Ryan*

"Everyone who is going to India, everyone who has been to India and indeed everyone who never plans to go to India should read this book." *Outsider Magazine*

ISBN 9780863223686; paperback original

LARRY KIRWAN
Green Suede Shoes

The sparkling autobiography of the lead singer and songwriter of New York rock band, Black 47.

"Lively and always readable. He has wrought a refined tale of a raw existence, filled with colorful characters and vivid accounts." *Publishers Weekly*

ISBN 9780863223433; paperback original

SEAN O'CALLAGHAN
To Hell or Barbados
The ethnic cleansing of Ireland

"An illuminating insight into a neglected episode in Irish history... its main achievement is to situate the story of colonialism in Ireland in the much larger context of world-wide European imperialism." *Irish World*

ISBN 9780863222870; paperback

GERARD RONAN
'The Irish Zorro' The extraordinary adventures of William Lamport (1615–1659)

"Comprehensive and enthralling... Burned at the stake by the Mexican Inquisition at the age of 44, after a 17-year imprisonment, Lamport's story is truly extraordinary... Sometimes historical biography can be a dry read. Ronan's is anything but. He provides interesting insights into the lives of large Irish enclaves in France and Spain in the first half of the 17th century along with harrowing ones of those accused of heresy and subjected to the auto-da-fé of the Inquisition. Ronan's passion and sympathy for his subject shine through so it reads like a novel. A 'must read'." *Irish Independent*

ISBN 9780863223297; hardback

MÍCHEÁL Ó DUBHSHLÁINE

A Dark Day on the Blaskets

"A wonderful piece of drama-documentary... entertaining and captivating. It's an evocative story, a portrait of a young woman and her times, and an engrossing description of a beautiful place at a turning point in its history." *Ireland Magazine*

"A fascinating insight into Blasket Island life, life on the mainland, and life in Dublin in the early part of the last century." *Kerryman*

ISBN 9780863223372; paperback

GEORGE THOMSON

Island Home

"Imbued with Thomson's deep respect for the rich oral culture and his aspiration that the best of the past might be preserved in the future. It is when the deprived and the disposessed take their future into their own hands, he concludes, that civilisation can be raised to a higher level."
Sunday Tribune

ISBN 9780863221613; paperback

JOE GOOD

Enchanted by Dreams
The Journal of a Revolutionary

A fascinating first-hand account of the 1916 Rising and its aftermath by a Londoner who was a member of the Irish Volunteers who joined the garrison in the GPO.

ISBN 9780863222252; paperback original

DRAGO JANČAR
Joyce's Pupil

"Jančar writes powerful, complex stories with an unostentatious assurance, and has a gravity which makes the tricks of more self-consciously modern writers look cheap." *Times Literary Supplement*

"[A] stunning collection of short stories... Jančar writes ambitious, enjoyable and page turning fictions, which belie the precision of their execution." *Time Out*

"[E]legant, elliptical stories." *Financial Times*

"Powerful and arresting narratives." *Sunday Telegraph*

ISBN 9780863223402; paperback original

AGATA SCHWARTZ AND LUISE VON FLOTOW
The Third Shore: women's fiction from east central Europe.

"A treasure trove of quirky, funny, touching and insightful work by 25 women writers from 18 countries in the former communist bloc. Flipped open to any page, it offers a window into unique worlds – some political, all intensely imaginative and often unexpectedly funny." *Sunday Business Post*

"These stories are exciting, intriguing and never predictable. For all their startling narrative tricks and puzzles these stories will appeal for their wide range and honesty." *Books Ireland*

ISBN 9780863223624; paperback original

NENAD VELIČKOVIĆ
Lodgers

"[A] beautifully constructed account of the ridiculous nature of the Balkans conflict, and war in general, which even in moments of pure gallows humour retains a heartwarming affection for the individuals trying to survive in such horrific circumstances." *Metro*

ISBN 9780863223488; paperback original

CHET RAYMO

Honey From Stone

"A travel book about the world of ideas. Raymo uses the natural setting of Dingle as a place in which he asks you to explore with him through his own private universe ... a beautiful book that is well worth reading." *Irish Echo*

ISBN 9780863222320; paperback original

Valentine

"This atmospheric, lyrical and sensual tale of epic proportions... Raymo's interpretation may be controversial, but he is a gifted storyteller and philosopher." *Irish Independent*

"[A] vivid and lively account of how Valentine's life may have unfolded... Raymo has produced an imaginative and enjoyable read, sprinkled with plenty of food for philosophical thought." *Sunday Tribune*

ISBN 9780863223273; paperback original

In the Falcon's Claw

"[A] novel of never-ending pleasure ... superbly innovative. It is a work of rare and irreverent intelligence." *Le Figaro Litteraire*

"A metaphysical thriller comparable to Umberto Eco's *In the Name of the Rose*, but more poetic, more moving and more sensual." *Lire*

ISBN 9780863222047; paperback original

STEVE MACDONOGH
The Dingle Peninsula

A comprehensive illustrated survey of the archaeology, folklore and history of one of Ireland's most fascinating regions.

"Far and away the best of the many books written about the area. A visitor who travels to Dingle without it is seriously deprived." *The Examiner*

ISBN 9780863222696; paperback original

Dingle in Pictures

"Wonderful colour photographs reproduced to perfection and with informative captions. All the text is printed in English, Irish, French and German. Gorgeous!" *Ireland of the Welcomes*

"A beautiful book... We stopped at many places featured in its pages and found that Steve MacDonogh's photographs wonderfully reflected the beauty that was there." *Irish Examiner*

"A stunning collection." *The Kingdom*

ISBN 9780863222795; paperback original

Open Book: One Publisher's War

"An intelligent, informative account of a life spent fighting for freedom of speech, a right which is still not adequately safeguarded." *Irish World*

"MacDonogh is without doubt the most adventurous and determined of the Irish publishers... This is an important book." *Phoenix*

"A fascinating and very important book." Brid Rosney, *Today FM*

ISBN 9780863222634; paperback original

LILY O'CONNOR
Dreams of Hope

"It's a wonderful read from start to finish. Forced out of Ireland in the 1950s in search of a decent wage, with a young husband and very young family she lived first in Luton in England and later in a small town in Australia, some fifty miles from Melbourne. Hurrah for the likes of Lily O'Connor and the families associated with them – they make a lot of the bright spots in this world." *Ireland of the Welcomes*

ISBN 9780863223587; paperback original

DESMOND ELLIS
Bockety

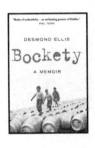

"Genuinely funny. It is enlightening to learn that, despite the censorious and tight-arsed approach of the Catholic Church and its lapdog politicians, working class people were quite subversive in their attitude to life back then. Straight-laced they certainly were not. *Verbal Magazine*

ISBN 9780863223648; paperback original

MAY O'BRIEN
Clouds on My Windows

"This is a wonderful book… May O'Brien says in her afterword that this is an ordinary book about Dublin life in the 40s. Maybe it is. But it's a story about an extraordinary woman, in any time."
Irish Independent

ISBN 9780863223358; paperback original